CHINESE AIR POWER IN THE 20TH CENTURY, Rise of the R

Andreas Rupprecht

CHINESE AIR POWER IN THE 20TH CENTURY

Rise of the Red Dragon

Andreas Rupprecht

HARPIA
PUBLISHING+

Consulting and inspiration by Kerstin Berger

Front cover artwork by Ugo Crisponi, Aviation Graphic shows a J-8II from the former 1st Air Division, 3rd Air
Regiment displaying its original 'Siberian Tiger' patch.
Rear cover artworks by Ugo Crisponi, Aviation Graphic show (from top to bottom): H-6A '50473' from the 36th
Bomber Division, 106th Air Regiment, J-7C '30164' from the former 15th Air Division, 43rd Air Regiment and MiG-15
'1765' from an unknown unit in the very first PLAAF markings.

Artworks by Ugo Crisponi, AviationGraphic

Editorial by Thomas Newdick

Layout by Norbert Novak, www.media-n.at, Vienna

Maps by James Lawrence

Printed at finidr, Czech Republic

Harpia Publishing is a member of

ISBN 978-1-9503940-0-5

中国人民解放军空军

Contents

Introduction

On 11 November 2019 a historic moment was celebrated, as the People's Liberation Army Air Force (PLAAF) celebrated the 70th anniversary of its foundation. However, the event was marked somewhat earlier with a dedicated airshow held between 17 and 21 October in Changchun, a city with historically significance for the air force. Attending the glamorous opening ceremony were General Ding Laihang, the current PLAAF commander-in-chief, and General Yu Zhongfu, the service's political commissar. In fact, this was the second remarkable event of the year – on 1 October the foundation of the People's Republic of China itself was celebrated with even more fanfare.

Led by President Xi Jinping, a spectacular ceremony was held over Tiananmen Square to mark 70 years of Communist rule in China and the country's subsequent rise to global superpower status. Amid this 'show of force', President Xi promised to the audience: 'There is no force that can shake the status of this great nation. No force can stop the Chinese people and the Chinese nation forging ahead.' All this reflects the facts that the People's Liberation Army (PLA) has not only evolved dramatically, but also that Xi Jinping has successfully spent years consolidating his grip on power to become perhaps the most influential leader since Mao himself.

This growing self-confidence is now clearly expressed and increasingly justified since China can indeed be proud of what it has achieved. Concerning the PLAAF, the development is all the more remarkable since it was previously always influenced by its status of subordination to the always dominant PLA Ground Forces. Once dependent on the overall armed forces doctrine and above all the political situation, the last 70 years have been presented more than a few challenges for the air force. While the PLAAF was still in its infancy, embroiled with its own build-up and organisational gestation, it had to prepare for a planned Taiwan campaign. This, however, was abandoned only for the service to stumble almost unprepared into its first full-scale war in Korea. What followed were periods of turmoil including the Great Leap Forward, the break with its most important ally, the Soviet Union, during the 1960s, and then the Cultural Revolution, after which the PLAAF was widely considered as traitorous. Following the Lin Biao incident in 1971, the air force was hit harder than any other branch of the armed forces, and it took many years before it again received the necessary political support. Despite the efforts to regain political stability, self-reliance and economic growth led by the country's leader Deng Xiaoping through the 1980s, little changed for the air force until Jiang Zemin initiated changes in standing and a modernisation programme following the Gulf War of 1991. Regardless of previous efforts, it was only with the election of President Xi – as General Secretary of the Communist Party and Chairman of the Central Military Commission – that a profound reform of the PLA's armed forces could begin. Until then, the PLA had existed largely as a paper tiger, not meeting the demands of modern military requirements, plagued by corruption and widespread nepotism, and severely hampered by the PLA's questionable ability to fight.

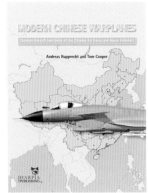

The way in which the PLAAF – and similarly the naval and army aviation arms – has been reorganised into a modern force is described in previous books in this series. Suffice to say, it evolved into numerically the largest air force in Asia, perhaps behind only the US Air Force in terms of overall capability– surpassing eventually even the Russian Air Force. Therefore, it is a suitable time for a historical review of the PLAAF, and this book serves as an introduction to a unique air force. Perhaps most interesting is the fact that China still remains a mystery for many – especially in the West. China has always been dynamic, quick to face challenges and – in contrast to the West – has always sought to resolve issues pragmatically. In the same way that China does not always understand Western thinking, the Chinese way of thinking can seem overly complex to Western observers. After many years spent studying the scene, it is the conclusion of this author that as China tends to take a holistic view and often thinks several more steps ahead of Western powers. In contrast to the West – and especially its politicians – the individual and its fate are assigned less importance. There are clearly limits on privacy and personal freedom and the same applies for information. Although China as a country is incredibly curious, all information is subject to restrictions. Transparency, as we know it in the West, is not important and there is far less space for speculation. Above all, there is a degree of secrecy around everything. And, in stark contrast to other countries, where political leaders proclaim and promote their plans, in China such things are seldom announced until they occur in reality. The same applies to the military, as demonstrated by the surprise unveilings during the 1 October anniversary parade in 2019, during which several previously unseen items – including the H-6N bomber and WZ-8 supersonic reconnaissance drone – were unveiled to the public. In general, the Chinese people are proud of their PLA, and while they are provided with a lot of information, any details are scarce.

In coming up with the idea for this book, I must thank Kenneth W. Allan. When I first became interested in Chinese aviation matters – and above all the PLAAF – I stumbled across his publication *China's Air Force Enters the 21st Century*. Published in 1995, this booklet was above all an academic research report primarily aimed at providing an analysis focused on the PLAAF's order of battle, latest procurement and force projections. But what was new was its interest to a wider audience, to which it brought details of a so far largely unknown air force. In particular, the historical review was tantalising and led to an even more impressive book: *Red Wings over the Yalu* by Xiaoming Zhang, published in 2002. Since then I began to collect information on the development of all possible types and anything else related to the PLAAF. I began to analyse and compare different sources and above all I started to revise the prevailing Western attitudes concerning the PLAAF. With the *Modern Chinese Warplanes* series, I aimed to fill an important void and focused on the then-current situation in 2012, the structure of this growing force, its order of battle, plus the latest types in service and under development. *Flashpoint China* followed in 2016 and aimed to put the relationship between China and its neighbours, as well as with the United States and its allies, into perspective. Finally, since 2018, three completely revised volumes aimed to supersede the original title. In consequence, and coinciding with the PLAAF's 70th anniversary on 11 November 2019, this volume returns the focus to the historical background. Providing a historical framework around the *Modern Chinese Warplanes* series, it examines the different periods, attempts to explain the consequences of major political events and how this all connects to military developments, as well as individual structures and capabilities within the different periods. Also included is a brief examination of how the political climate influenced the design and development of the country's major military combat aircraft – fighters, attack aircraft and bomb-

ers – since the Chinese aviation industry became established after World War II. In essence, this directory should serve as an illustrated, in-depth analysis and overview of the historical gestation of the PLAAF to the modern air force as we know it today.

Above all, I hope that this work serves as a useful tool for many observers outside – and perhaps also inside – the PRC who are curious and eager to understand the 'rising dragon' of Chinese military aviation. While I invested considerable effort into ensuring that the sources for all illustrations presented herein are properly credited, some of these remain unknown. By the same token, the author apologises in advance for any errors or inaccuracies in this work: these are all his own.

Andreas Rupprecht, November 2018

Acknowledgements

As with all my previous books, this project would not have been possible without the support of numerous individuals. I would like to express my gratitude to the various experts who provided invaluable assistance, support, guidance and – most of all – patience in the process of developing this project. My deepest gratitude is offered to a number of posters on various online discussion groups, especially on the internet sites China-Defence and Sino-Defence, as well as their forums, without whose knowledge and assistance this work could never have been realised. Sadly, many of them – especially those in China – prefer to remain anonymous.

I would like to thank all these individuals for their extensive help in the provision of references, sharing of literature, translations of original publications and documentation, research into the latest reorganisations and unit insignia, as well as their unstinting moral support. One, however, should be named individually – Kenneth W. Allen. His book *China's Air Force Enters the 21st Century* (1995) prompted my interest in this topic. Throughout the years he has been a most helpful advisor, explaining PLA terms, translating original Chinese texts and giving me a better understanding of the PLA and its aerial assets in general.

Last but not least, I would like to express my gratitude to my family, for their understanding and patience throughout the duration of what was a very intensive period of work.

Abbreviations

AA	anti-aircraft
AAA	anti-aircraft artillery
AAM	air-to-air missile
AC	air corps
AD	air division
AESA	active electronically scanned array
AEW	airborne early warning
AEW&C	airborne early warning and control
AGL	above ground level
ALCM	air-launched cruise missile
AR	air regiment
ARH	active radar homing
ARM	anti-radiation (radar) missile
AS	attack squadron
ASCC	Air Standardisation Co-ordinating Committee (US, UK, Australian and New Zealand committee for standardisation of designations for foreign [primarily Soviet and Chinese] armament; its standardisation code-names are usually known as 'NATO designations' and have meanwhile been standardised as such even though the ASCC is no longer active)
AVIC	Aviation Industry Corporation of China
BD	bomber division
BR	bomber regiment
BS	bomber squadron
BUAA	Beijing University of Aeronautics and Astronautics (also known as Beihang University)
BVR	beyond visual range
CAC	Chengdu Aircraft Industry Corporation
CAE	Chinese Academy of Engineering
CAF	Chinese Air Force (1942–45)
CAP	combat air patrol
CAS	close air support
CATIC	China National Aero-Technology Import and Export Corporation
CCP	Chinese Communist Party
CDF	China Defence Forum (www.china-defence.com/smf/index.php)
CEGC	Chengdu Engine Group Company
CFTE	China Flight Test Establishment (sometimes also called Chinese Flight Test Evaluation)
CHETA	China Hai-Yang Electro-Mechanical Technology Academy
C-in-C	commander-in-chief
CMA	Chinese Military Aviation Page (http://chinese-military-aviation.blogspot.com)
CMC	Central Military Commission
CMF	China Military Forum (www.centurychina.com/plaboard)

CNAF	Chinese Nationalist Air Force (title often used in the 1940s and 1950s to designate the air arm operated by the Nationalist Chinese during and after the Civil War in China)
COMINT	communications intelligence
CRT	cathode-ray tube
det	detachment
ECCM	electronic counter-countermeasures
ECM	electronic countermeasures
ELINT	electronic intelligence
EO	electro-optical
ESM	electronic support measures (sensors typically used for gathering signals intelligence)
EW	electronic warfare
FA	Flying Academy
FBW	fly-by-wire
FD	fighter division
FLIR	forward-looking infrared
FOD	foreign object damage
FTTB	Flight Test and Training Base
FTTC	Flight Test and Training Centre
GAIC	Guizhou Aviation Industry Corporation
GAIG	Guizhou Aviation Industry Group
GCI	ground-control/controlled interception
Gen	general (military commissioned officer rank)
GP	general-purpose (bomb)
GPS	Global Positioning System
HAF	Harbin Aircraft Factory
HAIG	Hongdu Aviation Industry Group
HAMC	Harbin Aircraft Manufacturing Corporation
HMS	helmet-mounted sight
HOTAS	hands on throttle and stick
HQ	headquarters
HUD	head-up display
IFF	identification friend or foe
INS	inertial navigation system
IR	infrared
IRST	infrared search and track
KnAAPO	Komsomolsk-on-Amur Aircraft Production Association
LCD	liquid-crystal display
LGB	laser-guided bomb
LLTV	low-light-level television
LMC	Liyang Machinery Corporation (assigned to Liyang Aero Engine Corporation, now a subsidiary of GAIC)
MAI	Ministry of Aircraft Industry
MAWS	missile approach warning sensor
MFD	multi-function display
MND	Ministry of National Defence

MoA	Ministry of Aeronautics
MR	military region
MRAF	military region air force
MRTB	military region training base
NAMC	Nanchang Aircraft Manufacturing Company
NPU	Northwestern Polytechnical University
NRIET	Nanjing Research Institute of Defence Technology
NUDT	National University of Defence Technology
OCU	operational conversion unit
OTU	operational training unit
PGM	precision-guided munition
PLA	People's Liberation Army
PLAAF	People's Liberation Army Air Force
PLAN	People's Liberation Army Navy
PLANAF	People's Liberation Army Naval Air Force
PRC	People's Republic of China
RCS	radar cross-section
RHAWS	radar homing and warning system
ROC	Republic of China (Taiwan)
ROCAF	Republic of China Air Force
RoEs	rules of engagement
RWR	radar warning receiver
SAC	Shenyang Aircraft Industry Corporation
SADO	Shenyang Aero-engine Design Office
SAEF	Shenyang Aero Engine Factory (now Shenyang Liming Aero Engine Company – Liming Engine Manufacturing Corporation)
SAM	surface-to-air missile
SARH	semi-active radar homing
SATCOM	satellite communications
SDF	Sino Defence Forum (www.sinodefenceforum.com)
SEAD	suppression of enemy air defences
SEF	Shenyang Aero-Engine Factory
SIGINT	signals intelligence
TACAN	tactical air navigation
UAV	unmanned aerial vehicle
UHF	ultra high frequency
UK	United Kingdom
UN	United Nations
US	United States
USAF	United States Air Force
USD	US Dollars
USSR	Union of Soviet Socialist Republics
VFR	visual flight rules
VHF	very high frequency
VVS	Voenno-Vozdushnye Sily (Soviet Air Force)
XAC	Xi'an Aircraft Industrial Corporation (also Xi'an Aircraft Company)
XAE	Xi'an Aero-Engine Corporation

PREQUEL: 1911–24

China's last imperial dynasty, the Qing dynasty – also referred as the Manchu dynasty – was overthrown in October 1911. China was declared a republic in January 1912, after the boy emperor Xuantong (Hsuan Tung) – also and popularly much better known as Pu-yi – was forced to abdicate. What followed was a period of instability throughout the early 20th century in which China suffered from both internal rebellion and foreign imperialism. Shortly after the declaration of the republic, Dr Sun Yat-sen – widely seen by both mainland China and Taiwan as the 'founding father' of the Republic of China – was elected the first elected provisional President of the Republic of China (ROC) in Nanjing on 29 December 1911. Sun Yat-sen was an inspirational figure in these very early days and the first beginnings of any modern Chinese military aviation were deeply influenced by him. As early as 1911, he initiated studies on how to use aviation technology in a military sense and also established the foundations of a later Chinese aviation industry.[1]

Nevertheless, until this was at least initiated, much ground had to be covered, since the provisional government was actually in a very weak position, with the Chinese Nationalists controlling only the southern and central provinces of the country, some of them having declared independence from the Qing dynasty. For example, this was the case for Mongolia, in 1912, with help from Russia, while insurrections also broke out also in Anhui, Hubei, Hunan, Jiangsu and Sichuan provinces. At best the political situation could be described as chaotic, with numerous warlords exerting their own influence over a vast territory, often using the force of their own armies and sometimes even establishing their own air forces.[2]

Therefore, Sun started his presidency under the most difficult conditions, especially since he lacked the necessary military strength to defeat the Qing government. In addition, in contrast to the south, most of the northern provinces had not followed suit and especially the later all-important capital of Beijing and northern China were under control of General Yuan Shikai, the very autocratic pro-republican commander of the Beiyang Army. Yuan came into power by the former Imperial Court and following Sun Yat-sen's promise to hand over presidency of the new republic, Yuan Shikai agreed and forced the emperor to abdicate. This change in presidency was accomplished in February 1912. However, because of Yuan Shikai's dictatorial methods and especially his ambitions to re-install monarchy with himself as emperor, Sun Yat-sen led an unsuccessful revolt against him in 1913. Sun was forced to seek asylum in Japan in November 1913, where he reorganised the Kuomintang (KMT), or Nationalist Party of China.

Immediately after that failed revolution, Sun Yat-sen attempted to form a group of aviators to build a force against Yuan Shikai.

Insignia of the Chinese Republic/Beiyang government 1914 to 1920s
For the first time Chinese aircraft saw action on several fronts between 1913 and 1917, including against Mongolia, fighting in the Hunan 'White Wolf' uprising and even operations against Sun Yat-sen's southern army. China's first military aircrafts, a dozen Caudron G.IIIs, were delivered in July 1913, and as their markings, they used a five pointed star and the traditional Chinese colours representing the five main ethnic groups: Han Chinese, Mongol, Manchu, Tibetan and Moslem. This is also known as the 'Five races under one union flag'. Later the five-coloured star was replaced by a roundel also showing the five colours before this air force broke up in the 1920s with the rise of different warlords and provincial governments.

The KMT's way – 'aviation as the nation's salvation' during chaotic times

In the end, Yuan Shikai indeed declared himself emperor of China in 1915 but since more and more provinces declared independence – China had therefore become divided between different local military leaders but left without a proper central government – he resigned as emperor in 1916 and died shortly afterwards. After his death, Sun Yat-sen was displaced by a succession of warlords that ruled different parts of a literally fragmented China, which – even with the central government continued functioning in Beijing – had little power outside the city. This chaotic period of warlordism at least allowed Sun to return from his Japanese exile to Guangdong province in 1917, where he advocated the reunification of China. With the help of a few loyal warlords he set up a self-proclaimed military government in Guangzhou and was elected Grand Marshal. An alliance of these provisional governments formed a united front between 1912 and 1927 to rival the Beiyang government in the north, which was internationally recognised as the legitimate Chinese government. Sun also re-formed the former KMT on 10 October 1919 as the new Nationalist Party of China (Chung-kuo Kuomintang or *Zhōngguó guómíndǎng*).

However, his government remained militarily weaker than the local warlords' armies and the Western powers denied the delivery of arms. The leading figure however during that time was General Chen Jiongming, then Governor of Guangdong – also known by its English name Kwangtung – and Commander-in-Chief of the Kwangtung Army[3]. In parallel, due to rising dissatisfaction in the Chinese population, an open and wide-ranging debate evolved regarding how China should react to an increasing fear for spreading Western influence and to replace Chinese culture. The government's weak response to the Treaty of Versailles – especially by allowing Japan to receive territories in Shandong, which had been surrendered by Germany after the Siege of Tsingtao in 1914 –, which was considered unfair by Chinese intellectuals, led to additional unrest including the May Fourth movement. On the other side, these nationalistic demonstrations also influenced the growing of Marxism and its ideas, which became more popular, eventually leading to the founding of the Communist Party of China in 1921.

Besides these constitutional obstacles of the founding period, the provisional government did not have military forces of its own, and its control over elements of the newly established army was quite limited. Moreover, there were still significant forces which were undecided, had not openly declared war against the Qing or were following their own aspirations. With this in mind Sun Yat-sen already noted the significance of aviation to gain effective control over the whole country[4]. Even further, he already pointed to the potential role of air power for future warfare, since in his belief only a well organised and strong political power backed by a substantial and loyal military force could ensure a minimum of security[5].

Following the establishment of a military government in Guangzhou – also and especially formerly better known as Canton – in 1917, the first steps towards an air force was the foundation of an aviation bureau within the Grand Marshal Office. Here also a first flying squadron and finally an aviation school were set up. Already between 1915–16 a group of Chinese students were sent to the United States with the aim to purchase aircraft and to receive basic flight training. For additional help Sun Yat-sen tried to obtain aid from the Western democracies but regrettably, these were ignored and additionally severely hampered by an international arms embargo, set in place to stabilise the political situation and prevent a civil war. As such, for some time the only aircraft were two Curtiss trainers and three World War I-era German aircraft acquired via commercial channels.

1   https://books.google.de/books?id=qle3CwAAQBAJ&pg=PA35&lpg=PA35&dq=Chinese+warlords+air+forces&source=bl&ots=OqU79bEwQg&sig=ACfU3U0M6LARK2xswSFm-GsGo1HxCccpvw&hl=de&sa=X&ved=2ahUKEwiC_b334oPhAhWFLlAKHWHlBOcQ6AEwDHoECAoQAQ#v=onepage&q=Chineseper cent20warlordsper cent20airper cent20forces&f=false and https://www.reddit.com/r/AskHistorians/comments/6u27c3/did_the_chinese_have_an_air_force_during_the/

2   via http://storm.prohosting.com/cwlam/part1.htm

    This is a short list of several known warlord, provincial and communist air forces, which operated an independent air arm between 1920 and 1949 often with individual and unknown markings:

    • Chen Jitong: Operated in Guandong province until 1936
    • Fukien People's Republic Air Force: based at Hangkow between 1933 and 1938, this air force appears to have inherited the inventory of Tsai Ting-kai as listed below
    • General Liu Wen-loILiu Hsiang: operated at Chengtu, Szechuan provinces between 1930 and 1932
    • Lung Yun: operated in Yunnan 1926–33
    • Tsai Ting-kai: operated between August and October 1933, location unknown Chinese White Army
    • Tuchun, son ot Ch'uan-Fang: based in Tchekiang province, 1926–27
    • Unknown Warlord: operated between Peking and Hangkow
    • Yen Hsi-shan: based in Shansi province at Taiyuanfu with Japanese flight Instructors 1921–1949

    See also ANDERSSON, L., *A history of Chinese Aviation – Encyclopedia of Aircraft and Aviation in China until 1949* (Taipei: AHS of ROC, 2008)

3   For more information see ANDERSSON, L., *A history of Chinese Aviation – Encyclopedia of Aircraft and Aviation in China until 1949* (Taipei: AHS of ROC, 2008)

4   See XIAMING ZHANG, *Red Wings over the Yalu*, chapter 1, pp 13–17 [based of Chen Xipi, ed., 'Sun Zhongshan nianpu changbian' (A long edition of the chronicle of Sun Yatsen)]

5   See BUESCHEL, R. M., *Communist Chinese Air Power*, 1968 – Part One/Chapter I 'Communist China finds Wings'.

EARLY YEARS: 1924–49

Interestingly, this arms embargo – originally imposed to end the civil strife in China – was only introduced and upheld by the Western powers. The Soviets, however – even with the same goal in mind – initiated a dual policy of support for both the KMT and the newly established Chinese Communist Party (CCP). In 1921, representatives of the Communist International (Comintern) proposed the foundation of a military academy to train the revolutionary army. In line with these proposed restructurings, the Soviets' military advisor and political commissar Mikhail Borodin was in China during September 1923 with the duty given by Sun Yat-sen to analyse and to reorganise the military forces. He not only initiated the establishment of the famous Whampoa Military Academy (later Huangpu-Military Academy and now Republic of China Military Academy) with Chiang Kai-Shek being appointed the first commander but also recommended the delivery of Soviet arms and military equipment to the KMT government in Canton. Even further, he proposed the united front of the KMT and CCP, when he urged the Chinese Communist Party to join forces with the Nationalists. This First United Front (also known as the KMT–CCP Alliance) was formed in 1922 as an alliance against the numerous warlords and to form a new central government in China. In parallel to the Soviet advisors, help in aviation matters was also sought from Germany.

After the KMT defeated General Chen Jiongming (Chen Ciung-ming) in 1923 in Guangdong the alliance was formed officially in 1926 as the so-called National Revolutionary Army, which was sent out during the famous Northern Expedition. However, the fight against the warlords was for both groups only a forwarded reason, since the real intentions for both groups were quite different: the Communists wanted to use the KMT's superiority in numbers to help spreading Communism and Marxism in China, while on the other side the Nationalists had the aim to control the communists from within. As such, the alliance was weak and unsustainable in the longer term. In the meantime, in line with the restructuring and military reform also first steps towards an air force were initiated: already between April and May 1923 a group of aviators, which had received their training in the US, were based at Sun Yat-sen's headquarters in Canton and several of the damaged aircraft were recovered and repaired. Additionally, an aviation bureau was founded.

With Sun Yat-sen's turn to the Soviets and the arrival of the first Soviet advisors in Canton during autumn 1923 – quite coincidently with the arrival of the first Germans instructors – Marshal Vasily Konstantinovich Blücher, better known as General Galen, became the appointed Chief Military Advisor. In 1924 the Aviation Bureau was reorganised into an aviation department and from 1925 on it was led – at least officially – by Wang Jingwei, then chairman of the KMT Political Council and second in com-

mand to General Chiang Kai-shek. The actual director however was still the Soviet advisor Victor P. Rogachev. This aviation department or aviation bureau as it is also often still known consisted of a flying school, which was founded in December 1924 at Tungshan equipped with Curtiss Jenny trainers. In addition, an army air squadron was formed, which was equipped with Russian-built Polikarpov U-1 Avrushka trainers (Avro 504K), Polikarpov R-1.M-5 reconnaissance bombers (de Havilland/Airco D.H.9A) and Junkers-Fili F.13 transports. Noteworthy in this regard is that the first class of aviator students were chosen from the newly established Whampoa Military Academy and five more were sent to the Soviet Union to receive their training there. By October 1926, the last German instructor was dismissed and as a consequence, Aviation in Canton was now in Russian hands.

Canton government – Shan Chung Aviation Team 1921–25
Predecessor to the later first central KMT air force was the so-called Shan Chung Aviation Team established by Sun Yat-sen in Canton. Reportedly following Sun Yat-sen's death on 12 March 1925 the Chinese characters were added and quite confusing both names 'Chung Shan' (as shown above) and 'Shan Chung' (with Chinese characters in reversed order) are known on several R-1.M-5, MS AR & FBA and Breguet 14.

Even after the flight training of both CCP and KMT members had begun jointly, it took place quite separated and both remained mostly with their own respective forces. Additional disagreements between the KMT general staff and the Russians led to the downgrade of their advisor status. New commander of the Aviation Bureau – and with this task also being appointed Chief of the Air Force – became Colonel Lim Wei-cheng (sometimes also written Lum Wai-sing or even Lam Huei-hsing). With these growing rifts between the Soviet advisors and the KMT, the air force of the revolutionary movement began to split into two groups: the first one following Chiang Kai-shek while the second one loyal to Mikhail Borodin and Marshal Vasily Konstantinovich Blücher.

By mid to late 1926 with now about 200 aircraft operational – main forces were the IV and VII Corps of the KMT armies – both parties jointly started the Northern Expedition on 1 July 1926 as an advance towards the north, defeating one warlord after the other. Following Chinese sources the KMT forces used 13 British-supplied de Havilland/Airco DH.9A reconnaissance bombers, but since Great Britain was a signatory of the embargo these were most likely Russian built Polikarpov R-1.M-5.[1] Especially the professionalism of the Russian-trained KMT pilots led to a high reputation among the own troops as well as the foes. Tragically Sun Yat-sen had died in the meantime in 1925, while the troops were preceding quickly capturing Wuhan (Wuchang) in late 1926, Hangzhou, Shanghai and Nanjing (Nanking) in early 1927 and finally Beijing in 1928. Sun Yat-sen's successor and leadership of the KMT became General Chiang Kai-shek, who was declared Commander-in-Chief of the Army, Navy and Air Force on 5 June 1926.

In retrospect, even if Sun Yat-sen was not able to see the fruits of his initiations, the PLAAF '...literally regards Sun as one of the few Chinese able to articulate an understanding of the potential role of air power, even though his view on the subject was indeed sporadic.'[2] Quite noteworthy, after Nanjing was captured by the KMT about halfway through the Northern Expedition in 1927, the city was declared to be the national capital despite other Nationalists had already made Wuhan the capital. This decision was not only strategic, but even more of symbolic importance, since it was here that the original republic was established in 1912, the original provisional government sat, and Sun Yat-sen was finally buried.

KMT/Central Government, Nanking 1925–38

Following Sun Yat-sen's revolution in 1923, the Nationalist regime began with the formation of a new central KMT air force at Nanking. A first step was already the establishment of an Aviation Bureau in 1925 with Soviet aircraft and training assistance. At around that time the well-known 12-pointed star and blue disc symbol was officially introduced, however already before 1927 one with a red outline – similar to the one of the Kwangsi Air Force – was still used. Later other warlords and provincial governments joined the central government in their effort to fight the Japanese following the Japanese invasion of China in July 1937. Typical aircraft seen in this livery were Corsair V65 and Douglas O2MC4.

Chinese Naval Aviation 1927–38

Besides the KMT central government's air force also a small naval aviation detachment was formed at Fuzhou (Foochow). This predecessor to the later PLA Naval Aviation was operated as the KMT Naval Air Service between 1927 and 1938, but in the end was not too successful. Markings were not uniformly applied, and several variations were used in addition to those of the Central Government.

Aircraft worth to mention were the Ning Hae 2 and Biing 1 (also listed as Aichi Experimental AB-3 Ning Hai 1 and Hsin-1 Ning Hai 2).[3]

Besides the 'official' Chinese government's central air forces, several local governments, regional commanders or even warlords established their own air forces. These were later – especially during the times of changing alliances and loyalties during the Civil War – often later united into the later Nationalist's CAF or the Communist forces and frequently existed only briefly.[4]

Kwangsi Air Force 1924–37

At the beginning, around 60 aircraft including Armstrong Whitworth Atlas, Avro Avian and Avro 631 Cadet were operated by Kwangsi Air Force, which opposed the KMT government. However, following the outbreak of war with Japan, the Kwangsi Air Force merged with the KMT forces in July 1937.

Shantung Air Force 1925–28

In 1925, Shantung Warlord Zhang Zongchang (Chang Tsung-ch'ang) set up an Aviation Training School, which was later expanded with the help of Manchurian Air Force. A few German Junkers aircrafts were obtained, including F-13 and K-53. Finally, in 1928 all air-

crafts were flown to Mukden and the Shantung Air Force was amalgamated with the Manchurian Air Force.

Manchurian Air Force pre-1931

Until 1925, Manchuria was ruled by the local Warlord Zhang Zuolin (Chang Tso-lin) and later succeeded by his son Zhang Xueliang (Chang Hsueh-liang or Chang Hsüeh-liang). In that same year, the province switched its allegiance to the central KMT government, although it maintained an autonomous air force containing several Breguet 19, Caudron G.III and de Havilland D.H.60G Gipsy Moth – at Mukden, the later Shenyang. It should also be noted that both Changs also maintained their own private air forces at Fengtein in addition to controlling the Manchurian Air Force. And to confuse the situation even further, Marshall Zhang Zuolin's commander-in-chief, Chan Tsung-chang, also maintained an air force at Tsinanpu. The insignia illustrated here are supposed alternative renditions of the Manchurian Air Force markings shown above. Quite unconfirmed it could also be that the example shown could be a misinterpretation of this variant in which the tail striping could also have been made up with the red band replaced with red, blue and yellow stripes.

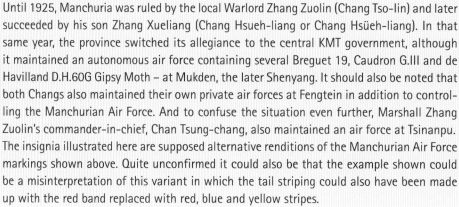

Sinkiang 1927–40

In Dihua (known today as Ürümqi or Ürümchi), the capital of Xinjiang in Northern China the warlord Sheng Shicai (Cheng-Chi-Tsai) also established a small air force that was receiving Soviet aid including aircraft like several Polikarpov R-5, I-15 and I-16.

Unfortunately, these first air force ambitions were still severely hampered by the overall political instability and with each military success, the split between the KMT and the CCP became ever wider. Following the successful Northern Expedition between 1926 and 1928, which culminated in the demise of the Beiyang government and the reunification, the KMT took over most of China's territories. Additionally, the KMT itself had begun to split into a left- and right-wing faction leading the CCP and the left wing of the KMT to move the KMT government from Guangzhou to Wuhan, where the Communists were dominating but leaving the nominal capital in Nanjing. Therefore, Chiang Kai-shek purged[5] the KMT – while the Northern Expedition was still half-complete – of leftists and hundreds of CCP members were arrested or even executed in the so-called April 12 Incident or Shanghai Massacre of 1927. As a result, and even further aided by the deepening of the social crisis, rising tensions between Japan and China, the First United Front was terminated. The ideological confrontation between both parties led to the KMT and the CCP turning against each other, which initiated the first phase of the Chinese Civil War in April 1927.

In parallel to these internal rivalries, this had resulted in a temporary move of the Soviet advisor staff to Nanchang in December 1926 but already on 27 April 1927, the Politburo in Moscow ordered all advisors to leave Canton and to serve now for the Wuhan government in Hankou (Hankow). This also led to the postponement of all aircraft deliveries and finally in July 1927 the Soviet advisors left China after the break of the CCP with the Wuhan Government. The aircraft, which were left over were immediately incorporated into the new Canton (Kwangtung) Air Force. For the aims in building up a functioning air force this meant again a severe setback and viable achievements were only possible after the embargo was lifted in 1929, even if the KMT leadership insisted again in the potential of an air force in uniting China under KMT control.

Manchukuo Air Transport Company (MKKK) 1932–45[6]

Occupied in 1931–32 by Japan, the Manchurian Air Force was partially revived in September 1931 at first, when the Japanese occupation forces established a para-military airline, Manchukuo National Airways (Manshū kōkū kabushiki gaisha or Manchu Kokuyuso Kabushiki Kaisha, MKKK) sometimes referred to as Manchukuo Air Transport Company. This however acted only as a puppet air force in support of Japan, with the task of simple air transport and photographic reconnaissance missions. As a 'national' symbol this air force revived the original five Chinese colours shown and known aircraft with this marking were a few Junkers Ju-86, Fokker Super Universal build under licence as the Nakajima Ki-6 and Nakajima Ki-34. Additionally several other types were flown in Manchuria/Manchukuo but often they cannot be assigned to any particular air arm.

Manchukuo Air Force 1938–45

A fully fledged Manchukuo Air Force – officially the Manchukuo Imperial Air Force – was formed then in February 1937 also by the Japanese. The aircraft including Nakajima Ki-27 Type 97, Tachikawa Ki-36 and Nakajima Ki-43 Hayabusa aircraft wore the horizontally striped roundels on the wings only. By 1944 this air force was struggling to survive, especially after Japanese surrender, although there are reports of operations against occupying Soviet forces even in August 1945.

Re-formed Government of China 1938–40

Again under the occupation-government, the Japanese Army organised a local army in order to defend the Nanjing Regime (Nanking) in 1938. This air force was called the Re-formed Government of China Air Force by 1938 and was equipped only with Japanese gliders and tasked with pilot training.

National Government of China Air Force 1940–45

The National Government of China was formed in 1940 by the combination of the Japanese controlled Nanking and Peking governments. Again, Japan allowed the formation of an air force, which had its roots in the Re-formed Government of China Air Force from 1938. As such it was renamed the National Government of China Air Force or Cochin China Air Force in 1940 and received – depending on source – several Nakajima Ki-34, Nakajima Ki-27b Tachikawa Ki-55, Tachikawa Ki-9 and Nakajima Ki-43Ia Hayabusa aircraft. However, other sources say that a unit equipped with the Ki-27 fighters was only proposed, but since the Japanese never trusted the Chinese enough, they were never delivered.

Canton Air Force 1933–36
Under General Wong Kwang-yu (?) the Canton Air Force operated around 90 aircraft including several Douglas O-2MC-4. During its brief existence, it used a typical KMT-like symbol with red-outlined roundels on wings and rudders. Finally, in July 1936 the complete air arm defected en-masse to the KMT.

Kweichow Air Force 1933–36
In February 1933 General Wang Chia-lieh (?) became governor of Kweichow and a Military Aviation School was established at Kweiyang led by Brigadier General Chou Yi-ping (Chow Yat-ping?), the commandant of the Kweichow Army Air Corps. Besides that a small number of US-made Fleet trainers were operated. Finally in January 1935 the Central Government of Nanking gained control over Kweichow and all remaining aircraft were incorporated into the regular air force.

Plans to establish a Communist air force in parallel

Again, the political situation during the Civil War between 1927 and 1937 was thus more than chaotic. Following the unsuccessful Autumn Harvest Uprising on 7 September 1927 in Hunan led by Mao Zedong to gain control back in cities like Changsha, Guangzhou, Nanchang and Shantou, the Communists were forced to retreat underground or to the countryside where they fomented a military revolt. Additionally the suppression of the CCP in Shanghai and other cities finally drove many supporters to rural strongholds like the Jiangxi Soviet led by Mao Zedong. These movements grew even stronger and by 1928 – filled with deserters and defecting KMT units, supplemented by peasants from these Communist rural soviets – the Chinese Workers' and Peasants' Red Army was founded.

On the other side, the Nationalists resumed their campaign against the warlords and captured finally Beijing – the old northern capital – in June 1928, renaming it to Peiping (sometimes then also known Peking). From now on most of eastern China was under control of the central KMT government in Nanjing. However, there were now three capitals in China: the internationally recognised republic capital in Beijing, the CCP's and left-wing KMT bastion at Wuhan and the right-wing KMT regime at Nanjing, which would remain the KMT capital for the next decade.

Concerning the establishment of a Communist air force, parts of the KMT forces broke away and assembled a new army in Nanchang under command of Marshal Zhu De, the later founder of the PLA. Sadly, the few aircraft in communists hand were soon destroyed or lost by accidents leaving all chances of building up an own Communist Air Force within the newly established Red or Communist Army of China, which later became the People's Liberation Army (PLA) had vanished. At about that time Zhu De and Mao Zedong (Mao Tse-tung) met for the first time.

Meanwhile, however, the Communists became strong in several parts of China, and in August 1927 they started an uprising against the KMT under leadership of Mao Zedong. While this war was raging back and forth, in 1931 the Japanese invaded Manchuria, where a puppet regime was installed that remained in power until 1940, ruling a state now named Manchukuo. Another similar regime was established in Nanking, after the Japanese continued their invasion deeper into China. Both regimes in Manchukuo and in Nanking were based on anti-KMT elements, mainly former warlords, but in 1940 they were superseded by the so-called Re-formed National Government of China, established at Nanking and led by Wang Jingwei, a former associate but now a rival of Chiang Kai-shek.

Following the success against the warlords, the KMT turned against the Communists between 1927 and 1937 – known in mainland China as the Ten-Year Civil War – in altogether five encirclement campaigns. During most of these campaigns, the KMT forces proceeded swiftly into the Communist-held areas, but because of the vast countryside they were easily engulfed, and it was not possible to consolidate their occupations. The Communists on the other hand reacted often only with guerilla operations or simply by avoiding major military clashes. In October 1934, under the command of Mao Zedong and Zhou Enlai, a massive military retreat of their Red Army (First Front Army of the Chinese Soviet Republic) – the forerunner of the later People's Liberation Army – finally began from the Jiangxi province until they reached the inner Shaanxi province; this became known as the famous Long March. Even if surely a massive retreat, with the Long March Mao Zedong's rise to unquestioned leadership begun, in line with a complete degrade of all other communist rivals.

Quite understandable these even more chaotic times opened up not the best possibilities to establish an air force, but especially under the emerging treats of both the Civil War against the Communists and the Japanese advance the build-up of an air force became again a top priority for the Nationalists. This was again discussed at a National Aviation Conference in Nanjing in April 1931 and since the embargo was lifted in 1929, this situation now permitted the delivery from all available sources, leading to a substantial number of Soviet as well as US and Italian aircraft being introduced during that time. Based on the eagerness of building a viable force within shortest time, also a new national training programme was initiated at the newly established Central Aviation School in Hangzhou in 1932 now led by American Colonel John H. Jouett and Italian advisors; this also marked the beginning to shift to Western assistance within the KMT, while the CCP still stood to the Soviet side.

As such between 1932 and 1936, the KMT Air Force operated 72 Douglas O-2MC attack bombers and 20 Vought V-92C Corsairs, as well as 24 Heinkel He 66Ch biplane dive bombers, which were used mainly for counter-insurgency as well as close support operations. Additional types were Curtiss Hawk II and III fighters, Northrop 2-E bombers and Vought V-65 light bombers as well as a few long-range bombers like the Martin B-10 and Savoia S.81.[7] Until then at least nine squadrons were operational flying around 600 aircraft of very different types.

However nearly all this progress was destroyed within the first weeks following the outbreak of the Sino-Japanese War in July 1937. By the end of the year only about 80 aircraft were left, but thanks to Russian assistance between 1937 and 1941 followed by increasing US help from 1942 on at least a minimal force could be held operational against the Japanese. According to Chinese sources[8] the Soviet Union delivered 222 Polikarpov I-15 and 75 Polikarpov I-153 biplane fighters and 197 Polikarpov I-16 fighters, 279 Tupolev SB-2 light bombers, 24 Ilyushin DB-3 medium bombers and 18 Tupolev TB-3 heavy bombers, which were complemented and replaced later by different US

Very little is known about the 'Marx'. This is the sole known image of the aircraft, with Lin Biao (left) and Nie Rongzhen (right) in front of it. (via Bai Wei)

Captain Long Wenguang was the pilot of the later 'Lenin'. Later he joined the ranks of the PLA.
(via Bai Wei)

The replica of the 'Lenin' as exhibited in the National Aeronautic Museum in Beijing.
(via Bai Wei)

types. Especially these US deliveries made the Nationalist not only the strongest air force but gave the KMT nearly a monopoly on air power against Japanese forces and the Communists as well. The later build-up and development of the ROC AF from now on will be ignored; it would be worth a book on its own.

On the other side the Communists were able to acquire only a few aircraft from local warlords during the early years of the Civil War including some Avro 594 Avian IV trainers but actually none of them was virtually useable for aerial combat operations. As such, the first real Communist combat aircraft – a replica of it is exhibited in the National Aeronautic Museum – became a captured CAF Vought Corsair V-65-C1 on 28 February 1930. It was forced to land after it run out of fuel and was painted light grey, as a national symbol a simple five-pointed star in red was painted on the wings and it was renamed 'Lenin' ('Lei Ning'). Operationally, it was used for about two years for leaflet-dropping, communication and reconnaissance missions. Interestingly, there are two different versions of its later fate: following the PLAAF, the 'Lenin' was dismantled in July 1932 and hidden in a remote mountain area until it was discovered only in 1951[9]. In contrast the Nationalists claim that the 'Lenin' was shot down on 5 October 1936 and a photograph is still on display at the Chinese Military Museum in Taiwan[10]. The second combat aircraft was then a former Nationalist Douglas O-2MC-4 'found' behind the Communist lines in Changzhou, Yan'an in April 1932 (other sources speak of a 'Moth'). Following a quick repair and rebuild it was re-named 'Marx' and handed over to Mao's Jiangxi Soviet, which was established in 1929. But it also was not used in combat and later abandoned.

Vought Corsair V-65-C1 renamed 'Lenin' ('Lei Ning')
First aircraft of the Red Army 1930
Most readers are quite familiar with the current PLAAF symbol: a red and yellow star-and-bar with a symbolised 'Ba Yi' meaning 1 August in remembrance of the founding day of the PLA on 1 August 1927. However, the current insignia was not the only one and also not the final one used by the Chinese Communist's Red Army of China in the early years until the founding of the People's Republic of China: even during the pre-PLAAF era at least five different national insignias were used.

1937-45: until the Second United Front during the Second Sino-Japanese War

Even during the Japanese invasion and following occupation of Manchuria, Chiang Kai-shek still saw the Communists as a greater threat and at first refused an alliance. However, this lasted until the so-called Xi'an Incident in December 1936 when Chiang Kai-shek was kidnapped by KMT generals – including Zhang Xueliang – and forced to form the Second United Front against the invading Japanese.

But since history often repeats itself, also this was not a real alliance and each party tried to gain as much territorial advantage for its own group as possible. It also led to major clashes between the Communist and KMT forces in late 1940 and early

1941 – especially the so-called New Fourth Army incident – and effectively ended any substantial cooperation in preparation of the inevitable following the civil war. In general, the overall political favour shifted to the Communists, since the resistance to the Japanese proved too costly to Chiang Kai-shek's Nationalists. By the end of this Sino-Japanese War, the Communists were in control of nearly all territories in northern China not controlled by Japan or its puppet forces.

A very rare image of two Polikarpov I-16s with Sinkiang Aviation School markings. (via CDF)

Besides this constant up-and-down of the KMT Air Force, the Communists too proceeded with their preparations to build up an air force, especially in mind of a strong Soviet presence in Xinjiang (Sinkiang), giving a new opportunity for a CCP-Soviet-cooperation. In May 1937 the CCP established a military academy called New Camp in Dihua – this town is known today as Ürümqi or Ürümchi, but also *Wūlǔmùqí* (Pinyin) or even Tihwa (Wade-Giles) – the capital of Xinjiang. Xinjiang was ideally suited, since it was the main overland route for the Soviet arms deliveries to the Nationalists and as such it was already a strong Communist base in northern China. Additionally, the CCP leadership suggested an alliance with the local warlord Sheng Shicai (Cheng-Chi-Tsai), who was also receiving Soviet aid including aircraft like several Polikarpov R-5, I-15 and I-16. The resulting unit is often referred as the Xinjiang Aviation Unit (or Sinkiang Aviation School). However even if until early 1941 virtually only a limited flight training was possible, and besides the fact that this cooperation was only briefly, when Sheng Shicai changed sides to the Nationalists in summer 1942, several Communists earned their wings within that unit. Even more important – at least in view of the PLAAF history – the Xinjiang Aviation Unit can be seen as the fundament of any later Chinese Communist Air Force and the close relations to the Soviet training system and doctrine[11].

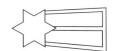

Sinkiang Aviation School 1936

The next 'national' symbol used by Communist forces was actually not a national symbol but more an organisational one or unit badge. Following an agreement between the government of the Sinkiang (now Xinjiang) Autonomy and Chinese Communist, a few officers were selected from Red Army units and sent to the Sinkiang Aviation School to receive basic flight training in 1936. Not many aircraft used this insignia but examples included several Polikarpov R-5s, I-15s and I-16s.

1946-49: the Yan'an Years and the end of the KMT Air Force

As already noted (and even if most readers might wonder, why the first part was mostly about reflecting so long the history of the Chinese Air Force under the influence of the Nationalists besides the mentioned short intermediate Communist episodes) it is nearly impossible to separate the 'hampered build-up' from the historical events and their consequences. Additionally, it is quite difficult to ignore pure KMT- or CAF-related steps from the Communists intention to create an air force, since often both are interdependent.

Besides all these most likely chaotic or parallel running timelines, the history of the real later PLAAF born out of the Communists steps to build an air force actually already begun in 1924 too, during the brief united phase of both the first KMT and the CCP, when in September Sun Yat-sen's Guangzhou Revolutionary Government established as an first initiative an Aviation Bureau together with a military flying school at the Huangpu Military Academy in Guangzhou. Within the next 12 months 50 members of both parties received a basic training between 1924 and 1925 in two classes. Later on, 18 of those cadets – 9 CCP and 9 KMT – were sent to the Soviet Union for advanced flight training, where this group stayed until March 1927. Members of this group were both later 'founders' of the PLAAF: Chang Qiankun and Wang Bi.

Interestingly, the driving factor behind these efforts on behalf of the Communists was not the creation of an air force, but simply the Communist party's struggle for and efforts to consolidate their power. Until September 1938 both Chang Qiankun and Wang Bi served in the Soviet Air Force, when they returned home and served as military instructors at Dihua in Xinjiang. About two years later in October 1940 they left to Yan'an and proposed the establishment of an aviation school to train their own air force members without dependence of Soviet assistance. Consequently, this phase is often called the Yan'an Years or Yan'an Period although Mao did not move to Yan'an until December 1936. At about the same time several members of those, who have been in the Soviet Union suggested a closer cooperation and the open request for arms delivery to the CCP but as Xiaoming Zhang states, 'Mao doubted, however, that Moscow would bypass the KMT, and was afraid the CCP could not pay for such help. He appreciated the aviators' enthusiasm but urged them to be patient'[12].

The first real steps towards the subsequent PLAAF were then initiated between 1941 and 1945, firstly with the creation of an Aviation Engineering School (also known as the Air Force Engineering School) – albeit without aircraft, pilots or airfields – in January 1941. Its aim was to teach the basics of aviation theory, mathematics, physics and most importantly the Russian language. However, with the civil war still raging, in early 1943 the studies had to be suspended with only one pilot – Liu Yuti, who later became an ace in the Korean War – having graduated. The second step, in early 1944, was the re-establishment of the once proposed school, now known as the 18th Group Army Engineering School. Additionally these efforts culminated in May 1944 with the establishment of a Central Military Commission's (CMC[13]) subordinated Aviation Section at Yan'an; a town in Shaanxi province, where the communists were based, with Chang Qiankun being appointed director (and the first commander) and and Wang Bi as vice-director and chief instructor of the school. The school itself was responsible for teaching the basics in aviation theory and aviation armament, whereas the Aviation Section – also known as Aviation Office – was tasked responsible for all national aviation matters – especially the rebuilding of airfield in Yan'an and the acquisition of aircraft and equipment – under the 18th Group Army's General Staff Department. The immense importance in Yan'an and Manchuria was because of the already established training facilities there left over from the former Japanese Kwantung Army's 2nd Air Army. Besides these organisational issues and the beginning flight training, one main aim was to gather as many aircraft and abandoned equipment from the Japanese forces since another civil war between the KMT and the Communists seemed inevitable.

By October 1945 however the newly established Aviation Section was disbanded again leading to a series of reorganisations one after another on the way to establish an operating air force. Also, efforts to regain abandoned aircraft resulted in altogether 120 aircraft being collected in Manchuria. Following this a specialised Aviation School was first set up as the Northeast Old Aviation School in Tonghua (also known as the Northeast Democratic United Army Aviation School) in the Jilin province, northeast China on 1 March 1946 as the very first PLA flying school. It was built around former members of the Japanese Air Force – especially instructors and ground support personnel – who remained in China after the Japanese surrender and equipped with about 40 Japanese aircraft[14].

Red Army of China Air Force 1944

Following the surrender of the Japanese forces in 1944, several aircraft were captured by Communist forces in northern China and introduced into the newly established Red Army Air Arm. For simplicity only Chinese characters were painted over the original red Japanese roundels in white, representing CHICOM (Chinese Communists). Most likely as an insurance to prevent Allied attacks, a standard KMT roundel with the blue-white 'Sun Yatsen-sun' was painted on the tail. Examples for this marking are former Japanese Army Air Force Tachikawa Ki-54.

Red Army of China Air Force 1946–47

The next step on the way to establishing the later PLAAF, a Communist Aviation School was setup in Manchuria. Presumably because of the same political reason all aircraft wore briefly the same National Chinese blue-white roundel together with four blue and three white stripes on the tail rudder.

Finally Japan's campaign was defeated in 1945, marking the end of World War II. This again resumed China's full-scale civil war between CCP and KMT forces only one year later, when negotiations failed in June 1946 (war broke out on 26 June); in China this war is known as the War of Liberation. Interestingly, in line with the CCP-KMT negotiations, Mao Zedong acquired his first 'personal' aircraft, when a former USAAF Douglas C-47 was given by the American Ambassador General Patrick J. Hurley to arrange the transfer of CCP members from Yan'an to Chongqing (Chungking). Later Mao Zedong did not return the aircraft, which was then used with Chinese Communist markings over the original olive drab as his personal transport and mobile headquarter during the civil war.

Most of the other additional equipment and aircraft then acquired, were from the Japanese forces following their surrender, when the Red Army overran the former Japanese-held territories in Manchuria. Nearly all Japanese Army aircraft were handed over to the Communists making the new 'Red Chinese Air Force' theoretically the strongest air arm in northern China with modern Nakajima Ki-43 Type 1 Hayabusa ('Oscar'), Nakajima Ki-44 Type 2 Shoki ('Tojo'), Kawasaki Ki-45 Toryu ('Nick'), Nakajima Ki-84 Type 4 Hayate ('Frank'), and Kawasaki Ki-61 Type 3 Hien ('Tony') fighters plus more than 100 Ki-30 ('Ann') Mitsubishi Ki-51 Type 99 ('Sonia') and Kawasaki Ki-48 Type 99 Sokei ('Lily') ground attack and light bombers. Even more important were the numerous transports – mostly Nakajima Ki-34 Type 97 ('Thora'), Tachikawa Ki-54c

Type 1 ('Hickory') and Mitsubishi Ki-57 Type 100 ('Topsy') – and trainers – especially Tachikawa Ki-54a Type 1, Tachikawa Ki-55 Type 99 ('Ida') and Manshu Ki-79 Type 2 (Ki-27), Kokusai Ki-86 (Bücker Bü 131) – from the major Japanese bases in Mukden (later Shenyang) and Harbin. However, of this vast number of airplanes, only 120 aircraft have been collected until December 1945 and about 40 were chosen to be made operationally useable. Another – especially political and psychological – important source for aircraft and trained personnel were defecting members of the 'former' CAF, who were dissatisfied with the government's corruption or incompetence. One example of this was a B-24J Liberator, which landed in Yan'an in June 1946, – albeit it was never used as an operational combat type[15]. Another maybe equal important issue was to persuade as many as possible former Japanese pilots and ground-crews to stay in China, because of the lack of own trained aviation personnel.

However due to KMT harassment and an offensive in Manchuria in early 1946, the Northeast Old Aviation School in Tonghua (dongbei lao hangxiao) had some troubled early years and needed to be relocated twice: it had to move in spring – 1 May 1946 – to Mudanjiang in the northern Manchuria, where the first class began in July with only four basic and a few additional Ki-55 Type 99 advanced trainers. In November it had to be moved even further north to Dongan near the Xingkai lake (also known as the Khanka Lake) near the Soviet border and finally from here it was relocated again back to Mudanjiang in November 1948. As such despite several problems – especially the lack of instructors – , the core of the real PLAAF was formed and many of the first PLAAF pilots were trained by Japanese in Manchuria during these years. Here also the fundament of the future PLAAF's trainings system and doctrine[16] was laid down.

Finding a common insignia for the PLAAF
Following the altogether four different insignias used during the pre-PLAAF era between 1930 and 1947 – in some cases even 1949 –, again four different insignias followed until the final star-and-bar symbol was selected.

1. Red Army of China Air Force 1946–49
Even if the 'faked' KMT colours might have the desired effect, they also led to confusion on the own forces. As a result, and in order to avoid misidentifications with KMT aircraft, all Communist aircraft had to wear this Red Army of China national marking between 1947 and 1950. It consisted of a symbolised star on the white red-outlined roundel again including the Chinese characters for 'China' Zhong'. However, it was used mainly by aircraft from the Communist Aviation School in Manchuria and those assigned to the 1st Squadron of the Air Combat Group. Again, these were former Japanese types like the Kawasaki Ki-45, Mitsubishi Ki.-30 Ann, Mitsubishi Ki-46 and Nakajima Ki-43 Hayabusa and Tachikawa Ki-55.

2. PLAAF 1946–49
Even before the real PLAAF was founded, three more concurring symbols were used between 1946 and 1949 or even 1950 in parallel to the one mainly used by the Aviation School in Manchuria. This one was seen on a few Ki-79a and Ki-79b trainers in northern China and Manchuria but also at the Sian Air Academy and consisted of again a simple red star with a slim white outline worn on the wings and fuselage.

3. PLAAF 1946–50

This second attempt also included this simplified curved star and circle roundel was used on several types between 1946 and 1950. This was the first national marking that included Chinese characters representing the 'Ba Yi' formation date of the Red Army of China on 1 August 1928. Representative types Kawasaki Ki-45, Mitsubishi Ki-30, Mitsubishi Ki-46, Mitsubishi Ki-51 and Tachikawa Ki-55.

4. PLAAF 1946–49

The final step to the definitive insignia as known today was this star insignia with four additional bars in Red and White. It made its first appearance as a national symbol at around 1946 and reportedly applied to several aircraft types including some very early MiG-15.

War is over and the retreat of the KMT to Taiwan

In line with these events, following the previous war-weary battles and because of a heavy inflation and political corruption, the central KMT government was never able to consolidate its power again especially in northern China. In contrast to them, the Communists were able to do so step by step and as such the period between 1937 and 1947 is often called the Yan'an Years. After about four years of fighting, by late 1948 the Communists captured the northern cities of Shenyang (Mukden) and Changchun seizing control of most of the northeast. On 21 April, the CCP forces crossed the Yangtze River and captured the KMT's capital Nanjing. By late 1949, the People's Liberation Army was pursuing remnants of KMT forces southwards in southern China resulting in a step-by-step retreat of the Nationalists from Nanjing in April to finally Taipei in December 1949, taking with them the remains of the former ROC Air Force. What the Nationalists left, was in most cases later introduced into the later PLAAF.

With the Communists now controlling the whole mainland China including the important Hainan Island by April, the major military hostilities were ending de facto in 1950[17]. Finally, on 1 October 1949, Mao Zedong proclaimed the new People's Republic of China with the capital Beijing, which was again renamed from Beiping. This date also marked the first major public appearances of the not yet established PLAAF, when on 1 October 1949 17 warplanes of the first aviation squadron of the PLA overflew the Tiananmen Square in Beijing in a military parade to celebrate the founding of the People's Republic of China. These included nine P-51D, two DH.98 bomber, three C-46 transports, two PT-19 trainers and one L-5 liaison aircraft.

In contrast, General Chiang Kai-shek and the Nationalists proclaimed Taipei – or better-known Taiwan – as the capital of the Republic of China as the sole legitimate government of China. Interestingly, until today no armistice or peace treaty has been signed and as such, there is still controversy as to whether the Civil War has legally ended.

1   See Xiaoming Zhang, *Red Wings over the Yalu*, p 16 and note 20.

2   See Xiaoming Zhang, p 15.

3   See http://cwlam2000hk.sinaman.com/cafx10.htm

4   For more information see also http://flagspot.net/flags/cn~round.html

5   'Century of Flight – Aviation during World War II', an online article on the 'Chinese Air Force'
    http://www.century-of-flight.net/Aviationper cent20history/WW2/china_force.htm

6   See http://cwlam2000hk.sinaman.com/manchu_1.htm

7   See Xiaoming Zhang, p 16 and note 25 based on Zhang 'Towards Arming China', p 317 and
    http://forum.axishistory.com/viewtopic.php?f=101&t=138717

8   See Xiaoming Zhang, p 17 and note 28 based on Wang Zhenghua.

9   See Xiaoming Zhang, p 19 and note 34. Photos of a replica of the aircraft are available on the Scramble and Air
    Britain ('Vought 65-C1 Lenin Plane') websites.

10 See Bueschel, R. M., *Communist Chinese Air Power* (Frederick A. Praeger, 1968), Part One/Chapter I 'Com-
    munist China finds Wings', p 10.

11 See Xiaoming Zhang, p 17 and note 46 based on Lü Liping.

12 See Xiaoming Zhang, p 22 and note 48 based on Wang Dinglie, et al. (Biography of General Lin Yalou)

13 According to Chinese-English dictionaries published in China, three terms – zhongyang junshi weiyuanhui,
    zhongyang junwei, and junwei – are used interchangeably to mean the Military Commission of the Central
    Committee of the Chinese Communist Party. Although these terms have always been used in Chinese, West-
    ern publications have translated them differently, and, consequently, certain Chinese publications printed for
    outside consumption have followed the Western practice. For example, Western publications originally trans-
    lated them as the Military Affairs Commission (MAC), but later changed to the Central Military Commission
    (CMC). (China's Air Force enters the 21st Century)

14 Following Allan, K. W, *China's Air Force enters the 21st Century* (RAND Corporation, 1995) p 36 these were
    actually only four basic trainers and some Tachikawa Ki.55 Type 99 advanced trainers (altogether slightly
    more than 30 captured were operated by late 1945 with the final 14 being retired in 1953).

15 See Bueschel, R. M., *Communist Chinese Air Power* (Frederick A. Praeger, 1968), Part One/Chapter I, p 17: of
    note: while the Nationalists claimed the bomber has landed because it ran out of gas and demanded the return
    of the plane, the Communists claimed that the pilot has defected. As a result this incident heated even further
    the already explosive situation.
    See also Xiaoming Zhang, p 22: of special note is the pilot Liu Shanben, who was trained in the United States
    and later became commander of the PLAAF' 10th Division. Altogether by June 1949 20 ROC-aircraft and 54
    trained members of the CAF changed sides.

16 See Xiaoming Zhang, pp 26–27: it seems as at first there were two concurring sides – the first supposing to
    adopt the Japanese system, whereas the second group (especially those, who were trained in the Soviet
    Union) favoured the Soviet system. In the end it was decided that the Soviet system fits better the PLA,
    because of the many not well educated conscripts.

17 This can for sure be discussed controversially, since the Communists' were eagerly preparing amphibious
    operations to capture the islands still in KKMT hands: see the successful conquest of Hainan in April 1950,
    the operations against the Wahshan Islands during May-August 1950 and finally the Zhoushan Island in May
    1950. Additionally several island remain under KMT control like the Kinmen, Matsu and Penghu and several
    smaller ones in the Fujianese Islands. This again formed the basic requirement for the first foreseen PLAAF
    operation.

FOUNDING PERIOD:
JANUARY 1949 TO DECEMBER 1953

The founding period of the PLAAF, the early years
and the Korean War

For Mao, the establishment of an air force was more driven by the political goal of defending a reunited China than by the same enthusiasm Sun Yat-sen shared. Anyway, he urged already in late 1947 – the civil war started just to turn to the communist's favour – the authorities in Manchuria to consider the founding of a future communist air force.

The final step in preparation to establish the PLAAF was the establishment of a dedicated Central Military Commission Aviation Bureau (junwei hangkong ju) located in Beijing on 17 March 1949 with Chang Qiankun appointed the Director and Wang Bi as the Political Commissar. With this the CCP demonstrated officially its will to construct a real air force and the tight connections to the political system was fixed by the still valuable twin-based system of a commander and a political officer. Additionally, within each of the six military regions (MR) an aviation division (hangkong chu) was established with subordinated aviation offices (hangkong bangongshi) – which became later the military region air force (MRAF) headquarters – were set up in Beijing, Changsha, Jinan, Nanchang, Shanghai and Wuhan, and each an Aviation Station (hangkong zhan) in Hangzhou, Qingdao, Tianjin, Taiyuan, Zhangjiakou and Xuzhou. Administratively the Aviation Bureau was structured strictly hierarchically led by the director and his appointed political commissar, both who led four divisions [Operations and Education Division (zuozhan jiaoyu chu), Aeronautical Engineering Division (hangkong gongcheng chu) and the Civil Aviation Division (minhang chu)] and two offices [Intelligence Office (qingbao ke) and Supply Office (gongying ke)].

Besides this, the main objective was to take over as much as possible of the former Nationalist aviation facilities, manufacturing plants, and especially trained personnel. Following Chinese sources 86 serviceable – of altogether 115 abandoned – Nationalist aircraft were captured between 1 July 1946 and 31 January 1949 including 15 by defecting pilots[1]. Confirmed by an US intelligence report from April 1949 these included three B-24M, three B-25, nine C-46, two C-47, nine DH.98 Mosquito, one L-15, one P-47, eight P-51, one AT-6, one AT-1 and two PT-19 aircraft. Additionally, 1,278 engines and 74,000 bombs were seized and altogether 2,267 technicians were listed. Of the numerous airfields at least 40 had been repaired. By October, the number of aircraft had increased to 113 aircraft.

But until all this was reached, some long ways had to be gone, since it had to be an air force for one special operation: the driving reasons to create a strong air arm was not only a military necessity – China's CCP had to consolidate its power – but also politically urgent. With the build-up of the armed forces, its industry and economy were thought to be developed quite quickly and additionally – maybe most important of all – there was Mao Zhedong's plan to 'de-liberate' Taiwan as soon as possible and already scheduled for summer 1950. With both these higher goals in mind and also, since the Northeast Old Aviation School had so far achieved only little success, the CCP decided to establish close relations to the Soviet Union. A first step – even before the official proclamation of the People's Republic of China – was a secret visit of Anastas Mikoyan to the CCP's headquarters during spring 1949 (between 31 January to 7 February), when Moscow offered a helping hand to this request. Anyway, by July 1949 the Aviation School had already trained 560 people including 125 pilots and 435 ground support personnel. In the end, the PLAAF emerged surely as an air force heavily influenced by the Soviet Air Force – especially in equipment and doctrine – however, the Chinese system of even closer political linkage to the CCP, always 'kept the development of the air force within a Chinese political, cultural und military context' as Xiaoming Zhang mentioned.

Especially trained personnel, pilots and technicians were the most urgent requirements. As such, already prior to a final decision by the Soviets, Zhu De supposed to send Chinese pilots to the Soviet Union in preparation of the Taiwan campaign. By July 1949 Liu Yalou – commander of the 14th Army Group at the time – was ordered to organise the creation of an air force capable of seizing Taiwan and to prepare the special requests to the Soviets. His proposals to the CMC besides massive imports of hardware in the Soviet Union itself were the complete transfer of 'his' army group's headquarters staff to establish the air force's headquarters, the delegation of PLA ranks to flight and combat training and the establishment of its own aviation schools. At around the same time Liu Shaoqi was in Moscow to negotiate the requested material, including about 100–200 Yakovlev fighters and around 40–80 bombers. Additionally, a large number of Chinese pilots and mechanics should receive training in the Soviet Union and Soviet advisors should be sent to China to assist the build-up[2].

To the surprise of many, Joseph V. Stalin agreed to all points but regretted that the CCP had not asked one year earlier for assistance and he proposed to establish aviation schools in China with Soviet help. However, in the meantime new estimated of the remaining CAF's strength showed that this first request would not grant superiority and now about 300–350 fighters and 350–400 pilots would be required within one year. Quite surprising again for the Chinese delegation, the Soviets had a preliminary plan ready by mid-August. Following this schedule, it was planned to train 350–400 pilots in the Soviet Union within one year and to establish six aviation schools. Additionally, at least 434 aircraft – 120 La-9 fighters, 40 Tu-2 bombers and 270 trainers (90 Yak-18, 90 Yak-11, 90 La-9UT and La-2UT) plus four Il-12 transports were acquired. At first one composite division should be set up. However, this assistance to build up an air force was only the beginning, with a memorandum approved on 5 October by Stalin calling for the immediate move forward of the Soviet Air Force, led by Major General D. Prutkov as the chief advisor to the new Chinese Air Force. Within a few years the PLAAF grew to one of the largest air forces virtually from nothing.

The PLAAF is born

Following the successful outcome of these Sino-Soviet negotiations, the CMC appointed Liu Yalou as the first PLAAF Commander, together with Xiao Hua the first Political Commissar and Deputy Commander. The final step in the foundation then occurred on 11 November 1949 – as this year to celebrate the PLAAF's 70th anniversary on 11 November 2019 – when the CMC disbanded the Aviation Bureau and formally established the People's Liberation Army Air Force (PLAAF) with the move from Wuhan to Beijing. The core of this new air force was built by using elements of the Fourth Field Army's 14th bingtuan.

However, this again led to some changes in command, when both former leaders of the CMC Aviation Bureau Chang Qiankun and Wang Bi – interestingly, since at that time both were the last officers who had received their training in the Soviet Union – were re-appointed as Deputy Commander and Director of the Training Department, and Wang Bi as the Deputy Political Commissar and Director of the Aeronautical Engineering Department, responsible for aircraft maintenance.

Formation of an air division and delivery of aircraft

The reason for this subchapter lies in its importance to understand, how the PLAAF grew during its early days and how the combat units were formed. During these early formative years, the PLAAF acquired aircraft primarily for defensive duties most of all to be able to provide an adequate air defence capability for its major cities and industrial areas. After that, all subsequent locations were based on the considerations to prepare for the Taiwan campaign, which was then superseded by China's intervention into the Korea War and the massive support by the Soviet Union. Later on – and again typical for the development of the PLAAF and the dislocation of its operational units – all changes were mostly related to operational considerations like the Sino-Indian border conflict, the Vietnam War and finally after the break with Moscow, the new adjacent threat in the north. This is quite similar to the recent developments to gain control and spread influence over the South Chinese Sea (oil) and the Indian Ocean (to oppose India). Finally, an as important factor in the assignment and creation of new units is the acquisition process of aircraft.

Following delivery of the first few aircraft to the PLAAF in July 1949 in Beijing Nanyuan, this unit was in reality nothing more than a mix of captured aircraft like the B-24, B-25, DH.98 Mosquito and P-51D. Quite understandable – since only a stop-gap until the new Soviet aircraft were available – this unit existed not for long and was disbanded as early as November 1950.

Date	Base/ location	Unit	Sub-units	Aircraft types	Notes
1949 July	Beijing Nanyuan	With 3 flights?	2 fighter flights 1 bomber flight	P-51 (6) DH.98 (2) PT-19 (2)	

1949 October	Beijing Nanyuan	With 4 flights?	2 fighter flights 1 bomber flight 1 transport flight	P-51 (19) DH.98 (3), B-25 (1) PT-19 (2), C-46 (3), C-47 (2)	
1950 January to August	Beijing Nanyuan	With 4 flights?	2 fighter flights 1 bomber flight 1 transport flight	La-9 (13) DH.98 (3), B-25 (1) PT-19 (2) C-46 (3) C-47 (2)	Disbanded in November 1950 following the assignment of a Soviet MiG-9 unit to Beijing; following the Tibet campaign, the transport flight received altogether 12 C-46 & C-47 later complemented by Il-12 to be called the 13th Air Division

With both new commanders one of the biggest obstacles for any future independent development was set right from the beginnings: since both were officers from the People's Liberation Army (PLA), none of them having any experiences in aviation matters, its commanders had problems – if they ever had the will to do so – to develop independent doctrines, tactics, requirements or even operational procedures and the PLAAF became never an independent service besides the army and later navy (only established in September 1950 by consolidating regional naval forces)[3]. As such, the PLAAF became only – like John Golan stated 'the PLA's lowly dog on the chain of the PLA commanders'[4] – a supporting unit to provide assistance to the combating troops on the ground. Additionally, air power was only seen – again deeply influenced by simply adapting the Soviet system – in its tactical sense of providing close air support, supply, air superiority and air defence and in no way in a whole strategic sense[5]. This was even deeper manifested by Mao's personnel decree to designate the new CCP Air Force, the Chinese People's Liberation Army Air Force (PLAAF); giving it the status of an army group within the PLA's chain of command. There was never ever an intention to establish the PLAAF as an independent branch.

This, however, was clearly a politically intended move by the CCP leaders, even if the General Staff Department originally proposed the name Chinese People's Air Force, in order to indicate its greater independence. As such, the administrative structure mirrored in most cases the PLA's one and was organised along each of the six military regions (MR) – northeast, north, east, south-central, southwest and northwest – within the five established field army (FA) operations areas. Besides this 'regular' army air force, the CMC also established the so-called PLA Air Defence Headquarters (fangkong siling bu)[6] on 23 October 1950 with the aim of protecting all major cities[7] – among them, Beijing, Shanghai and Shenyang – with Zhou Shidi as the commander and Zhong Chibing as political commissar.

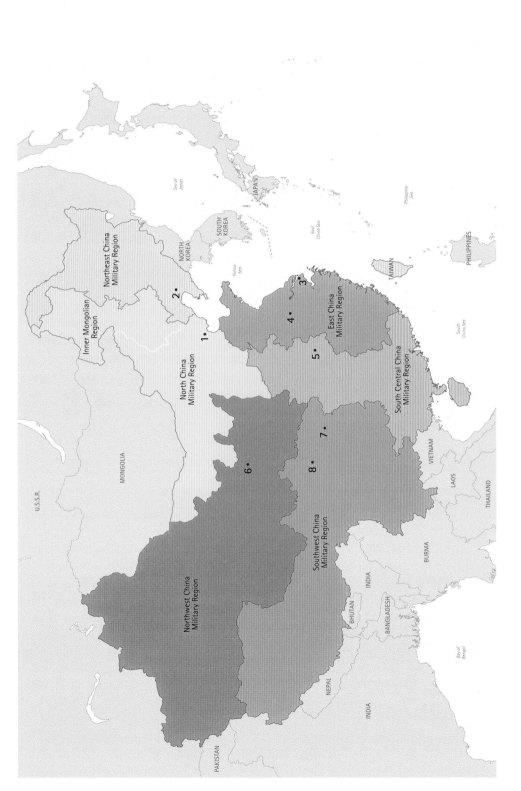

Command Posts
1. Beijing
2. Shenyang
3. Shanghai
4. Nanjing
5. Wuhan
6. Lanzhou
7. Chongqing
8. Chengdu

Map showing the organisational structure of the six military regions between 1949 and 1950.
(Map by James Lawrence)

In line with these build-ups, a first administrative reform was undertaken, when the existing three levels of the Headquarters Air Force (HQAF) – headquarters, political, and logistics – were expanded to six – headquarters, political, training, engineering, logistics and cadre/personnel by the end of the first year. Additionally, the PLAAF Party Committee was established in July 1950.

However, yet another reorganisation was initiated between August 1950 and September 1951, when the original Aviation Offices established in early 1949 became the MRAF Headquarters. As such administratively, each MRAF Headquarters had six departments: headquarters (siling bu), political (zhengzhi bu), logistics (houqin bu), aircraft maintenance (jiwu bu) and cadre/personnel (ganbu bu).[8]

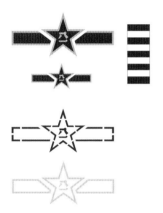

The current PLAAF insignia: 1949–present

Following the numerous attempts to introduce a common national symbol that no longer represents a simple derivate of the former KMT symbol nor can be misidentified with the famous Soviet red star and includes typical Chinese characteristic as well, the now familiar red and yellow star and bar national insignia made its first appearance in 1949. It represents a development of the last insignia with a reduction of the horizontal stripes to only one bold bar and a yellow outline. Still retained are the Chinese 'Ba Yi' characters representing the formation date of the Red Army of China on 1 August 1927.

Later in its development the PLAAF also experimented with and introduced toned-down markings on some types. A blue version was for many years used on the fuselage of regular H-6A bombers and there were even light grey versions similar to the recent variant.

The first unit and aircraft

Even with this massive organisational build-up and the pressing need to establish the aviation schools in preparation for the upcoming Taiwan campaign, the PLAAF was for most of these early days an air force without any operational forces.

Due to the pressing need to train Chinese pilots and ground crews to man and maintain the aircraft, the CMC had also approved to establish seven flying schools and in August 1949 the Soviet Union had agreed to sell 434 aircraft of different types (see above) and to provide technical advisors for the schools. As such the 1st and 2nd Aviation Schools were established on 30 October in Harbin and Changchun to train bomber crews, while the 3rd to 6th Aviation Schools at Jinzhou, Shenyang, Jinan and Beijing were dedicated to fighter crews. Slightly later the 7th Aviation School was added at Mundanjiang for transport crews. Additional problems however were the low educational standard of the new cadets and most of all the language barrier between the Chinese and their Russian instructors. As such the progress was relatively slow and the standard had to be – much to the concern of the Russians – lowered. This all led to a low training standard and a fearful high accident rate[9].

Even when the Civil War ended with the Communist victory in October 1949 and the retreat of the Nationalist Kuomintang to Taiwan – also known as Formosa – the PLAAF possessed only 159 foreign aircraft of 21 different types but 542 airfields. Yet another problem besides these logistical nightmares was the personnel composition of

Images of the very first types in PLAAF service in 1949 are very rare. The left image shows two B-25s with a C-46 in the background and the right image – a wider view of the same scene – reveals a line-up of several P-51Ds and B-25s, with C-46s and a C-47 behind. (Both via CDF)

the force, since only about 3,000 persons were trained aviation personnel[10]. The lack of experienced personnel was not only devoted to pilots but also ground crews and especially officers, leading to the decision to transfer PLA personnel to the PLAAF; again, manifesting the PLAAF as a branch of the PLA only. A stopgap solution was the 'acceptance' of former Nationalist and even Japanese pilots and technically trained personnel, which remained in Manchuria after 1945 and were part of the original contingent of instructors at the Northeast Old Aviation School.

As for the combat units, by then altogether 115 (other sources say 113 or even 159) former KMT aircraft together with large stocks of engines and ammunitions were acquired, collected or confiscated together with the repair of about 40 airfields. Overall, there were 542 airfields available but only 94 of them were repaired and modernised until 1953. In addition, the ratio of pilots to mechanics was uncomfortable. This however led to additional problems in maintaining and operating a wide variety of different aircraft types (about 21) and attempts were made to standardise the equipment during the early days until Soviet supplied types were delivered in sufficient numbers.

The PLAAF's first operational squadron (zhongdui) was established only in July 1949 at Beijing Nanyuan, with three flights at first consisting of two fighter, one bomber with the operational types of six North American P-51 Mustangs, two de Havilland DH.98 Mosquito bombers and two Fairchild PT-19 trainers. Until October, the fighter units were able to operate 19 P-51 and one additional Mosquito and one B-25 were added to the bomber unit. Additionally, a fourth flight for transport was formed slightly later and equipped with three C-46s and two C-47s. During August 1950, the fighters were replaced by the first La-9 delivered by Moscow and in November this unit was disbanded after being replaced by a Soviet MiG-9 equipped fighter unit.

Besides the preparation to seize Taiwan, especially the continued vulnerability to Nationalists air strikes[11] dictated the PLAAF's main operational task: to provide air defence of the largest cities such as Beijing, Shanghai and Tianjin, major troop-concentrations and the most important industrial centres from Nationalist bombardments. The Nationalists still controlled the skies over southeast China as far as Shanghai – for example an attack on Beijing on 4 May 1949 or in February 1950. As such the main emphasis was laid in establishing air defence and fighter units: a first plan from early 1950 called for the establishment within the next six months of only two fighter regiments and one bomber regiment but this was slightly later revised to seven fighter regiments and four bomber regiments. Because of the lack of combat-ready pilots, the number of aircraft within each unit – originally planned with 40 aircraft per regiment –

Images of operational C-46s are very rare, especially during their early operational career. These stills were taken from a CCTV report.
(Via CCTV)

had to be reduced to 30 fighters in a fighter regiment and only 20 bombers in a bomber regiment. In the meantime, Major General Prutkov was replaced by General Korotkov in October 1950. In a report from September 1950[12] the PLAAF issued its first development plan for the years 1950 to 1953, which called for establishing about 100 aviation regiments, repairing over 100 airfields and setting up 11 aircraft repair factories. The plan called to establish 11 regiments (330 aircraft) in 1950, 12 regiments (480 aircraft) in 1951 and finally 31 regiments in 1952 (750 aircraft). Altogether 54 regiments with 1,560 aircraft between 1950–52. This plan however was revised again with the outbreak of the Korean War to 11 regiments in 1950, 12 regiments in 1951, 45 regiments in 1952 and finally 28 regiments in 1953 for altogether 4,507 aircraft including 2,640 combat aircraft. Overall this was to bring the size of the PLAAF to about 290,000 and by the end of 1953 most of these goals were accomplished.

Yet another interesting fact of that time was the dislocation of these air forces, which were concentrated mostly in the northeast of China and close to major cities like Beijing, Nanjing, Shanghai and Tianjin to protect them from still possible Nationalist Air Force air raids. This was not changed in majority until after the First Taiwan Strait Crisis in 1958, when PLAAF units were moved to the Fujian and Guangdong provinces. A similar relocation was done further into the western Chinese regions following the 'liberation' of Tibet and the in preparation of the border war with India in 1962. Southern China received its first major air force units only during the Vietnam War and after 1969 following the Sino-Soviet border clashes. Finally, by the mid-1970s, the PLAAF had a permanent presence throughout China. These expanded operational areas again however necessitated yet again another change of the PLAAF's administrative command and control structure.

Following the signing of several cooperation agreements between China and the Soviet Union, the first Soviet Air Force air division arrived in northeast China in August 1950 to provide air defence and assist with the PLAAF's training, since the developing PLAAF was not capable to do so. Additionally, one Soviet combined aviation group arrived in Nanjing, Shanghai and Xuzhou even earlier in February 1950 also for air defence duties. In the following months until December 1950 hundreds of new aircraft were delivered to the PLAAF and altogether 13 Soviet Air Force divisions (ten fighter, two ground attack, and one bomber division) to four China's military regions – Dongbei, Huabei, Huadong, and Zhongnan – were stationed in China. Iinterestingly, the Soviets began returning home already in July 1951 and most of their equipment was simply handed over to the PLAAF. However, it is not clear when the last Soviet unit left China.

Altogether the deliveries to the PLAAF between November 1950 and early 1954 occurred in seven batches. As a result, there is not a strict system behind the number of a division, since in this phase with each batch of new aircraft, new divisions were formed. This 'system' can at best be seen by the first 28 divisions:[13]

1st batch

Following closely to the first unit based at Beijing Nanyuan the first new operational unit was formed in June 1950 in Nanjing as the 4th Mixed Brigade (huncheng lu). This unit consisted of the 10th and 11th Fighter (quzhu) Regiments, the 12th Bomber (hongzha) Regiment and the 13th Attack (chongji) Regiment. Already in October this brigade was relocated to Shanghai and renamed the 4th Fighter Division. Nearly immediately after renaming it was disbanded and split to form the first three air divisions.

Date	Base/location	Unit	Sub–units	Aircraft types	Notes
1950 June (16 June)	Nanjing	4th Mixed Aviation Brigade	10th Fighter Reg. or reversed? 11th Fighter Reg. 12th Bomber Reg. 13th Ground Attack Regiment	38 MiG-15? La-11 or La-9 (39) Tu-2 (39) Il-10 (25)	Altogether 155 aircraft (including 14 trainers); relocated from Nanjing to Shanghai during October for air defence duties; there the unit was renamed to 4th Fighter Brigade and only weeks later to 4th Division
1950 October	Shanghai Longhua	4th Division	10th Fighter Regiment or reversed? 11th Fighter Regiment 12th Bomber Regiment 13th Ground Attack Regiment	38 MiG-15? 39 La-11 or La-9 39 Tu-2 25 Il-10	Split in November 1950

Founding an aviation industry

In March 1950 the newly established Ministry of Heavy Industry decided that a modern national aircraft industry was to be created from scratch, which in truth was an extraordinarily ambitious objective. Consequently, right from the beginning two parallel approaches were made – first, the delivery of equipment from the Soviet Union, and second, the establishment of a modern aviation industry assisted by the Soviet Union. Fighter aircraft received a very high priority right from the start – especially bearing in mind a planned campaign in Taiwan – and the first jet fighters to be operated by the PLAAF were Soviet designs (China's first jet fighter was in fact the Soviet MiG-15).

In many ways the early years of the developing Chinese aviation industry were influenced by the PRC's newly established political system and the decisions made by its Communist Party leaders. As a result, several important goals were set in the First Five-Year Plan, but the principal aim was to build up an indigenous and competitive aviation industry.

Even if the C-47 was the main transport type during the Tibet crisis in 1950, a lack of airlift capabilities was one of the main reasons for the acquisition of these Il-12s from the Soviet Union.
(Top81.cn)

In fact, with the assistance of China's bigger 'Soviet' brother, the First Five-Year Plan was actually completed ahead of schedule in 1956 and this led political leaders to think about rather more ambitious objectives for the Second Five-Year Plan.

Tibet 1950: the PLAAF's first campaign

Following this, in the eyes of most external observer surely confusing organisational dominated build-up, the next phase which influenced the early history of the PLAAF were the first combat operations, which speeded up a massive build-up both numerically and in regard to quality.

Right in the middle of the phase of establishing a functioning air force, the Chinese government ordered in January 1950 via the CMC to 'liberate' Tibet. There are surely different perceptions, if this was a means of unification of what was always united or a military occupation. Regardless the point of view, following the Kuomintang (ROC) government's perception and so the Communists too always maintained that Tibet was integral part of China. Consequently, to liberate Tibet was as much a top priority as to incorporate Hainan Island, the Pescadores Islands and most of all Taiwan into the PRC either peacefully or by force.[14] Therefore this reincorporation is either called the Chinese invasion of Tibet (by the Tibetan Government in Exile) or a Peaceful liberation of Tibet, in China. De facto it is an annexation even if the Government of Tibet and the social structure remained in place until the 1959 Tibetan uprising.

Preparations started already in December 1949 and even if the PLA crossed the Jinsha River only on 6–7 October 1950 resulting in the captured the border town of Qamdo on 19 October, the amassing of troops begun in February. Due to underestimated difficulties to provide supply, Mao ordered the PLAAF to help. The formation of the PLAAF's transportation troops resulted in this issue, since by then only 12 C-46 and C-47 were operational to provide air supply. For this mission, 6 transports were deployed to Chengdu to carry out airdrop operations. Overall air operations started in April 1950 and lasted until November 1952, with up to 25 routes across the Tibetan Plateau established. During this time the PLAAF allegedly flew 1,282 missions and dropped 51t of supply. Soon after the campaign, this unit gained Il-12 transports and was re-formed in December 1950 as the 13rd Transport Division.

The C-47, later supplemented by the Soviet Li-2, as seen here, was in service much longer than the C-46. A total of 41 Li-2s were purchased for both military and civil use before finally being retired in 1986.
(via CDF)

Not directly related to the Tibet campaign, further missions were flown by the PLAAF from December 1952 on, when the PLAAF took part in several combat missions against terrorists and 'armed bandits' in the Gansu and Sichuan provinces. This campaign lasted until July 1953 and included five La-9 fighters, six Tu-2 bombers and a few Il-12s.[15]

Creation of the PLAAF's Airborne Troops

In parallel to the ongoing preparations and massive build-up, the PLAAF begun on 26 July 1950 with the establishment of dedicated Airborne Troops (kongjiang bing). Concerning its history, there are still some misconceptions and it earliest traces are linked to 1949, when the Ninth Column was reorganised and pre-designated the 15th Corps. As such it traces its lineage to an infantry army within the Fourth Field Army – and not as erroneously reported from Deng Xiaoping's Second Field Army – to which in fact this corps was later transferred in 1950.[16] As an infantry army it only became an airborne troop on 26 July 1950, when the PLA's 1st Airborne Brigade was raised for special mission operations. Following the usual Soviet practice, this it was at first assigned to the 1st Marine Division (luzhan diyi shi), before it eventually became an airborne division (kongjiang bing shi). Only briefly later, the brigade's headquarters moved on 1 August to Kaifeng, while Kaifeng and Zhengzhou, Henan province, were designated as the brigade's training bases. On 17 September 1950 the PLA re-formed this unit as the PLAAF 1st Airborne Brigade. In the time that followed it was re-designated several times, becoming also the Air Force Marine 1st Division, the Paratroops Division (sanbing shi) of the Air Force and finally an airborne division (kongjiang bing shi). Operationally it was deployed to Korea in February 1951 and – quite confusing – even if already subordinated to the air force, it fought as part of the 3rd Army Group in April 1951 resulting as an elite unit. In the early 1960s, the 15th Army was reorganised as an airborne army and subordinated to the PLAAF's headquarters in Beijing. Until the late 1960s the 15th Army's three organic divisions – the 29th, 44th, and 45th – had retained their numerical designators. Quite remarkably the 29th Division seems to be an exception and – even if not entirely clear anymore – it is highly likely that elements of this division merged with the original PLAAF's 1st Airborne Division at Kaifeng to create the 43rd Division. In consequence in May 1961 the Central Military Commission reassigned the Army's 15th Army (15 jun) into the PLAAF 15th Airborne Army (kongjun kongjiang bing di 15 jun) and subordinated the PLAAF's original airborne division to this new army. Since then all the PLA's paratroop units belong to the PLAAF. In the following decades, the 15th Airborne Army received an aviation transport regiment in October 1964 and in December 1969, the first helicopter regiment was assigned to the airborne troops. In parallel, the number of personnel and equipment was steadily increased until 1975, when the airborne troops underwent a force reduction however in parallel with the introduction of new types of weapons. For many years, the PLAAF airborne corps or airborne forces were better known as the 15th Airborne Corps, which was and still is the PLA's primary strategic airborne unit. In its current form it is part of the newly established rapid reaction units primarily intended for airborne and special operation missions. De facto their role is similar to that of the US Army's XVIII Airborne Corps/82nd Airborne Division.

For many decades, the main transport for the airborne forces was the versatile Y-5.
(via CDF)

Soviet deliveries and a massive build-up

Even if these operations gave the PLAAF a first operational insight, the main objective for any future campaign remained always Beijing's intention to 'liberate Taiwan'. However, this had to be shelved because of the Korean War between 1950 and 1953, an operation the PLAAF had never anticipated it would be capable of at such an early stage. As such the Korean War gave the all-important impetus to the massive build-up of the PLAAF. Following the establishment of the provisional first operational unit in July 1949 in Beijing, the very first combat ready unit was then actually formed on 19 June 1950 in Nanjing. This unit was called the 4th Mixed Aviation Brigade – to remind of Mao's Fourth Army during the fighting in the Jinggang Mountains and is most commonly known as the PLAAF 4th Combined Brigade (hunchenglu). The brigade used the 90th Infantry Division as its base and later moved to Shanghai on 8 August, thus being assigned to the East China Military Region. On 28 October 1950, the 4th Combined Brigade became the PLAAF 4th Fighter Brigade and changed again on 31 October 1950 to the PLAAF 4th Division. The four regiments were split and became the backbone of the four aviation divisions. On 30 March 1956, the 4th Division changed its name to the 1st Air Division with the 1st, 2nd, and 3rd Regiments.[17] Interestingly, as a combined brigade it consisted of – in analogy to modern terms a quite sophisticated mixed super-wing – the 10th and 11th Fighter Regiments (39 La-9s and 38 MiG-15s), the 12th Bomber Regiment (39 Tu-2s) and the 13th Attack Regiment (25 Il-10s) with altogether 155 aircraft (including 14 trainers).

These regiments were subordinated to the East China Military Region and formed later the backbone of the first four PLAAF divisions. After only a three-month conversion phase, the brigade – later re-designated as a division – it was relocated from Nanjing to Shanghai during October for air defence duties. But even far from being operational combat ready it gave valuable experiences in training and operations to the regional commanders in preparation to the later war they had to fight. Besides that, already in January 1950 the next important unit was formed as the PLAAF transportation aviation troops following the requirements to supply the troops involved in Tibet Campaign. The first aircrafts operated by this unit were altogether 12 C-46s and C-47s based in Beijing but soon after the campaign additional Ilyushin Il-12 were acquired via the Soviet Union. Later the unit was renamed the 13th Air Division.[18]

As a result even during the start of the war, the PLAAF was in fact not in a good shape: the all-important build-up of the command structure was still under way and the available aircraft were merely a 'hodge podge of existing aircraft'[19]. As such the few regiments were surely no real operational combat units. Even worse, one common

Although the MiG-9 was ordered earlier, the first MiG-15s were actually delivered first. On the left is one of the few images showing operational MiG-9s, while the MiG-15s on the right wear the very early PLAAF national markings. (Both '728K6' via CDF)

joke was to call the PLAAF a 'Kongjun' (regular PLAAF = *Kōngjūn)*, which literally means a 'skeleton force'. That however should have changed soon.

In regard to the planned aircraft purchase and following the original intentions, which were officially negotiated in 1950 during Mao's visit to Moscow and finally signed the Treaty of Friendship, Alliance and Mutual Assistance, China placed four separate orders in early 1950 – 11 and 15 February, 8 March and 13 April – and requested altogether 586 aircraft. However, this was soon expanded to 628 and later on complemented by the last two orders for additional advisors and to help organising the first combat units. Following the Chinese intervention in Korea, which further strengthened the Sino-Soviet relations, the first Soviet deliveries of weapons, equipment and especially the assignment of technical advisors to assist the build-up of the military and the defence industry begun in late 1950, so that the PLAAF expanded quite rapidly by increasing its strength to more than 650 combat aircraft.

2nd batch

The second batch of aircraft was delivered to the PLAAF between October and November 1950 (depending sources) to establish the 3rd Fighter Brigade in Shenyang, consisting of the 7th, 8th and 9th Regiments. Additionally, the 4th Fighter Brigade was formed in Liaoyang, Liaoning province out of the 4th Combined Brigade's 10th Fighter Regiment and the 3rd Fighter Brigade's 7th Regiment. In Liaoyang it was renamed the 12th Regiment. The final unit to be formed with this second batch was the 2nd Fighter Brigade in Shanghai built out of the remaining 4th Combined Brigade's 11th Fighter Regiment.

Right after their establishment, all three fighter brigades underwent several significant changes, when they were upgraded to divisions (kong # shi / # = number of division). In line with this, each division reduced the number of regiments from three to two and the name denoting the operational purpose of the regiment (fighter/attack/bomber) was dropped from the name.

Date	Base / location	Unit	Sub-units	Aircraft types	Notes
1950 October	Shenyang, Liaoning	3rd Fighter Brigade changed to 3rd Division	7th Regiment 8th Regiment 9th Regiment	MiG-15	7th Regiment moved to Liaoyang to form the 12th Regiment/4th Div.
	Liaoyang, Liaoning	4th Fighter Brigade changed to 4th Division	10th Regiment 12th Regiment (ex 7th Rgt)	MiG-15	Built out of 10th Regiment/4th Mixed Aviation Brigade and 7th Regiment/3rd Fighter Brigade Re-established in March 1956 the 1st Division in Anshan, Liaoning

Date	Base/location	Unit	Sub-units	Aircraft types	Notes
1950 November	Shanghai/Longhua	2nd Fighter Division	4th Regiment 6th Regiment	La-9, MiG-15	Built out of 11th Regiment/4th Mixed Aviation Brigade to become the 2nd Fighter Division

3rd batch

The third batch of aircraft was delivered between November and December 1950 (depending sources) to establish five divisions:

Date	Base/location	Unit	Sub-units	Aircraft types	Notes
1950 December	Kaiyuan, Liaoning	5th Ground Attack Division	13th Regiment 15th Regiment	Il-10	
1950 November	Anshan, Liaoning	6th Fighter Division	16th Regiment 18th Regiment	MiG-9 MiG-15?	
1950 December	Dongfeng Xi'an, Jilin	7th Fighter Division	19th Regiment 21st Regiment	MiG-9 MiG-15?	
1950 December	Siping, Jilin	8th Bomber Division	22nd Regiment 24th Regiment	Tu-2	
1950 December	Jilin, Jilin	9th Fighter Division	25th Regiment 27th Regiment	La-9	Transferred to Naval Aviation as 5th ND on 7 December 1955; re-established as 9th Div. in Guangzhou in March 1956

However, this quite flourishing period had not only the positive build-up but quite understandable it created several problems. The first and most important one was the lack of experienced officers to command the newly established units. Even if besides the ongoing negotiations and orders, the delivery of Soviet aircraft – flight training on Yak-18 started actually already in January 1950 – permitted the graduation of the first pilots in October (with an average of only 63 flying hours on Yak-11 and Yak-18) and most of them were dispersed immediately to the first combat units. With these first two classes it was planned to organise the first 15 regiments (now organised into about six to seven divisions) and quite understandable the accident rate remained very high during these days. As such numerous additional personnel has been recruited from regular PLA ground forces units. Another side effect of this necessary move was yet another manifestation of the PLAAF as a PLA branch.

The second severe problem was the financial side and the question how to establish these military acquisitions, since – at least officially – the Soviet founds of USD300 million[20] were restricted to humanitarian and civil purposes. Following the original plan, China placed four separate orders in early 1950 – on 11 and 15 February, 8 March and 13 April – for a total of 586 aircraft. These included 280 La-9s, 198 Tu-2s and 108 trainers, plus miscellaneous types. As early as February, the original request was expanded to 628 aircraft and included a further requirement for additional advisors to help organise the first divisions. This however changed completely right after China had entered the war: China immediately ordered altogether 2,470 aircraft of various types and the Soviets fulfilled these orders in most cases by simply transferring their aircraft based in China plus associated equipment directly to the newly established units. In addition, the internal political support of the air force grew to an unprecedented priority. The PLAAF – at the expense of the PLN – was allowed to finance its programmes without restraints, but an additional, and important, contribution was the collection of funds by the so-called 'Federation of Chinese People to Resist the United States and Aid Korea', which called for patriotic donations. This resulted in no less than enough funds to purchase 3,710 fighters, after this campaign had ended in June 1952.

Following the ongoing build-up, several divisions each with two regiments were formed and by late 1950, the 4th Mixed Brigade was divided up to build the core of another three fighter, one ground-attack and two bomber divisions. Additionally, the steady deliveries of aircraft in altogether seven batches between November 1950 and early 1954[21] permitted the establishment of a growing number of divisions. Besides the PLAAF also the PLA Naval Aviation created six air divisions and five independent regiments between 1952 and 1955 and established three more divisions during the 1960s. Following a report from Zhou Enlai to Mao Zedong dated 3 September 1950 it was scheduled to create 11 regiments in 1950 (330 aircraft), 12 regiments (480 aircraft) in 1951 and 31 regiments (750 aircraft) by 1952. However, after war broke out, the PLAAF leadership expanded this quite moderate plan to 23 regiments in 1950 and 1951, 45 regiments in 1952 and finally 29 regiments in 1953. Altogether it was planned to reach a full operational strength of 97 regiments by late 1953 of about 290,000 troops and 4,507 aircraft of which 2,640 were combat types.[22]

Until mid-1951 altogether 17 divisions with 34 regiments were operational with 1,050 aircraft. Of these 17 divisions there were 12 fighter divisions (equipped with La-9, MiG-9 and 445 MiG-15), two attack divisions (with Il-10) and two bomber divisions (with Tu-2) complemented by one transport division (with C-46, C-47 and Il-12). At around the same time, the main focus on flight training shifted. From now on the Chinese began to establish their own training system and – even still completely reliant to the Soviet technology and supplies – decided quite independently from the Soviet advisors. Consequently, especially when the Soviet advisors left the aviation schools from July, they were relegated in preparation of the combat units. This altogether led to several conflicting situations, when the local commanders refused the Soviet's advises which in consequence resulted in wrong decisions, which again raised sharp criticism from the PLAAF leadership.

By late 1952 the overall size of the PLAAF was even more increased, when not only the number of aircraft was expanded to 1,487 [including 950 MiG-9 and MiG-15 jet fighters), 165 propeller fighters (P-51 and La-9), 100 newly delivered Il-28 jet bombers and 65 older light bombers (Tu-2) and 115 attack aircraft (Il-10) as well as 90 transports],

In common with other early types, images of La-9s in PLAAF service are very rare. This is also due to the fact they were an interim fighter, bridging the gap between the very first P-51s and later MiG-9 and MiG-15 jets. (via CDF)

but also the number of operational divisions were dramatically increased. In parallel the PLAAF was establishing its organisational and command structure, its personnel training and education institutions and overall the logistics on equipment and aircraft maintenance support structure. When the war ended with the signing of the armistice on 27 July 1953, the PLAAF had 28 divisions with 56 regiments with about 3,000 aircraft operational. Nearly as important by late 1953, 13 aviation schools were formed, which had already trained 5,945 flight crew members and more than 24,000 maintenance personnel and not to omit the PLAAF had created its first airborne unit in 1950, which it continued to expand until these were formally designated an airborne corps in 1960. Slightly later or in parallel, the next phase of expansion was initiated by increasing the strength of each division from two to three regiments with about 25 aircraft each.[23]

Another major issue was a rising rift between the Chinese PLAAF command and the Russian advisors. These problems started with the fact that the Russians lived under better conditions. In addition, most Chinese students had a very low education, rarely spoke the Russian language and the Russians in return had no experiences in teaching, since they were drawn from combat units. Consequently, everything had to be translated but these translators barely had any knowledge in aviation. Therefore, to no surprise, the initial goals were not reached. Additionally, the programme to train and educate was soon expanded dramatically beyond the original plan so that too few advisors and teachers lectured a large number of students. Moreover, these issues mentioned did not even include social and cultural issues like the way to criticise or even rate a Chinese student.

Korean War 1950–53

As already mentioned, the Korean War gave an all-important impetus to the build-up of the early PLAAF. Interestingly, in original Chinese sources, the reasons to step in were seldom (if ever) discussed. Besides that, it is not called the 'Korean War', but the War to resist America and aid Korea following the outbreak of the Korean Civil War from 25 June 1950 on. As such it was – at least not officially – not the PLAAF, which was involved but the so-called Chinese People's Volunteer Air Force (PVAF) or simply the People's Volunteer Army (PVA), which included the PLAAF (as its primary force), the small North Korean Air Force and pilots from the Soviet Air Force.

Even if it would be beyond the capabilities of this book to review the PLAAF's involvement in Korea[24] the most important factors and consequences – especially the interrelations between the Soviet Union's and the Chinese decisions – and how these events influenced the further development will be included.

As already noted, the PLAAF was by June 1950 – as originally scheduled – under preparation for the Taiwan campaign as of national unification, when the North Korean Army invaded the South and therefore the majority of the PLAAF forces were bases in southern China, where reportedly 16 armies were preparing the invasion. As such originally, neither the Chinese government nor Chairman Mao were eagerly interested in an intervention in Korea. Additionally, the PLAAF had severe concerns about a lack of air support, which in turn again would have required Soviet support and most of all the Chinese government did not expect the US to step in. In contrast, it seems as if the

Soviet Union urged China to send troops, which in turn were promised to receive air support from the Soviets.

However as a direct consequence to the North Korean invasion, the Truman administration immediately sent the United States Seventh Fleet to the Taiwan Straits, not only as a show of force but also to protect the Nationalist Republic of China (Taiwan) from the People's Republic of China (PRC).

This in turn led on 4 August 1950 – with the Taiwan campaign postponed for the moment – to a report by Mao Zedong to the Politburo that China would intervene in Korea. However, still undecided at that time was the question of air support and the necessary reorganisation of the prepared Taiwan invasion force into the PLA Northeast Frontier Force. What followed were several consultations – which due to the lack of public documentations even today give only a vague picture if and to what content the Soviet Union actually promised to provide air support – and the decision to restructure the training programme to provide sufficient numbers of Chinese pilots. Overall it seems as Stalin's main strategy was to 'avoid committing Soviet troops to fighting the Americans,' while at the same time urging 'the Chinese to move towards entering the war.'[25]

The Il-10 was the first dedicated ground-attack type in PLAAF service and saw extensive use in various campains. This one was allegedly damaged at Kimpo, Korea in 1950.
(via CDF)

A line-up of Tu-2 bombers - most likely from the 8th Bomber Division, 24th AR - prepares for the next mission. (Both via Top81.cn)

As such, the weeks between September and October 1950 were quite crucial especially after the Soviet Union was still delaying the requested military assistance. In parallel the Politburo authorised Mao's proposal of Chinese intervention in Korea on 2 October 1950 right the day after the ROK Army had crossed the 38th parallel and finally after long consultations on 4 and 5 October the CCP Politburo decided to step in to 'fight America and assist North Korea'. In turn again it seems that Stalin was still undecided – by trying to avoid a direct military confrontation with the US – and urged Kim Il Sung to be patient depending further consultations with the Chinese. In consequence, Soviet Union limited their assistance at first only to air support north of the Yalu River and deliveries of materiel to minor quantities of 'non-essential' supplies like trucks, grenades and machine guns. Finally on 8 October 1950, Mao Zedong rebranded the PLA Northeast Frontier Force as the Chinese People's Volunteer Army (PVA) under the leadership of Marshal Peng Dehuai. At around the same time, on 14 October, also the Soviets issued an order to provide four fighter divisions with some 248 MiG-9s. Only two weeks later, another four MiG-9 fighter divisions, one La-9 division, one Il-10 and one Tu-2 divisions were deployed to China. Additionally, and due to a shortage of MiG-9, the MoD suggested the delivery of two MiG-15 divisions. Until December 1950 altogether 11 Soviet air divisions – comprising six MiG-9, two MiG-15, one La-9, and one Il-10 and Tu-2 divisions each – were assigned to China in order to provide air defence and training Chinese aircrews.[26]

In regard to PLAAF operations – PLA actions which succeeded the secret crossing of the Yalu by the PVA 13th Army Group on 19 October should be studied in depth by other sources – the book *Red Wings over the Yalu* is highly recommend – and as such will not be covered in this book, but overall it the most important aspects are mentioned.

PLAAF operations – a brief summary

Following the official historical reviews,[27] the PLAAF accomplished 26,491 sorties over Korea and engaged 366 aerial battles during that time. It claims to have shot down altogether 330 aircraft – 211 F-86, 72 F-84 and F-80 and 47 others – but also damaging 95 additional enemy aircraft. In contrast, a loss of 231 aircraft – 224 MiG-15, 3 La-11 and 4 Tu-2 – including 116 airmen and a damage of 151 aircraft through aerial combats were acknowledged. Additionally, 168 aircraft were lost due to other non-combat cir-

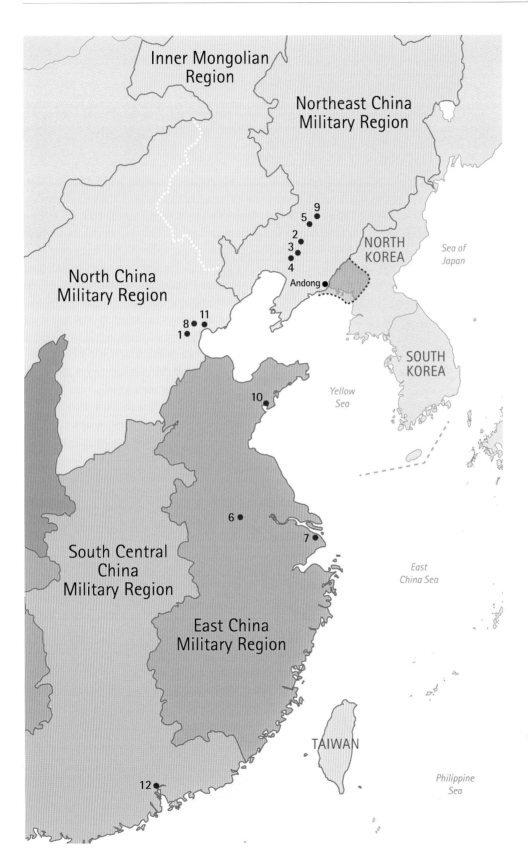

MiG Alley

● **Aviation Division Base**
1. 2nd Division, Zhuoxian
2. 3rd Division, Shenyang
3. 4th Division, Liaoyang
4. 6th Division, Anshan
5. 8th Division, Siping
6. 10th Division, Nanjing
7. 12th Division, Shanghai
8. 14th Division, Beijing
9. 15th Division, Gongzhuling
10. 16th Division, Qingdao
11. 17th Division, Tangshan
12. 18th Division, Guangzhou

This map shows the theatre of operation during the Korean War, including the so-called MiG Alley and the home bases of the individual divisions, which were concentrated at Andong.
(Map by James Lawrence)

cumstances. Overall 12 air divisions – 10 fighter divisions with 21 regiments and two bomber divisions with three flying groups – including about 800 airmen plus 59,700 ground personnel were fighting in Korea and as such gained valuable combat experience.

In retrospect, the PLAAF history describes the involvement in Korea divided in two phases: during the first phase between September 1951 and May 1952, the operations were quite limited to air defence along the Russian colleagues and can be seen as a pure learning phase.

By late 1950 the PLA had to recognise that the ground campaigns would not succeed without the necessary and promised air support as such the PLAAF leadership under the command of General Liu Yalou was ordered to develop a plan to support the ground forces supposed to start their offensive in spring 1951. However similar to Stalin's concerns in regard to a direct US-Soviet confrontation, the PLAAF was restricted by several political and operational boundaries: first of all the fear of retaliation strikes on Chinese bases in the event of attacks started from China the PLAAF was ordered not to strike UN forces in the south. This in turn limited the effective range of strikes, since the range of the operational aircraft allowed only attacks to targets within about 100 miles (161km) off their bases. Additionally, this phase was most of all limited by the lack of suitable bases within the Korean theatre of operation and the general operational inexperience, cautiousness and especially lack of skilful pilots.

To overcome this in order to create a cadre of experienced pilots, the PLAAF remodelled their training cycle to a system now consisting of five phases: four to gain operational experiences with increasing complexity – an effort not without some heavy losses, set-backs and sacrifices – and a fifth of rest and relaxation in order to summarise the gained experiences.[28] Following a careful introduction from December 1950 on of young pilots by the rotation of smaller units detached to Andong to gain combat practice the PLAAF leadership again urged by Stalin but assisted by the delivery of MiG-15 and the build-up of the necessary infrastructure in North Korea continuing throughout 1951 and 1952 – felt confident enough by mid-1951 to enter the war. Following these efforts aided by the build-up of an extensive network of early warning and ground-control intercept (GCI) radar sites, the employment of MiG-15bis' during daylight operations and mixed forces during night missions, the PLAAF was able to develop and perfect their integrated CGI techniques into their air defences; something that later led to the amalgamation of the PLAAF and Air Defence Forces.

Very early in their career the MiG-15s were unpainted, with simple two-digit serial numbers and often wore political slogans. This MiG-15 also carries a rarely seen slipper tank.
(via CDF)

Finally, the second phase lasted from about June/July 1952 until the end of the war on 27 July 1953. Within this phase, the PLAAF operated increasingly independent and finally fulfilled – at least by the PLAAF's own retrospect – the expectations. However it has to be reminded that these experiences – and overall in comparison the general involvement – remained quite limited, since the PLAAF was almost incapable to provide direct air support to ground forces and only a few occasions were known.[29]

Additionally, the PLAAF units operated in the theatre seemed to appear in a 'predictable three-month training and operational cycle', which also made it hard to explore their full potential. Furthermore, it is quite difficult to extract the Russian contributions out of the overall successes[30] and even besides the undeniable achievements claimed by the Chinese authorities; it has to be set in comparison to the overall number of missions flown or aircraft operated. Especially in this regard, the PLAAF and Soviet Union were overwhelmingly outnumbered by the UN forces, which had an average about 1,200 aircraft in theatre and which flew about 1.04 million sorties. For example, whereas the USAF averaged around 900 sorties daily, the PLAAF was only able to provide around 50 sorties per day additional to a similar amount flown by the Soviets. In order to overcome this and compensate the low range of their aircraft, the PLAAF tried to establish own bases within North Korea throughout 1951 and 1952, which in the end failed. But this also is the main reason, that Chinese pilots never were able to effectively provide close air support to their ground forces.

As such even the PLAAF had to admit that they were only able to provide a serviceable air force with the Soviet aid – which itself limited its involvement to air defence duties in the rear – they were limited by the lack of experiences pilots and ground crews, the lack of forward-located bases in North Korea and the limited range of the aircraft involved. With these limiting factors in mind, the PLAAF was never able to supply air support of the ground forces, nor to gain air superiority. Additionally, they were only able to react and never equipped to assume the initiative and as such shifted their primary missions to air defence and single point protection of valuable locations and areas. This again manifested the later essential defensive air doctrine, which limited the PLAAF from acting as an independent service rather than being at first a subsiding service for the PLA Ground Forces. However, it proved that the overall system was mature to train and educate the PLAAF personnel independently in aviation schools, the combat units were qualifying their pilots on their own and finally these 'warriors' were fighting and succeeding against experienced US pilots. Anyway, the basic principles of air operations, strategy and tactics were critically inspired by this baptism of fire between 1950 and 1953.[31]

Conclusions: the Chinese view

In retrospect and surely understandable, one of the most interesting conclusions drawn by the PLAAF reports or reviews of the war is the fact that it differs quite a lot from UN or USAF analysis. This might be seen as a lack of capabilities to analyse the conflict properly and accurately and, especially, to negate the performance and effectiveness of air power or even as a creation of myths, but can also be seen as a 'mirror-image' of the historical context and the political situation. With this in mind it seems as even until the 1980s it was to hold the line behind the own doctrine by deluding themselves

A rare undated image showing a line-up of MiG-15 fighters in an unusual black colour scheme. (via CDF)

about the capabilities and performance of their aircraft.[32] However, there were some interesting 'lessons learned' drawn by the own operations and at least published in an official report[33]:

One of the first lessons was the fact, that the PLAAF acknowledged the higher quality and technological advance of the material the UN forces had available. As such, it was concluded – and became a justification of the further modernisation of the air force – that the quality of the equipment was pivotal for success. However, it was also concluded that the human factor was even if not more important. Since the young Chinese soldiers came from the army or ground forces, they were known to handle difficult situations or even to scarify their live for China. This second point again gives proof for the political standing of the PLAAF or better the PLA, since their own forces were from the ground forces, they were deemed superior even if the UN forces were equipped with higher-quality equipment. This as a third reason – and to even deeper manifest this 'man-over-machine' doctrine – of special importance was the system of a political commissar alongside the real commander to serve the political work and standing within the troops to boost the morale of the fighting soldiers. Finally, fourth additional lessons specified the requirement of a high technical skill among pilots and the maintenance personnel and the need to improve the command structure.

An attempt to draw an objective conclusion in retrospect – myths & consequence

In consequence, the frequently published simple comparisons of kill-loss ratios are often misleading and it is still difficult to judge especially without the historical content behind in mind, the view of what goals or schedules the PLAAF leadership wanted to achieve together simply by measuring on the own – Western – expectations, intentions, values or yardsticks. However especially the superiority of the 'man-over-machine' doctrine and the overall standing of the PLAAF within the PLA led to that strange 'perpetuated misunderstanding and ignorance about the role of air power for more than forty years'[34]. In fact it lead to the creation of myths and a deluded glorification of the PLAAF's achievements, which seems sometimes – in the eye of external observers seem to be distorted, outlandish and most of all self-delusional. Like Xiaoming Zhang stated, 'for too many Chinese air force veterans, the PLAAF's role in Korea nestled in their memories as an unbroken string of victories and heroism', when young and inexperienced Chinese pilots 'bravely challenged their much more experienced American counterparts and defeated them.'[35]

Yet another important factor for the next decade was the crack the relationship to the Soviet Union received: with Stalin's reluctance to step in the war unrestrictedly, the Chinese political and military leaders had to learn that the Soviet Union – regardless the delivery of materials – might be an unreliable alley. Especially in mind of the own material and human losses, the PLA had to bear, China accepted to emphasise on self-reliance, which later led to the split with the Soviet Union, the inner-political turmoil and the long-lasting international isolation until the late 1980s.

As such, one might ask, if most of these conclusions were finally wrong, what could be drawn from them? First of all in retrospect they are reason to explain the next steps since they deeply influenced the further development of the PLAAF, the general doctrine and even more important the relationship to the Soviet Union. Additionally it shows that the PLAAF is only recently – now, exactly 70 years after their foundation – on its way to throw-over the former strategy, which has limited itself to defensive missions only. In retrospect the PLAAF after the Korean War became one of the largest air arms but according to Western standards it was for decades and still might be far from a true modern force. However the events around the Korean War led to a huge positive self-perception of the PLAAF, it shows – again stated by Xiaoming Zhang – that the PLAAF 'can be counted to fight valiantly, despite military insufficiencies, by drawing on pride and the need to protect national security' and most of all 'the will of the Chinese People, not the nation's military capabilities, will likely continue to play a vital role in China's national security decision making.'

But the question is not only what has the PLAAF finally learned from Korea and how the PLAAF will use its only recently newfound military strength, but also what conclusions could any potential adversary draw out of the Korean War. Again, we too should not be so ignorant by simply pointing to the Chinese mistakes and lessons-to-learn but also draw our own conclusions like the Chinese military historian Shu Guang Zhang[36] posted again quoted by Xiaoming Zhang: 'The U.S. military paid scant attention to the strategic thinking of the Chinese Communists. This lack of interest in developing an understanding of a 'non-Western' military philosophy, or the tactics of 'an irregular army', may have been contributing factors to the fatal clash between China and the United States in Korea' but also in other recent and still ongoing conflicts.'

Another rare image taken during the early years of the PLAAF showing a MiG-15 with a Tu-2 in the background.
(via CDF)

Build-up continues

Besides the ongoing operations in Korea, the PLAAF continued with its expansion. By mid-1951 already 17 divisions were created operating around 1,050 aircraft and until late 1952 and early 1953, when the armistice was signed this number had grown to 28 divisions attaining a strength of 1,485 aircraft. The time until early 1954 was dominated by expanding the PLAAF merely by expanding the number of regiments rather than by creating new divisions. Additionally the PLAAF established these first 28 air divisions between 1950 and 1954 nearly solely in preparation to deal with the Korean War and most of these new units were concentrated in the northeast of that vast country and around major cities like Beijing, Nanjing, Shanghai and Tianjin to protect them from Nationalist Air Force air raids. The Korean conflict loomed large as a galvanising event in PLAAF history. After this phase was finished the PLAAF had 29 divisions and 70 air regiments listed, with about 3,000 aircraft.

In parallel to this massive build up in process, the PLAAF established the necessary command structure to control the rapidly increasing number of air divisions, independent regiments and especially aircrafts. As such at first five air corps – in short, an organisational headquarters between a military region and an air division – were founded and in parallel the seven MRAFs were established to control larger geographic areas. However, these were only sometimes aligned to the ground force regions. Overall, these deployments were therefore arranged into seven groups of air divisions and independent regiments. Additionally 13 air corps were established to control one or more air divisions within each MRAFs, and several more command posts to control the aircraft and air defence assets deployed to or operating in a specific area. Even if the once primary 'target' Taiwan had to be postponed, one more air corps was created in the mid-1950s opposing Taiwan. Nevertheless, it was not until First Taiwan Strait Crisis in 1958 that the PLAAF established a constant presence in both the Fujian and Guangdong provinces.

By the end of May 1951, the PLAAF had 17 air divisions, including 12 fighter divisions, two attack divisions, two bomber divisions, and one transport division. Each of the divisions had two regiments.

4th batch

The fourth batch of aircraft was delivered between December 1950 and May 1951 (depending sources) to establish nine divisions:

Date	Base/location	Unit	Sub-units	Aircraft types	Notes
1951 January	Nanjing, Jiangsu	10th Bomber Division	28th Regiment 30th Regiment	Tu-2	Formed out of the 12th Bomber Regiment/ 4th Mixed Aviation Brigade
1951 February	Xuzhou, Jiangsu	11th Ground Attack Division	31st Regiment 33rd Regiment	Il-10	Formed out of the 13th Ground Attack Regiment/ 4th Mixed Aviation Brigade
1950 December	Xiaoshan Xi'an, Zhejiang	12th Fighter Division	34th Regiment 36th Regiment	MiG-9	
1951 April	Xinjin Xi'an, Sichuan	13th Transport Division	37th Regiment 39th Regiment	Il-12	Formed out of the very first transport flight
1951 February	Beijing Nanyuan	14th Fighter Division	40th Regiment 42nd Regiment	La-9	
1951 May	Gongzhuling Huaide, Jilin	15th Fighter Division	43rd Regiment 45th Regiment	MiG-15	
1951 February	Qingdao, Shandong	16th Fighter Division	46th Regiment 48th Regiment	MiG-15	
1951 April	Tangshan, Hebei	17th Fighter Division	49th Regiment 51st Regiment	MiG-9?	Transferred to Naval Aviation as 4th Naval Division on 1 June 1951; re-established as 17th Division in Beijing in March 1956
1951 May	Guangzhou, Guangdong	18th Fighter Division	52nd Regiment 54th Regiment	MiG-15	

5th batch

The fifth batch of aircraft was delivered between September 1951 and May 1952 (depending sources) to establish seven divisions and the first two specialised independent regiments:

Date	Base / location	Unit	Sub-units	Aircraft types	Notes
1951 October	Wuhan, Hubei	19th Fighter Division	55th Regiment 57th Regiment	MiG-15	
1951 September	Bengbu, Anhui	20th Bomber Division	58th Regiment 60th Regiment	Tu-2	
1951 November	Shanghai Dachang	21st Fighter Division	61st Regiment 63rd Regiment	?	later Mudanjianhailang
1951 September	Hengyang, Hunan	22nd Ground Attack Division	64th Regiment 66th Regiment	Il-10	
1952 January	Nanchang, Jiangxi (?)	23rd Bomber Division	67th Regiment 69th Regiment	Tu-2	
1952 January	Zunhua, Hebei	24th Fighter Division	70th Regiment 72nd Regiment	MiG-15	Later Yancun
1952 May	Huxian, Shaanxi	25th Bomber Division	73rd Regiment 75th Regiment	Tu-2 Tu-2U	
1951 November	Nanjing	1st Independent Reconnaissance Regiment		?	
1951 November	Nanjing	2nd Independent Reconnaissance Regiment		?	

6th batch

The sixth batch of aircraft was delivered between December 1952 and March 1953 (depending sources) to establish three divisions and two additional specialised independent regiments:

Date	Base/location	Unit	Sub-units	Aircraft types	Notes
1952 Dec	Liuzhou, Guangxi	26th Fighter Division	76th Regiment 78th Regiment	La-9, La-11	Later Chongming
1952 Dec	Tongxian, Hebei	27th Fighter Division	79th Regiment 81st Regiment	MiG-15	Later Laohekou
1952 Dec	Gucheng, Hebei	28st Attack Division	82nd Regiment 84th Regiment	Il-10	Later Jiaxing
1952 Dec	?	3rd Independent Transport Regiment		?	
1952 Dec	Shijiazhuang, Hebei	4th Independent Bomber Regiment		Tu-4?	Other sources state March 1953

The number of divisions expanded quite rapidly within one and a half year, so that by March 1953 28 divisions and 56 regiments were formed. Additionally yet another change occurred at around the same time after 1953, when the PLAAF began to upgrade all of its divisions to three regiments, as originally indented. Even if this resulted in a massive numerical build-up, it has to be noted, that only two of these regiments were regarded operational or 'combat ready' and the third one was usually used a training regiment.

However, the expansion to three regiments was also a bit different to the early days: when the PLAAF began to establish its first air divisions, most of them had already three regiments, of which in most cases at least one was later relocated and reassigned after the build-up was completed to form the next division (see table). As a result after this first phase was concluded, most of the divisions operated only two regiments, which were usually stationed at a single airfield. With this expansion, in most cases at least one regiment was relocated to another base; a habit until the latest reform to brigades. And to make things even more confusing, between 1964 and 1970, the name of each regiment was changed in 1963 for a short time to a group only to be reinstituted as a regiment in 1970.

7th batch

The seventh batch of aircraft was delivered in early 1954 to establish only one division and one additional specialised independent regiment:

Date	Base / location	Unit	Sub-units	Aircraft types	Notes
1954 January	Jiaxing, Zhejiang	29th Fighter Division	85th Regiment 86th Regiment 87th Regiment	La-11	Later Quzhou
1954 January	Yuanshi, Hebei	5th Independent Reconnaissance Regiment			

In parallel, Naval Aviation established six air divisions and five independent regiments between 1952 and 1955 and added three more naval air divisions during the 1960s.

Aircraft types

For an in-depth account covering the earlier types operated by Chinese Communist Forces in the pre-PLAAF era, especially during the war with Japan and the period up to 1949[37][38], readers might like to look at Lennart Andersson's encyclopaedia *A History of Chinese Aviation*. Consequently, the description of the individual types, operational within the PLAAF will be covered from the first combat unit on right after the foundation of the PLAAF[39]. Transport types like the very first C-46 and C-47 and their Soviet replacements will be omitted, since this book concentrates only on 'combat types'.

Consolidated Vultee B-24M Liberator

During the Second World War, the B-24 was widely used in the Pacific and China theatres. Attempts to acquire the B-24 were initiated by the KMT during summer 1943, and after the Sino-Japanese War, some were used in the civil war. The Communists got one aircraft in June 1946, when a B-24M from the ROCAF revolted and landed at the Yan'an air base, but it was later blown up by KMT's forces in August. A second similar event occurred in February 1949, when two B-24Ms defected and made a safe landing at Shijiazhuang and Beijing air base. At least one was officially introduced in November 1949 with the second one awaiting repairs but due to a constant lack of spares, it was retired in 1952.

The B-25 was a standard bomber in the Far East theatre throughout World War II and it was no surprise that it was also the PLAAF's first bomber. (via CDF)

North American B-25J Mitchell

The B-25 was also widely used in the Far East theatre and became most famous during the 'Doolittle Raid' in April 1942. The first B-25 arrived in China in 1943, and well over 100 B-25C/Ds and 131 B-25Js were supplied during World War II under a Lend-Lease contract. The USAAF also operated several examples during the Sino-Japanese War.[40] Some were used for various missions in the civil war and the Communists received their first B-25J – some sources say six examples – when the Nationalists fled to Taiwan and abandoned them; three more were provided via defections by 1954. Within the PLAAF, one example was in service in August 1949, and when the PLAAF was founded in November, four were reportedly available. They were later used by the Northeast Aviation School until retirement in 1952.

Images of the few DH.98s in PLAAF service are extremely rare. One is visible in the background, but even examples in ROC markings are hard to find. (via CDF)

de Havilland DH.98 Mosquito Mk 26

The DH.98 came to China after the KMT government had ordered in 1947 nearly 200 FB.Mk 26 fighter bombers to be used in the civil war, even if in the end only 137 were actually imported. The PLA seized the first DH.98 in autumn 1948 and gained the second one in March 1949, when the KMT AF's 1st Brigade revolted and descended the Shijiazhuang air base.

In August 1949, both were assigned to the PLAAF and were tasked from September onwards with the air defence of the capital. Allegedly, three more airframes – of 108

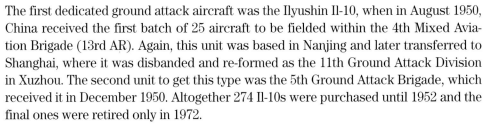

abandoned aircraft found – were awaiting repairs and eventually repaired but already in late 1950, this type was retired.

Ilyushin Il-10 (ASCC 'Beast')

The first dedicated ground attack aircraft was the Ilyushin Il-10, when in August 1950, China received the first batch of 25 aircraft to be fielded within the 4th Mixed Aviation Brigade (13rd AR). Again, this unit was based in Nanjing and later transferred to Shanghai, where it was disbanded and re-formed as the 11th Ground Attack Division in Xuzhou. The second unit to get this type was the 5th Ground Attack Brigade, which received it in December 1950. Altogether 274 Il-10s were purchased until 1952 and the final ones were retired only in 1972.

Operationally, the Il-10 was used during the Zhejiang Island campaign 1954–55. Together with the regular Il-10s, also at least 25 Il-10UTI trainers were purchased.

Il-10s prepare for another mission.
(via CDF)

Ilyushin Il-28 (ASCC 'Beagle') and Il-28U (ASCC 'Mascot')

The successor to the Tu-2 was the Ilyushin Il-28, of which an initial batch of 60 was ordered in September 1952 by the Chinese authorities in September and the first aircraft were delivered already by late October. China obtained a total of 171 Il-28s from the Soviet Union up until 1956, but it is not confirmed if this number included all of the 78 Il-28s (plus 12 Il-28U trainers) which were taken over by Naval Aviation from Soviet troops in 1954 when they left the Dalian-Lüda area.

Alongside the regular bomber version China also ordered several Il-28U trainers in September 1952 and a total of 22 were acquired by 1956.

A rare image of an Il-28. This particular aircraft from the 8th Bomber Division was flown by Li Xianbin, who defected to Taiwan on 11 November 1965.
(via CDF)

Lavochkin La-9 (ASCC 'Fritz') and La-9UTI

One of the first Soviet fighters ordered via the Sino-Russian arms agreement from January 1950, were 129 La-9 fighters. In July, this agreement was expanded to even include licence manufacturing of the aircraft and its engine but it seems as if this deal was changed and allegedly the mid-1949 order included only 120 aircraft to be complemented by a second contract signed in early 1950 about 280 more, which however was no longer fulfilled.

As a first unit, the PLAAF's 1st Fighter Brigade was re-equipped in mid-August 1950 with 13 or 14 La-9s replacing the P-51D/Ks and tasked with air defence duties until they were decommissioned in 1959. Included in this deal was also the delivery of the La-9UTI trainer and by the end of 1949 and China received 60 La-9UTI airframes. Flight training begun in January 1950 and in June that year the 4th Mixed Fighter Brigade (10th and 11th Regiments) became the first operational unit.

The second unit to receive this type was the 9th Division in December 1950. Overall, this type flew quite long as a trainer and was retired only in 1966.

A very rare image of a La-9UTI in PLAAF service. Two-seaters were included in the first batch delivered.
(via CDF)

Lavochkin La-11 (ASCC 'Fang')

Soon after the La-9, the PLAAF begun to introduce the improved La-11, so that already in October 1950, the just converted 4th Mixed Fighter Brigade (11th AR in Nanjing, but some mention also the 10th AR) received 39 La-11s in order to assist Soviet units with air defence of Shanghai. With the re-formation of this regiment, this unit became the PLAAF's 2nd Air Division.

Altogether 163 La-11s were purchased between 1950 and 1953. Operational wise, the La-11 was used in Korea and during the 1954–55 Yijiangshan campaign, when they escorted PLAN ships and Tu-2 bombers but also provided reconnaissance. The final La-11s were decommissioned in 1966.

Succeeding the P-51 and La-9, the La-11 was also an interim fighter, but saw extensive use in several campaigns.
(via CDF)

Mikoyan MiG-9 (ASCC 'Fargo')

The Yak-17s were soon supplemented by a larger number of MiG-9s, which arrived between November and December 1950. Although supplied as a fighter, the MiG-9 proved to be severely limited in performance and suffered from poor manoeuvrability so it too was mostly used as a trainer. Altogether, 369 MiG-9s were delivered with the objective to equip at least six fighter regiments. However, in March 1951, and with the Korean War broken out, it was clear that it was no longer adequate to match opposing Western fighters.

Even Stalin had to admit this and as a result a further 372 MiG-15 were subsequently delivered to the PLAAF free of charge to replace the MiG-9s. Anyway, they were flown until 1959.

Images of operational MiG-9s are extremely rare, especially those showing them in flight or in service. This example is undergoing maintenance.
(via CDF)

Mikoyan MiG-15 (ASCC 'Fagot') and Mikoyan MiG-15UTI

Quite surprisingly, the first MiG-15s were delivered to China already in August 1950, and so even before the first MiG-9. In line with preparations to organise the type's service introduction into the PLAAF the Soviet Union sent to total of 847 engineers and specialists to China. Additionally, by December 1951 plans had been made to implement local production of the MiG-15bis variant at Shenyang and production of the aircraft's engine to be undertaken at Harbin. However, this decision was amended in October 1954 in favour of the later MiG-17.

The MiG-15 became operational in October 1950 due to the pressing need for the Korea War and all delivered were of Soviet origin, either new build or 'second hand' having previously served with Soviet units. Later on, additional ones were supplied until 1961 as attrition replacements. Even if the exact number is not known (one source states 1,460 MiG-15s) it is known that the first delivery comprised 654 MiG-15s in 1950 and 1951 and additional 360 MiG-15 (with 12 MiG-15UTIs) free of charge to compensate the deficiencies uncovered with the MiG-9. Following the MiG-15, in June 1952 the request for improved MiG-15bis fighters was agreed and altogether 482 were provided (348 in 1952 and 134 in 1953).

Between 1951 and 1958 also 357 Mikoyan MiG-15UTI trainers were acquired and at least 83 MiG-15UTIs were delivered from Czechoslovak Socialist Republic (CSSR)

Another line-up of MiG-15s from the Chinese People's Volunteer Air Force – the air arm of the PVA that deployed to Korea. Later in the campaign, these jets received a red nose and North Korean markings.
(via CDF)

production lines. Interestingly, with the MiG-15 and MiG-15bis being replaced by the MiG-17 a project was initiated in 1958 to convert them to trainers and the first prototype was finished in November 1959 possibly as the MiG-15UM. Later in their career, they were gradually transferred to reconnaissance units, aviation schools and also to replace the Ilyushin Il-10 in the attack role until the Nanchang Q-5 arrived.

The final examples ended up as target drones until their final retirement in 1986.

Republic P-47D Thunderbolt

The P-47D was originally left over to the CAF after being used by the USAAF during 1944 in the Sino-Japanese War to support Chinese troops. Soon thereafter, the remaining airframes (allegedly 102) were transferred to the KMT Air Force in 1946 to replace obsolete P-40 Warhawks. Altogether 80 Thunderbolts – 29 P-47D and 51 P-47N – were operational by 1948, and 34 additional P-47N were delivered later.

During the chaotic final days of the CAF, one of them diverted or even defected in June 1949 to the Henan Anyang air base and was officially introduced into the PLAAF in November 1949. However, the awaited repair did not occur and it was finally abandoned in early 1950.

North American P-51 Mustang

The P-51 was certainly one of the most capable fighters in the PLAAF's early days, but due to a lack of numbers it only briefly saw service.
(via CDF)

Similar to the Thunderbolt, the P-51 entered the WW II after 1943 in the Far East Asia Theatre and during the later period of the Sino-Japanese War, units of the USAAF were equipped with P-51s. The CAF received their first P-51B in November 1944 and later also some P-51C, P-51D and P-51K, so that altogether 261 Mustangs were available. After the Sino-Japanese War, the KMT made extensively use of the type during the civil war, with P-51Ds operating from Shenyang Beiling Air base in January 1946.

During 1948, three P-51s defected to the Communists and were transferred to the Northeast Aviation School. Until the end of 1948, several more were seized at the Jinzhou Air base and at the Shenyang Beiling Air base, where a repair shop was established. A first was repaired until 30 December 1948 and altogether 39 P-51s were operated by the PLAAF, most of them of the P-51D fighters, but also a few P-51K for reconnaissance. As noted, the PLAAF's first unit at Beijing Nanyuan Air base consisted of six P-51, which were tasked with air defence of the capital. Later this number was increased to 17.

A very rare colour image of two Tu-2s. In contrast with the fighters, which were rarely painted during this period, the bombers wore dark green colours and white numbers.
(via CDF)

On the PLAAF's founding day on 1 November 1949, 22 P-51 fighters were operational with nine more in repairs. There are reports, that following the delivery of La-9s, several were transferred to the 7th Aviation School, and in 1951 13 were converted into two-seater trainer before being retired in September 1953.

Tupolev Tu-2 (ASCC 'Bat')

At the end of 1949, the PLAAF received 23 former Soviet AF Tu-2 bomber, so that by January 1950 flight training could begin. Other sources mention, that only 20 arrived in

June 1950, with nine more being delivered in October again to the 4th Mixed Aviation Brigade (12th AR). From then on, they assisted Soviet Forces in Shanghai, where this regiment was disbanded and re-formed as the 10th Bomber Division later at Nanjing. The second unit to gain this type, was the 8th Bomber Division in December 1950 and finally the 20th Division at Bengbu. Already in July 1950, the Soviet Union had provided the licence manufacturing rights including its engine, which however was not executed. Altogether 311 Tu-2s were purchased until 1952 and that type was used extensively during the Zhejiang and Yijiangshan Island campaigns in 1954 and 1955.

When the PLAAF introduced the Ilyushin Il-28 in 1954, the surviving Tu-2s were gradually reassigned to other roles including aerial reconnaissance. Therefore, they were equipped with an AFA-IM camera and NAFA-6/50-1 night-capable cameras. Even a few were reportedly re-equipped with the MiG-15 RP-5 radar to serve as specialised Tu-2P/PF night-fighters. After a very long operational career, the final ones were retired in 1982. Together with the regular bomber, also 33 UTB-2 and 29 Tu-2U trainers were used since late 1949 on and the trainers were retired in 1965.

Tupolev Tu-4 (ASCC 'Bull')

This image shows one of the few re-engined Tu-4 bombers, which were used as dedicated drone carriers. The WZ-5 shown in front is a reverse-engineered AQM-34N Firebee. (via CDF)

PLAF started to consider long-range aviation late in 1949 with negotiations to acquire Tupolev Tu-4 bombers during Chairman Mao's visit to meet Stalin. The type was discussed again in 1952 at a time when the Soviets had difficulties to supply Il-28s as quickly as the Chinese wanted, and as a stopgap they offered 120 retired Tu-4s. This was not taken up but only 10 Tu-4s were delivered, although two further examples followed slightly later as a special 'birthday present' from Stalin to Mao. Soviet instructors, technicians and manuals were also sent and the first aircraft arrived in February 1953.

Operationally the Tu-4 was rarely used as a regular bomber, but also as a WZ-5 – and test wise for the WZ-6 UAV carrier aircraft. Besides that, one aircraft was converted to the KJ-1 AEW and there was allegedly also an EW variant. In addition, examples participated in nuclear tests both as drop aircraft and for taking air samples after an explosion.

In PLAAF use the Tu-4s served until 1971, but due to the low serviceability of the original Shvetsov Ash-73TK radial engines as they approached the end of their service life, it was decided in March 1966 to replace them with four more powerful and reliable Zhuzhou WJ-6 turboprops (a copy of the Ivchenko AI-20K). Allegedly, 11 Tu-4s were refitted between 1970 and 1973 before that type was retired in April 1988.

Yakovlev Yak-17 (ASCC 'Feather') & Yak-17UTI (ASCC 'Magnet')

Since October 1950, the PLAAF assisted Soviet forces in Shanghai, and in order to ease the problem of training for Chinese pilots to fly and operate jet fighters like the soon to be delivered MiG-9s, several Yak-17s were delivered. Reports are varying and some sources say that Moscow transferred a total of 43 Yak-17s – eventually including one Yak-17UTI trainer – between 1950 and 1951, whereas other mention only Yak-17UTIs.

The final examples were decommissioned in November 1956.

1   See Bueschel, R. M., *Communist Chinese Air Power* (Frederick A. Praeger, 1968), Part One/Chapter I 'Communist China finds Wings', p 17.

2   See Xiaoming Zhang, *Red Wings over the Yalu*, p 33ff: planned were 120 pilots plus 500 mechanics to visit Soviet aviation schools as well as three to five high-ranking officers.

3   This only changed with Wang Hai (commander from 1985–92), who was the first pilot to command the PLAAF (see *China's Air Force enters the 21st Century*, p 37).

4   See John Golan 'China's hidden Air Power', *Combat Aircraft* volume 11, number 4, 2010.

5   See Xiaoming Zhang, p 38: based on discussions about the Soviet Air doctrines (note 17).

6   See Allen, K. W. et al., *History of the PLA Air Force* (May 1991)
    (http://www.globalsecurity.org/military/library/report/1991/plaaf-ch2.htm) and
    'Early Administrative Structure' p 376 ff (from Chapter 9. PLA Air Force Organisation by Allen, K. W.).

7   At that time this consisted only the cities the Communists had 'liberated' from the KMT so far but especially not the Fujian province and the Eastern part of the Guangdong province
    (see: *China's Air Force enters the 21st Century*, p 37).

8   See Allen, K. W. et al., *History of the PLA Air Force* (May 1991)
    (http://www.globalsecurity.org/military/library/report/1991/plaaf-ch2.htm)

9   See Xiaoming Zhang, p 42ff und also
    http://www.globalsecurity.org/military/library/report/1991/plaaf-ch20.htm
    By then, they had also collected 113 KMT aircraft and on 6 October the CMC approved the following seven aviation schools (hangkong xuexiao/hangxiao) with the 1st through 6th Aviation Schools split and began classes from on 1 December on. Already on 5 January 1950, the 7th Aviation School began with their training in classes.

10 The around 3,000 persons included only 202 pilots, 30 navigators and 2,373 mechanics plus three aviation engineers. Besides that, Communist (88 per cent of pilots but only 15 per cent of mechanics) had to work together with 'accepted' Nationalists (85 per cent of mechanics) and still about slightly more than 100 former Japanese pilots and ground personnel had to be integrated. By 1953 only 94 of these airfields were repaired for operational use, (see: *China's Air Force enters the 21st Century*, pp 38–39 and 'China Today', 1989a, pp 37 and 89)

11 See *China's Air Force enters the 21st Century*, p 38 and 'China Today', 1989a, p 109

12 See Xiaoming Zhang, p 45

13 See note 918 by Yao Jun, pp 163–164

14 Goldstein, M. C; Rimpoche, G., *A History of Modern Tibet, 1913-1951: The Demise of the Lamaist State* (University of California Press, 1989) ISBN 978-0-520-06140-8, pp 679 and 740.

15 See *China's Air Force enters the 21st Century*, pp 39-40.

16 Via Chinese Military Science Academy (2000): History of War to Resist America and Aid Korea, Volume II, Beijing: Chinese Military Science Academy Publishing House, ISBN 7-80137-390-1, p 249.

17 See Allen, K. W. et al., *History of the PLA Air Force* (May 1991)
    (http://www.globalsecurity.org/military/library/report/1991/plaaf-ch2.htm)

18 See *China's Air Force enters the 21st Century*, p 40

19 See Yao Jun, pp 163-164 (via: Yao Jun, Dangdai Zhongguo Kongjun and Lin Hu).

20 See Xiaoming Zhang, p 51 – about 1/3 of the annual sum was allocated to the build-up of the PLAAF and PLN.

21 For a complete review see Chapters 3 to 5 and Appendix II in this book, including a detailed history of the deliveries and individual units.

22 See Xiaoming Zhang, p 45.

23 See: *China's Air Force enters the 21st Century*, p 44, which itself is compiled from data out of 'China Today' (1988a).

24 See Xiaoming Zhang from Chapter 3 onwards (p 55ff).

25 See Xiaoming Zhang, p 62 based on Kathryn Weathersby 'New Russian Documents on the Korean War', *Cold War International History Project Bulletin*, nos. 6 & 7 (Winter 1995-96), pp 30–86.

26 See Xiaoming Zhang, p 84ff.

27 See: Xiaoming Zhang, pp 201–202 based on Wang Dinglie et al., *China Today: The Air Force*, (Beijing. China Social Science Press, 1989), pp 200–201 and Deng Lifeng, *A complete Record of Military Operations since the founding of the State*, (Taiyuan: Shanxi People's Press, 1991), p 313.

Additionally quite noteworthy the PLAAF has published two different sets of figures for the number of claimed shot-down aircraft, which is primarily contributed since the PLA operated the Air Defence Force independently until February 1957. As such the number of 3,818 kills – accumulated of all combat operations flown until 1969 – includes all aircraft shot down and damaged by both the PLAAF and the Air Defence Force. No single PLAAF publication provides a consolidated breakdown of the total that equals 3,818.

28 See *China's Air Force enters the 21st Century*, p 47 ff.

29 See *China's Air Force enters the 21st Century*, p 550ff and drawn by material from Futrell, 1983, p 415.

30 Overall the Soviet pilots flew reportedly 63,229 sorties over Korea, they fought 1,683 combat missions and claimed 1,309 UN aircraft kills, including 30 at night and 212 downed by AAA. Overall their own loss was 225 MiG's including 120 pilots, of which 319 aircraft and 110 pilots were committed combat losses. Of note is that it seems as if the Russians used a stricter system to confirm an aerial kill, which had to be confirmed by an additional source and not only by the pilot's report or a gun-camera film.

See Xiaoming Zhang, page 202 based on Kotlobovskiy, A. V., 'Twenty Years of Combat: A history of MiG-15 Fighters in Combat' Pt. 1., *Aerohobby*, No. 2 (1994), pp 25–29 and Pt. 2 *Aerohobby*, No. 3 (1994), pp 33–37.

31 See Xiaoming Zhang, Chapter 7 and 8 (p 143ff)

32 See *China's Air Force enters the 21st Century*, p 52, but also *Xiaoming Zhang* from Chapter 9 on (p 201ff)

33 Following the end of the war until 1955, the PLAAF leadership had collected 3,653 individual combat reports, which were summarised in the official 'Air Force's Combat Experiences in the War to Resist U.U. Aggression and Air Korea' – Wang Dinglie, et al in *China Today: The Air Force* (1989a, pp 203–211).

34 See Xiaoming Zhang, Chapter 9 (pp 212–213).

35 See Xiaoming Zhang, Chapter 9 (pp 212–213).

36 Shu Guang Zhang, *Mao's Military Romanticism: China and the Korean War, 1950-1953* (Lawrence: University Press of Kansas, 1995) p 261.

37 Based on C. W. Lam's excellent internet page Early Chinese Aircraft
(http://cwlam2000.0catch.com/index.htm).

The page itself is based on a series of articles from Chinese Air Force magazines and Lennart Andersson's encyclopaedia. The parts on imported US/Canadian and Soviet types were actually published in Aerospace Knowledge.

38 Additional sources for that early period are:
• Håkan Gustavsson Aviation Page 'Sino-Japanese Air War 1937-45'
(http://surfcity.kund.dalnet.se/sino-japanese.htm)
• Special 3 – Military Aircraft in the Chinese Civil War (Taipei) ISBN 957-8628-02-1
• 'Chinese Air Force in Action' series (Taipei: Yunhao Press, 1990)
• Ryan, M.A; Finkelstein, D. M and McDevitt, M. A., (ed.), *Chinese Warfighting: The PLA experience since 1949* (East Gate Books, 2003) ISBN 978-0-7656108-7-4

39 Based on C.W. Lam's excellent internet page on 'Early Chinese Aircraft' (http://cwlam2000.0catch.com/index.htm). The page itself is based on a series of articles in Chinese Air Force magazines and Lennart Andersson's encyclopaedia. The parts on imported US/Canadian and Soviet types were actually published in 'Aerospace Knowledge'

40 https://www.skytamer.com/North_American_Mitchell_II.html

OVERALL DEVELOPMENT: JANUARY 1954 TO APRIL 1966

After the war, several agreements were made with the Soviet Union to align not only the political cooperation but also even more the military developments of both Communist states. The main initiator of these changes on Chinese side was the then appointed minister of defence Peng Dehuai. Under his leadership, a period of greater professionalism was initiated for the PLA. As such and closely following the Soviet lines another reorganisation of the national defence assets; the command structure and the operating doctrines were introduced after 1954. The first one was the establishment of the National Defence Council and the Ministry of National Defence.

The second part of the reform was aimed more to the administrative structure, since the PLA was organised along different regional zones: following the territorial consolidation of all Communist armed forces under the leadership of the CCP in July 1947 the army forces were structured into five field armies (FAs). These however – following the intention to reorganise the Chinese military, its command structure and especially strategy along Soviet lines in 1954 – and the briefly existing six military regions (MR) were reorganised into 13 military regions. This was held until 1970 – following the next major reorganisation – when the number of MRs was reduced to 11 and finally to seven ones again in 1985.

The PLAAF Military Region

Followed by the PLAAF HQ, which is more or less an administrative chain or at least the connection between administrative and operational chains – the next step down the PLAAF tier are the military regions. Geographically spoken, the PLAAF is structured along so-called operational areas, which were long also known as air force districts (AFD). These mirrored the so-called military regions (*jūnqū*) and in contrast to the PLA they did not match for quite a long time. The reason for that was the historical unparallel expansion of both the PLA and even more the PLAAF and was only changed in 1985, when the military regions of both branches were consolidated. Only then, the six military region air forces (MRAF) were aligned to the seven general MR, so the boundaries finally matched each other/together only quite late in the PLA/PLAAF's development.

Adding again some confusion to this structure is the fact that for the PLA Ground Forces each MR was divided into several 'military districts' for command purposes, which usually match the administrative provinces. The PLAAF, however, was structured slightly different along each MR and in most cases – for assets near the head-

quarters – they are administered directly by the MRAF. For a long period, an intermediate command organisation in form of either a command post (CP) or air corps (AC) was included, but the PLAAF disbanded this intermediate tier during the PLA's 2003–04 force reduction. Only then within that hierarchy the most important organisation within the PLAAF's structure are the aviation divisions (AD), which are divided even further into the tactically most important command level or combat unit, the aviation regiments.

Another – historically based – problem is a nearly constant restructuring and reorganisation, what Kenneth W. Allen put this just simply together in 2002, when he summarised: 'Since the PLA was formally established from the components of the Red Army in the late 1940s, China has been divided into various operational areas to control the ground, air, and naval components of the armed forces. Over the past fifty years, some PLAAF command organisations (MRAF, Air Corps, Command Posts, and Bases) have been downgraded, upgraded, or disbanded as the PLAAF consolidated and reorganised its regional control capabilities.' And he continues with: 'Trying to track individual command elements is not always easy. There are several instances where some Air Corps were formed, moved to another location to form the basis for an MRAF headquarters, disbanded, downgraded to a Command Post, or re-established later in a new location.'

For many years the JJ-5 was the standard jet trainer, before it was replaced by the JL-8 in the late 1990s. As such it was a genuine anachronism: although fourth-generation fighters were already in use, basic training was still completed on these old aircraft.
(via Top81.cn)

Military Region Air Forces (MRAF)

The long-standing military region air forces and their respective MRAF headquarters make up the second tier within the PLAAF's operational structure and, interestingly, the PLAAF' organises each MRAF according to its missions and battlefield environment. In consequence, the PLAAF does not organise each MRAF the same and a quick view to the ORBAT tables show that not each MRAF has the same number of units, kind of units and missions. However, besides the 'aviation' units each MRAF has to a more or less similar decree subordinated SAM brigades or regiments, AAA regiments as well as radar, communications and support units and subunits. One exception to the general rule that all combat units in each MRAF are under the direct control and command of the MRAF headquarters, are the already mentioned 15th Airborne Corps and 26th Air Division, which were under direct control of the PLAAF HQ following the PLA's 2003–04 force reduction.

Historical review

As already noted, there have been several changes within the PLAAF's operational tier since 1949. Immediately after its founding – after the former aviation offices were renamed – six MRAF headquarters (junqu kongjun) existed between October 1950 and May 1955; these were originally designated by the geographic region for which they were responsible. From May 1955 onwards the MRAFs followed suit, when they were reapportioned and renamed – in this way, they received the names by which they are more commonly known.

For the PLAAF – which used a different system of MRs – the result reflected the main operational task of providing air defence, with the logical merger of the separate branches of the PLA Air Force and the PLA Air Defence Force (fangkong jun). This led to several changes for the MRAF headquarters after 1949. It should be remembered that in contrast to the PLA Ground Forces – which originally had 13 MRs, 12 by February 1955, only to be reduced to 11 in 1970 – the PLAAF did not follow these mergers. The overall situation was thus left largely unchanged, besides the usual movements: to assist in the restructuring of the Chinese air defences, a Soviet Combined Aviation Troop Group stayed in China between February 1950 and July 1951. This resulted in another change, when in May 1955, the six MRs (see table above) and their corresponding MRAF headquarters (junqu kongjun) were reapportioned and renamed. While four of the MRAF headquarters remained in the same location, two of them moved. The Zhongnan MRAF in Wuhan moved to Guangzhou and became the Guangzhou MRAF, wile the Xinan MRAF in Chengdu moved to Wuhan to become the Wuhan MRAF.

Only in August 1985, and in line with the overall consolidation – when the PLA reduced its number of MRs to seven – the Chengdu MRAF Headquarters (junqu kongjun) was established as the seventh PLAAF MRAF. It simply replaced the former Chengdu MRAF Command Post, while the Kunming MRAF Command Post never enjoyed the status of a full MRAF headquarters. Additionally, both the Fuzhou MRAF and Wuhan MRAF – which were only founded as part of preparations for the Taiwan campaign – were disbanded.

In addition, in order to control the aviation and air defence units within a certain geographical area, during the 1950s and 1960s the PLAAF created 13 air corps and several command posts. Yet another internal restructuring in line with these measures was the expansion in the number of departments from six to 11 until May 1955. These comprised: headquarters, political, personnel, military training, schools, engineering, procurement, airfield construction, logistic, finance and the directly subordinated political departments. This structure was then mirrored in each subordinated level.

Original Aviation Office	Founding dates	Location	New MRAF HQ	Founding dates	Location (1950)	Becoming MRAF (1955)
Dongbei (Northeast)	1950 January	First Beijing, later Shenyang	Dongbei (Northeast)	1950 August	Shenyang	Shenyang MRAF
Huabei (North China)	1949 April	Beijing	Huabei (North China)	1950 October	Beijing	Beijing MRAF
Huadong (East China)	1949 September	Shanghai	Huadong (East China)	1950 August	Nanjing	Nanjing MRAF
Huazhong (Central China)	1950 February	Wuhan	Zhongnan (South Central)	1950 September	Wuhan	Guangzhou MRAF
Xibei (Northwest)	1949 November	Lanzhou	Xibei (Northwest)	1950 September 1951 December?	Lanzhou	Lanzhou MRAF
Xinan (Southwest)	1950 January	Chongqing	Xinan (Southwest)	1950 September	Chengdu	Wuhan MRAF

Post 1957: PLAAF and Air Defence Force merge

The history of the ADF dates back between April 1949 and October 1950, when the CMC began organising the army's air defence assets such as anti-aircraft artillery (AAA), searchlight and radar units into an integrated air defence structure. The AAA branch itself was established already in 1946 as part of the ground forces. When then in August 1955 the CMC formally established the PLA Air Defence Force as one of the PLA's four services, the new force was simply created by merging the ground forces' AAA, search-light, observation, and radar units. On 23 October 1950, the PLA Air Defence Headquarters (fangkong silingbu) was formally established – based on a similar structure to the PLAAF – with Zhou Shidi as the commander and Zhong Chibing as the political commissar. During these early years several AD divisions and regiments were integrated into four MR air defence headquarters (Huadong, Huabei, Dongbei, and Zhongnan), which again were structured into air defence divisions (fangkong chu) and air defence command posts (fangkong zhihuisuo). Upon March 1955, Yang Chengwu became the integrated Air Defence Troops (*fangkong budui*) commander and from August 1955 on, the PLA Air Defence Troops became the PLA Air Defence Force (ADF/*fangkong jun*). As such they were designated an independent service (*junzhong*) equivalent to

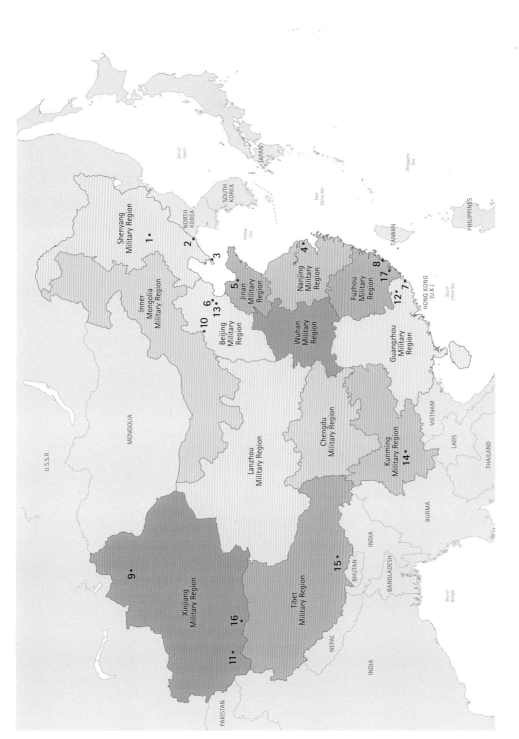

Command Posts
1. Changchun, Jilin
2. Andong, Liaoning
3. Dalian, Liaoning
4. Shanghai
5. Weifang, Shandong
6. Yangcun, Hebei
7. Shantou, Guangdong
8. Jinjiang, Fujian
9. Wulumuqi, Xinjiang
10. Datong, Shanxi
11. Hetian, Xinjiang
12. Xingning, Guandong
13. Shijiazhouang, Hebei
14. Kunming
15. Lhasa, Tibet
16. Xinjiang, Tibet
17. Zhangzhou, Fujian

China and its 13 military regions in the period 1954 to 1970.
(Map by James Lawrence)

As well as aircraft, in early 1960 the PRC procured a limited number of Soviet S-75 surface-to-air missiles as well as an agreement to produce them under licence. The domestic production variant was manufactured as the HQ-1 and was replaced from 1966 by the improved HQ-2.
(via CDF)

the air force and navy. However in May 1957 both services – the ADF and PLAAF – were merged under the air force's leadership, and all command posts were merged into a unified Air Defence Operations Command Post (*fangkong zuozhan zhihuisuo*), led by a mixed leadership of both branches. When this happened, there were 11 AAA divisions operational. Following the establishment in 1952 of the SAM force, the AAA divisions were gradually downgraded to brigades or regiments until today, where the PLAAF has no remaining AAA divisions.

However, with this administrative reorganisation after May 1957, lead only to a briefly fixed PLAAF structure at all. The May 1955 HQAF reorganisation which provided for 11 first level administrative departments reflected the needs of the three general departments (san zongbu): General Staff Department (GSD), General Political Department (GPD) and General Logistics Department (GLD). When the PLAAF and ADF merged, the AD-orientated departments – the AAA Command Department (gaoshepao bing zhihui bu), the Radar Department (leida bing bu), and the Searchlight Department (tanzhao deng bing bu) – were simply added as well as additional Departments in the following years between 1958 and 1965.

Finally, the HQAF had 11 first level administrative departments from 1966–1969. Besides that – and maybe one the most important weak points – the whole structure was aligned to perform the air force's main mission – air defence – which prevented the build-up or establishment of structures to support the PLA's ground forces. The non-alignment of the army and air force headquarters and especially the MRs further separated both services and laid the foundations of the following two severe defeats. Which in return further weakened Peng Dehuai's position, who was later purged and replaced by Lin Biao.

1954–55: the First Taiwan Crisis/Yijiangshan campaign

The 'liberation of Taiwan' which was and surely and is still regarded by many Chinese Red Army officers simply a 'renegade' province was following the Korea War the PLA's next most important emphasis. The biggest problem – and a thorn in the eye of the PLA – was the fact that the Nationalists still controlled several small islands – like Matsu (Mazu), Quemoy (Kinmen/Jinmen) and the Dachen and Yijiangshan Islands – near the coast of the Fujian and Zhejiang provinces and the surrounding airspace over the Fujian, Eastern Guangdong and Southern Zhejiang provinces, which facilitated air raids. Additionally, even worsening the situation for the PLA during that time, the PLAAF maintained not enough air bases or had an overall insufficient strength of units deployed within that region.

Interestingly, this campaign was the first combined operation for the PLA[1] and begun – on besides of the aviation units – with the relocation of several air force units with around 200 aircraft to five forward operating bases. These units included altogether three PLAAF fighter divisions (3rd, 12th and 29th Divisions with La-9?) and three additional PLA Naval Aviation fighter divisions (4th and 6th Division with MiG-15bis and J-5/J-5A), one ground attack division (11th Division with Il-10), parts of one bomber division (20th Division with Tu-2) and two independent reconnaissance regiments. To command the operation, the PLAAF established a forward CP under command of Nie Fengzhi, the then commander of the East China MRAF.

Preceding the military's action, China waited until the May-June 1954 Geneva Conference – with the intent to settle outstanding issues resulting from the Korean War and the First Indochina War – was over. Shortly thereafter, the PLA and the Nationalists in return started a nearly eight-month campaign of artillery, naval and aerial skirmishes. From September 1954 on it was planned to conduct the operations in two phases: the original plan for the air assets was to gain air superiority at first and then to assist the attack on ground targets. Also, it was planned, to use bomber and ground attack planes to target any potential supply ships from Taiwan, to conduct aerial reconnaissance and assistance to the army and naval forces during the amphibious assault. That however proved difficult, since the air force had virtually no capabilities to hit hardened targets and specially to perform pinpoint attacks, the weather situation was not suitable as well and there were no experiences in flying in bad weather, over open water and at night. On the positive side however and even if the Nationalists were flying F-47s and F-84s (the F-86s were still under preparation) there was virtually no air threat, since these islands were far too far off Taiwan's bases.

As a result, first bombing raids during the morning on 1 November 1954 on Yijiangshan performed by Il-10 and Tu-2 had only minimal effect. Officially 288 combat sorties were accomplished on that first day – 168 by MiG-15s, 72 by Tu-2s, and 48 by Il-10s – and 851 bombs being dropped and 3,741 rounds of ammunition fired. These campaigns were continued at a similar tempo, until 20 December but only against land targets. Finally the first operations against sea targets were performed on 10 January with the sinking of five vessels and in preparation of the landing assault, which finally begun on 18 January 1955 again aided by Il-10 and Tu-2 attacks. As such – and even with the recognition of the mentioned obstacles like the lack of coordination between the services – this campaign, which ended with the occupation of the Yijiangshan Island on 25 February 1955, was the first – and also only – 'successful' support for ground and naval forces. Altogether, the PLA lost 19 aircraft during that campaign due to AAA and only 35.9 per cent of the bombs hit their targets, but Yijiangshan was back under Chinese control, and subsequently the Dachen Island group had to be evacuated. In regard to aircraft programmes, the most noticeable fact was the initiation to develop the later Q-5 attack aircraft, which was deemed necessary since there was virtually no capability to attack hardened targets on the ground and since the current types lacked the appropriate combination of range, speed and weapons load while flying both over sea or in adverse weather.

For the PLA however it was only seen as the beginning in the 'liberation of Taiwan'. The next step – especially on behalf of the PLAAF – was the construction of several new air bases during 1956 in the Fujian, Guangdong and Zhejiang provinces in preparation of the air force expansion and by the end of that preparation, the PLAAF had a network of around 40 air bases within Taiwan's range or the aimed offshore islands.

The original four-digit serial system is still not understood. It is shown here on a flight of four J-5s from an unknown fighter unit.
(via CDF)

Units re-established/newly established in March 1956

Date	Base / location	Unit	Sub-units	Aircraft types	Notes
1956 March	Anshan, Liaoning	1st Division	1st Regiment 2nd Regiment 3rd Regiment		4th Division became 1st Division
1956 March	Liaoyang, Liaoning	4th Division	10th Regiment 11th Regiment 12th Regiment		4th Division re-established, later Dalian
1956 March	Ganzhou, ?	9th Division	25th Regiment 26th Regiment 28th Regiment		9th Division re-established; later Foshan?
1956 March	Beijing	17th Division	49th Regiment 50th Regiment 51st Regiment		17th Division re-established; later Tangshan

As a result, quite sadly for the time after the Korea War, not as much information is available as for the earlier period. However quite characteristic for this period is the re-establishment of the divisions, which were transferred to the PLA Naval Aviation and finally the 1st Division, which was formed by the renamed 4th Division. Additionally it is known that already in 1953 the aviation troops were rated as 1st, 2nd and 3rd level 'groups' (dadui) based on their respective training level. Eleven years later this system was even more manifested by adding a ranking-letter – 'A' (jia), 'B' (yi), and 'C' (bing) – to the individual group. Again and quite typical for the chaotic times during the Cultural Revolution, this system was suspended until 1977 only to be reinstalled again and by 1978 even complete 'A'-level regiments (jia lei tuan) were formed. One of the requirement to be rated 'A'-level was the ability to perform all kind of operational missions under both day- and nighttime visual flight regulations (VFR) and instrument flight regulations (IFR) conditions.

Anyway, this general lack of information – even where the units were established and what type of aircraft they flew – continued into the late 1960s and early 1970s. Yet another problematic point is the fact that even if most units were founded on one base, several of the early divisions and their regiments were relocated – sometimes more than once – in order to meet the PLAAF's changing operational needs. As such several units have been established, were merged or later disbanded again based on the criteria to have either a military presence in a particular area, following the introduction of new aircraft types with new capabilities or mission requirements and finally with a re-evaluation of the main and secondary strategic directions.

This happened – similar to the late 1950s to stand Taiwan – during the 1960s especially in response to the Sino-Indian border conflict. Following the 'liberation' of Tibet and as a consequence to China's 1962 border war with India, the PLAAF moved forces into the western regions; a shift from the previous basing concentrations. Slightly later, more units were deployed to the southern region during the Vietnam War, such as in the Guangzhou MRAF and the final shift in basing priorities occurred after the 1969 Sino-Soviet border incident.

Known however is the standard 'table of organisation and equipment' (TOE): since the 1950s a fighter division consisted of 80 aircraft (72 operational fighters plus 8 trainers). For these assets, 120 pilots were assigned, giving a 1:1.5 ratio. As such, each of the three fighter regiments had 24 aircraft and 40 pilots assigned.

For a bomber division the TOE was slightly different with 44 aircraft and 90 flying crews, permitting a 1:1.7 ratio. This resulted in a strength for each regiment of 18 aircraft and 30 crews. In recent times these numbers has been reduced again.

A standard consignment of a typical (fighter) unit during these days was:

1 air division	3 air regiments			75 aircraft
	1 air regiment	3 air groups		24–27 aircraft
		1 air group	3 squadrons	8–9 aircraft
			1 squadron	2–3 aircraft

1958–60: The Great Leap Forward[2]

Besides these military preparations, the political situation changed dramatically both within China and in relation to its most important alley. Even if additional Sino-Soviet cooperation contracts were signed right after the Korea War, a rift between this mutual alliance began gradually to emerge; at first over questions of Communist ideology but later also on international politics and economic development. Especially Mao was quite uncertain about the Soviet policy of economic, financial, and technical assistance to China and believed – as described in the conclusions after the Korea War – that the Soviet help fell not only far short of his expectations and the Chinese people's needs but he was also wary of the political and economic dependence in which China might find itself. For example, China owed about three billion Chinese *yuan* plus one billion more worth the weapons and equipment received by the Soviet Union – equivalent to about USD 1.3 billion[3] – and Moscow kept an careful eye on these rising depts. As long as the partnership was intact, this had no effect, but with these ideological differences rising until 1960, it was yet another contribution for the final split and China was only able to pay these dues in 1964.

As a consequence – but most likely even more as in internal anti-rightist drive – the CCP initiated in 1958 a radical militant approach toward economic development as The Great Leap Forward campaign under the new General Line for Socialist Construction. Even if the party leaders were apparently quite satisfied with the accomplishments of the First Five-Year Plan (1952–57?), many of the more radical members including Mao believed that even more could be achieved in the Second Five-Year Plan (1958–62) if the people would be ideologically aroused and if the domestic resources could be utilised more efficiently for the simultaneous development of industry and agriculture. Therefore – under the Xiafang movement (down to the countryside) – cadres were sent to factories, communes, mines and public works projects for manual labour and first-hand familiarisation with grassroots conditions in order to create a new socio-economic and more responsive political system created in the countryside and in a few urban areas.

However, this intensive mobilisation of the peasantry and other mass organisations, which received ideological guidance and political indoctrination by technical experts and political commissars led to creation of about 23,500 communes with each averaging about 5,000 households or 22,000 people. Each commune was organised along paramilitary and labour-saving lines and was to operate as the sole accounting unit. In consequence, The Great Leap Forward was not only an economic failure, which resulted in a severe shortage of food – even more worsened by natural disasters like the devastating famine between 1960–61 – but also a 'Great Leap Backward' for the developing industry and an immense waste of resources. This resulted – especially hard hitting the developing aviation industry – in a shortage of raw materials for the industry, an overproduction of poor-quality goods, a deterioration of industrial plants through mismanagement and an exhaustion and demoralisation of both the peasantry and the intellectuals, not to mention the party and government cadres at all levels.

In consequence, throughout 1959 efforts were initiated to modify the administration of the communes in order to partly restore the few achievements made so far and to decentralise control. Politically Mao as the main initiator of that failure had to bear the consequences and he stepped down from his position as chairman of the People's Republic in April, though he remained chairman of the CCP. As Mao's successor, the National People's Congress elected Liu Shaoqi.

Besides these change in leadership, the Great Leap Forward policy came under open criticism especially led by the Minister of National Defence Peng Dehuai. He – allegedly encouraged by Soviet leader Nikita Khrushchev to oppose Mao – had already pointed to adverse effects of Mao's policies on the modernisation of the armed forces and – quite modern in his sightings – he argued that 'putting politics in command' was no substitute for economic laws and realistic economic policy. This however was too much of criticism especially after the defeat in the Second Taiwan Strait Crisis and Peng Dehuai was deposed in the summer of 1959. Peng Dehuai was replaced by the radical and opportunist Maoist Lin Biao, who initiated a systematic purge of Peng's supporters from the military, which in the end would contribute to yet additional havoc in the near future.

1958: the Second Taiwan Crisis/Quemoy crisis and a severe humiliation

- ● Major cities/towns
- ● Base

Locations
1. Fuzhou
2. Jinjiang
3. Liancheng
4. Longtian
5. Shantou
6. Zhangzhou

▶ Map showing the operational theatre for both Taiwan crises between 1954 and 1958. (Map by James Lawrence)

These militancy tendencies on the domestic inner-political front were echoed as well in the international scene and external policies and became a complete reversion from the former 'soft' foreign policy based on the Five Principles of Peaceful Coexistence to which China had subscribed during the mid-1950s to a hard line beginning with 1958. Already throughout 1956 and 1957 occasional clashes between PLAAF and Nationalist fighters occurred – additionally provoked by regular reconnaissance missions flown by the ROCAF over Chinese territory – but finally in 1958 the Communists saw their chance for a combined invasion. Following lengthy discussions by the CMC between May and July 1958 it was planned to move the PLAAF to Fujian at first in parallel to resumed massive artillery bombardment of the Nationalist-held offshore islands of Matsu (Mazu) and Quemoy (Kinmen/Jinmen) between August on through October by

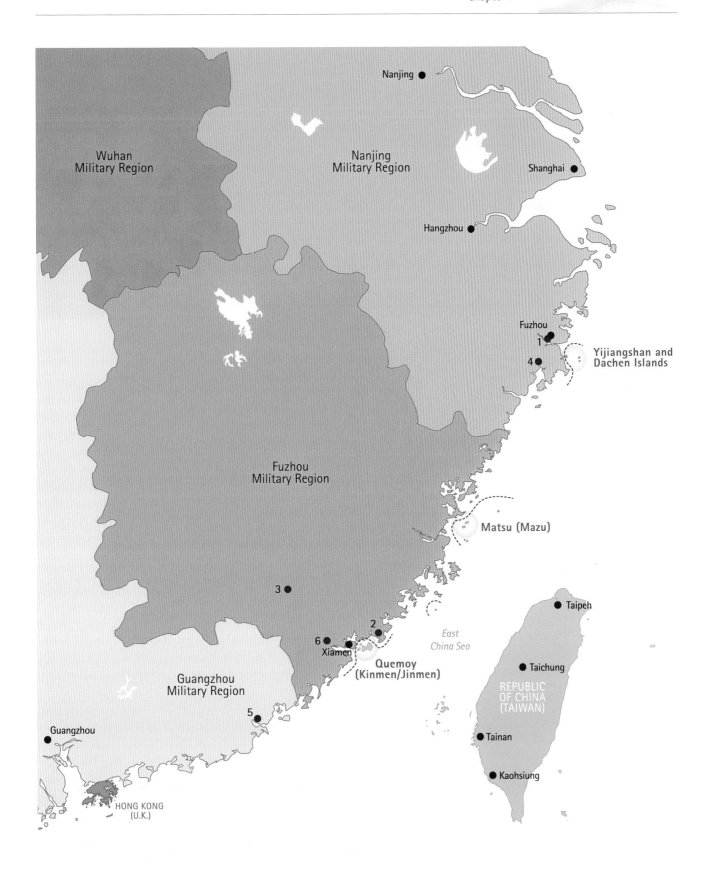

Two typical images of the period, showing several Il-28 and/or early H-5 bombers on the flight line and the usual political education in front of the aircraft.
(Both via CDF)

the PLA. This was accompanied by an aggressive propaganda assault on the United States and a declaration of intent to 'liberate' Taiwan.

In contrast to the successful first Taiwan campaign – which was in the end only a limited operation – the Chinese government had several additional reasons to the believe of an even more successful final liberation: at first they were confident that the US will not step in because of the preoccupation with the Middle East crisis. As such, the shelling of a 'minor important' offshore island was a test for any potential US reaction. Second, they thought once air superiority was reached and especially the sea interdiction became effective, these off-shore islands became isolated without supply and would surrender after a short time and finally this campaign was to aid two other political goals. At first it was to stimulate a greater internal strive for the declining enthusiasm of The Great Leap Forward movement and – maybe most important – it would demonstrate a greater independence from the Soviet Union, since the ally was not informed from the beginnings.

In order to prepare for the upcoming campaign – and even more since wide parts of that area were still a free-flight zone for the ROCAF – the PLAAF established several new air bases since 1956. In addition, the PLAAF begun to practice much more intensively to fly over the Formosa Straits, what in return lead to few aerial encounters between PLAAF and ROCAF fighters. Early in the preparations, the PLA secretly deployed two fighter regiments (10th AR/4th NAD and 46th AR/16th Division PLAAF with 74 MiG-17s).

The involvement of the PLAAF[4] within that campaign can be divided in two phases: within the first one between 27 July and 22 August to move in to the Fuijian Guangdong area and quickly to achieve air superiority. For this the 1st Air Corps from Fuzhou used as a core and filled up by experienced Korean War and Yijiangshan campaign veterans from the 5th Air Corps from Hangzhou were moved to establish a command structure in Fujian. For that purpose, the so-called Fuzhou MRAF was organised in August 1958 to command PLAAF units in Fujian and Jiangxi and the preparations were completed until mid-August, when the PLAAF and PLA Naval Aviation transferred huge amounts of material including aircraft, air defence systems like radar, anti-aircraft artillery and searchlights into the theatre. The following aircraft came from at least five PLAAF fighter divisions (1st, 9th, 14th, 16th and 18th Divisions with MiG15bis, MiG-17F and J-5?), two bomber regiments (Il-28 and Tu-4) and parts of the 4th PLAN Naval Aviation Division later complemented by four more divisions including ground attack units (Il-10) deployed to Fuzhou, Jinjiang, Liancheng, Longtian, Shantou and Zhangzhou. Finally, altogether six regiments formed the first ring of front-line of units – with about 200 aircraft – and 17 more the second line. During this phase, the PLAAF vigorously tried to achieve air superiority in four air battles but finally failed. Altogether, the PLAAF and PLA Naval Aviation deployed 691 aircraft for that operation. Right from the beginning of this phase, the PLAAF intensified its flights over the Formosa Straights, again provoking several encounters with ROCAF fighters; the first air battle took actually place on 29 July over Shantou[5] (18th AD/54th AR). Apparently, the appearance of MiG-17s, which was in fact not known by then, caused considerable surprise to the allied forces and as a direct consequence, the United States delivered their latest AIM-9B AAMs to the ROCAF. This was even more surprising, since that missile was just introduced into US Navy service. On Taiwanese side, F-84Gs and RF-84Fs, were used respectively for naval strikes and reconnaissance missions over the mainland. These types were escorted by F-86s in order to counter PLAAF and PLA Naval Aviation operations. According to PLAAF reports, the ROCAF flew about 100 sorties each day. On the PLAAF's side, officially 1,077 sorties were logged in Phase 1 until 22 August. Altogether these were flown in 255 groups engaging in four aerial combats with four claimed kills, damaging five more while losing one. Also of note, the PLAAF issued three major rules of engagements established during the preparations for the assault, namely that the pilots should avoid the high seas, bombing of Matsu and Quemoy should not occur as long the ROCAF did not bomb the mainland and finally PLAAF were strictly forbidden to engage any US military unless US aircraft did not enter Chinese airspace.

The first phase ended on 22 August – even if originally scheduled to last only until 24 July – with the shelling of Quemoy on 23 August. Overall this second Phase showed some certain differences on both sides: for example, the ROCAF begun to operate the AIM-9B AAMs, the USAF introduced around 140 (144?) F-100 and F-104 in the Taiwan theatre and the PLAAF begun to introduce the J-5 – a licenced variant of the MiG-17F – albeit most likely in limited numbers only (eventually only two regiments). Especially the use of AAMs – for the first time successfully in history on 24 September over Jingmen[6]. In addition, more aircraft were deployed to airfields in Fujian and eastern Guangdong, also the PLAAF doubled the number of fighter divisions on the frontline from one to two – and the intensity of the aerial battles increased with sometimes between 30 to 80 aircraft involved on ROCAF's side flying 100 to 200 sorties per day. The PLAAF responded also with an increase with 250 sorties in three separate engagements. As a pre-emptive measurement in case, the ROCAF would retaliate with bombing raids against mainland bases, the PLAAF and Naval Aviation had transferred several bomber regiments – one Tu-4 regiment and two Il-28 regiments – to Zhangzhou. To complement the true bombers also two MiG-15 and one Il-10 regiments were deployed, however since the Nationalists did not attack, the PLAAF did not retaliate.

In contrast to the first phase, the second one lasted from 23 August to mid-October and was characterised by the PLAAF's and Naval Aviation's attempts to use their superior numbers in order to contain the Nationalists. Also, the PLAAF lost one J-5 (piloted

A rare image, the caption of which mentions the unit: these J-5s are allegedly from the 18th Fighter Division. (via CDF)

by Liu Wiming from the 9th Division, 27th AR) via friendly fire by PLA anti-aircraft artillery over Zhangzhou. It was most of all characterised by several more and larger air battles – altogether three major ones – and the deployment of additional aircraft to several airfield in Fujian and Guangdong in order to blockade Quemoy and provide air cover for the naval operations and army artillery shelling. Similar unsuccessful like the first phase in achieving its pre-set goals, the PLA was never able to completely stop the supply of the Quemoy garrison within the second phase. As such after a stalemate was reached by the end of October, with the Nationalists still controlling the air over the Taiwan Strait and the PLAAF over the Fujian, Zhejiang and Guangdong provinces a temporary ceasefire was implemented.

Conclusion

Measured by the own originally set goal – the 'liberation' of Taiwan to bring back home the 'renegade' province – the PLA and particular the army artillery and the PLAAF suffered a hefty defeat which is still seen as severe humiliation. In consequence, it weakened further the already waggling position of Minister of National Defence Peng Dehuai, which finally led to his demission in the summer 1959.

Interestingly, and similar to the review of the Korean War, PLAAF and US reports vary quite widely with overall a different toll of victories and losses[7]. PLAAF sources report of altogether 3,778 sorties flown by 691 aircraft. Their fighters were engaged in 13 air battles and downed 14 enemy aircraft plus damaging another nine. The PLAAF admitted the loss of only five aircraft and five more being damaged. Additionally, the AAA units were involved in seven battles, downing two aircraft and damaging two more.

USAF sources in contrast list 25 air battles and the downing of 32 PLAAF aircraft plus probably three more and damaging ten. The Nationalists allegedly lost only four – other sources speak of three or five – aircraft. So even if the PLAAF gained additional combat experience, this failed coup revealed still several severe shortcomings, since the PLAAF was not able to capitalise their numerical superiority: first of all, with more than 500 aircraft deployed the PLAAF still lacked any capability for deep strikes. Second, the coordination between PLAAF and ground-based defences was far from optimal resulting in the downing of at least one MiG-17F and the revision of the AAA guidelines for future air and ground combat operations and most of all PLAAF logistics fell short of its expectations.

Kenneth Allen calculated by 'assuming that only the six regiments (about 200 aircraft) deployed along the front line conducted these sorties, each fighter flew an average of five sorties over the 23-day period – one sortie every four days. If the number of aircraft was greater, the number of sorties declines accordingly.' Consequently, even if not openly admitted, the success was rather disappointing and fell short of the expectations, allegedly due to still severe limitations within the PLAAF's logistical support capabilities.

However, the probably most positive effect for the PLAAF was the lessons learned from the review: revised training syllabi and an increase of the number of PLAAF schools to 29 and during this period as well as the writing of new regulations and teaching materials based on its own combat and operational experience proved valuable for the next period.

Nevertheless, it can be seen as a minor victory, that the ROCAF lost its dominance over the southeastern and southern Chinese airspace over the Fujian, Eastern Guangdong and Southern Zhejiang provinces and the PLAAF established finally a permanent presence opposite to Taiwan. And last, it proved that the United States was unwilling to directly engage PLA forces as well as its military support to Taiwan was restricted – at least for a longer time – to technical assistance and logistics, even more limiting the ROCAF's operational capabilities.

As already mentioned, the non-informing of Moscow prior to the finally failed coup helped to hasten the split between China and the Soviet Union. However, China received still valuable military assistance – the early delivery of MiG-17F is one example – and even received its first S-75 (ASCC SA-2 'Guideline') missiles (altogether five launchers and 62 missiles) for air defence in October, which facilitated the establishment of the PLAAF's SAM forces in 1958. The very first SAM battalion was based near Beijing and in line with this newly established force. The PLAAF founded a specialised missile school at Sanyuan in the Shaanxi province. Interestingly, the SAM forces are referred by the PLAAF as 'second artillery' in order to distinguish them from the AAA troops, which are regarded as 'first artillery'. This however often causes confusion, since the 'second artillery' also refers to the PLA's ballistic missile force. In addition, similar to the first successful operational use of AAMs in aerial combat, on 7 October 1958 a Nationalist RB-57D flying over Beijing at an altitude of 20,000m (65,617ft) was downed as the first ever successful SAM engagement.

For many decades the PLAAF used underground air bases or tunnels, which were not only used as aircraft shelters but for concealed preparations ahead of operations. These three Il-28s or H-5s are at an unknown location. (via CDF)

Tibet and India

Even if Taiwan was the most important flashpoint since ever, there was yet another one in the complete opposite direction – in Tibet and India. Chinese control over Tibet had originally been reasserted in 1950 and finally in May 1951 China has granted Tibet and the adjacent Xinjinag province the status of an 'autonomous region'. In reality, Beijing was responsible for all foreign affairs and the former Tibet's army was incorporated into the PLA. The socialist revolution that took place thereafter however became increasingly a process of 'Sinicization' for the Tibetans. The ongoing and always suppressed tensions culminated in a revolt between 1958-59 in which the Dalai Lama, the Tibetans' spiritual and de facto temporal leader, fled together with thousands of Tibetan refugees to India. This additionally deteriorated and complicated the already tensed relationship to India, since a lot of sympathy for the rebels aroused. Even worsening the situation and finally culminating in the brief Sino-Indian border war in October 1962, there were several border incidents in 1959 – China acclaimed sovereignty to Aksai Chin, a territory India regarded as its own like parts north of Jammu and Kashmir, Uttar Pradesh and Aruachal Pradesh.[8]

Even if the war – in which China achieved all its policy objectives of securing borders in its western sector and retained de facto control of the Aksai Chin with now a de facto borders being 'stabilised' along the Line of Actual Control (LAC) – was only a ground war fought by the PLA, it remained a hot spot for decades to come and consequently led to a constant presence of all PLA branches in that area. Several more skirmishers occurred in late 1967 – like the Nathu La Incident and the Chola Incident – in 1987 and again only recently in 2017 in a military standoff. Most surprising for

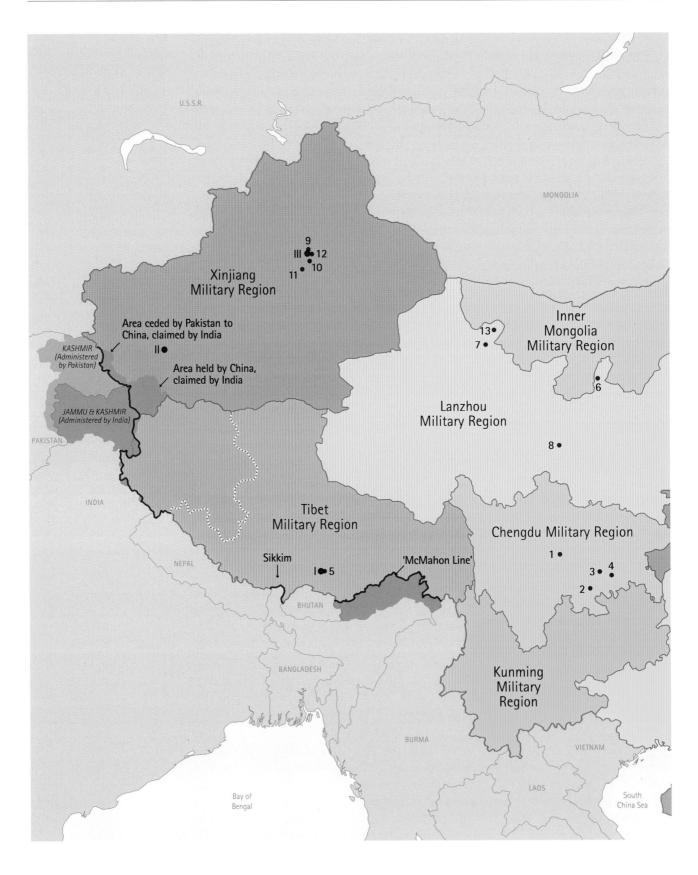

the Chinese political establishment however was that Moscow gave India its moral support in the dispute, which contributed even more to the growing tension between Beijing and Moscow.

The 1960s: break with the Soviet Union[9]

Even if this Sino-Soviet dispute was slowly growing through the late 1950s – itself a most momentous period of development and expansion for the PLAAF – the subsequent decade is characterised by the break with the Soviet Union. It finally escalated in 1960 and as usually was contributed by several factors. Right after the establishment of the People's Republic, Mao travelled to Moscow to negotiate the 1950 Sino-Soviet Treaty of Friendship, Alliance, and Mutual Assistance. Known and repeatedly quoted is the military support, the weapons deliveries and the large amounts of economic and technological assistance, including technical advisers and machinery China received under this agreement. However, in return – besides a growing toll of dues – China gave the Soviet Union certain rights, such as the continued use of a naval base at Luda in the Liaoning province.

It was quite clear from the beginning that China was only a junior partner under Soviet leadership in which China would initially only adopt and learn from the models of economy, society and especially military. This was deepened further through the Korean War even if seen from the outside China again became more dependent from a foreign country than before. However, with the lessons learnt in Korea, China desire to achieve self-reliance and independence and most of all with emerging questions over ideology and economic development, Beijing became more and more dissatisfied with several aspects of the Sino-Soviet security relationship.

The maybe final cut came with the Soviet change in leadership to Nikita Khrushchev and the following de-Stalinisation. While in the Soviet Union this lead to a more conciliatory policy of 'peaceful coexistence with the West', Mao became more radical than before in his beliefs that 'the East Wind prevails over the West Wind' and proceeded with a far more militant policy toward the non-communist world. This again led to an unyielding position on the issues of anti-imperialist struggle, an increasing competition for influence in the Third World and a rising rivalry within the international communist movement in general.

In 1966, the CCP finally cut all ties with the Communist Party of the Soviet Union, which was only restored by mid-1987. This – quite logically – had to lead to sever disagreements and even more to a series of situations, where both communist states collided with their opinions: the first example was the Soviets unwillingness to give China undisputed support on the Taiwan question especially during the 1958 campaign. During the same year the Soviet proposed a joint naval arrangement, which would have put China only in a subordinate position and in mid-1959, the Soviets terminated an agreement signed in late 1957, which was to assist China in its ambitions to develop its own nuclear weapons and missile projects. Finally, the Soviet neutrality during the tensions on the Sino-Indian border the same year were interpreted by Beijing even more as a moral and political support to India.

Sometimes mentioned are also territorial issues, which became more intense by 1963 when China explicitly raised the question about territories lost through 'unequal

Key

● PLAAF Command Posts

● PLAAF Bases

— Disputed Borders

▪ Disputed Territories

Command Posts

I   Lhasa CP

II   Hotan CP

III   Wulumuqi CP

PLAAF Bases

1. Qionglai (HQ)
2. Luzhou
3. Dazu
4. Chongqing-Shashiyi/ Baishiyi (HQ)
5. Lhasa/Gonggar
6. Yinchuan (HQ)
7. Jiuquan Qingshui
8. Lintao
9. Changji
10. Malan/Uxxaktal
11. Korla-Xinhiang
12. Ürümqi South (Wulumuqi)
13. Dingxin 14th Air Base

◀ Map showing the operational theatre for Tibet and the Indian crises in 1962 as well as the disputed territories.
(Map by James Lawrence)

treaties' with the Tsarist Russia. The following consultations in 1964 to solve this issue led to an increased Soviet military build-up along the Sino-Soviet border well into the 1970s and finally culminated in the bloody Sino-Soviet Border Conflict during 1969. The final nail to the coffin of this communist brotherhood was surely the devastating attempt to break away from the Soviet model of economic development during the already mentioned Great Leap Forward movement between 1958 and 1960, which led Moscow to withdraw all Soviet technicians and advisers from China in August 1960[10]. With this step the Soviets reduced or cancelled all economic and technical aid to China, which not only was a strong political sign but also an even more severe setback for all development efforts in industry and high-technology issues, most of all the nuclear programmes and especially the aviation industry. In retrospect, this discord became most important for any future developments in Chinese foreign relations – including the brief Sino-US honeymoon during the mid-1980s – and finally in the long term – after yet another disappearance from the international scene until Deng Xiaoping's rehabilitation in 1978 – outweighed the benefits Beijing had received as Moscow's junior partner.

Consequences for the aviation industry, its projects and the PLAAF

The Korean conflict proved to be an important factor in getting this programme on the move but no examples of the fighter variant were built in China, although repair factories were set up at Harbin, Shenyang and Zhuzhou. The second fighter to be brought into service was the MiG-17F and from 1961 onwards, work began on the licence manufacture of the MiG-17PF interceptor. As noted in the previous sub-chapter the Soviet withdrawal of all technical advisers and consultations had not only severe consequences on the political but even more on the operational side, since the following years proved to be a most difficult period for the PLAAF and even more to the just recovering Chinese aviation industry, which almost collapsed even if this setback and decline in retrospect was nothing in comparison the PLAAF and aviation industry had to face during and after the Cultural Revolution.

In many ways the early years of the developing Chinese aviation industry were influenced by the PRC's newly established political system and the decisions made by its Communist Party leaders. As a result, several important goals were set in the First Five-Year Plan, but the principal aim was to build up an indigenous and competitive aviation industry. In fact, with the assistance of China's bigger 'Soviet' brother, the First Five-Year Plan was actually completed ahead of schedule in 1956 and this led political leaders to think about rather more ambitious objectives for the Second Five-Year Plan. Now the aim was to concentrate on the development and series production of indigenous aircraft designs, the weapons and missiles that would arm them, and also ground-based missiles. Actually, just like the Soviet Union and every Western nation with its own aircraft industry, in the mid-1950s there were substantial discussions inside China towards putting missiles into service instead of aircraft. Some Chinese experts insisted that every effort should be made towards developing and producing missiles alone, but others argued for the simultaneous development of missiles and aircraft. A third group had also suggested that the First Five-Year Plan should concentrate on missiles while the Second Five-Year Plan would cover aircraft development. After much debate and argument between many aviation specialists, including Gao Fangqi, Qian Xuesen, Ren Xingmin, Shen Yuan, Wang Bi and Xu Changyu, the decision was reached to proceed with both aircraft and missiles, since each direction seemed to have its strong and weak points.

The Third Ministry of Machine-Building was one of the central offices within the PRC's administration and was responsible for overseeing the country's aviation industry. It was actually established in April 1955 but its roots go even further back to the Aviation Industry Administration Commission established on 17 April 1951. Interestingly, besides the discussion on missiles versus aircraft, there was a great deal of discussion between China's political and military leaders and the various design institutes, construction teams and manufacturers as to which direction to take in terms of new indigenous fighter types. One group favoured a more careful and progressive path by using original Soviet designs and manufacturing techniques and to accept Soviet assistance, whereas the other preferred a totally radical approach which was typical of the spring 1958 period during the Great Leap Forward. The objective of the Great Leap Forward was to use China's vast population to rapidly transform the country from a primarily agrarian economy dominated by peasant farmers into a modern, agriculturalised and industrialised communist society. This could be summed up by a political propaganda slogan which said 'It is better to take good heed of 300 poems from the Tang Dynasty rather than to follow a single theory from Mikoyan'.

In March 1958 the Bureau of Aviation Industry (then called the Fourth Bureau, No.1 Mechanical Industry Department) proposed a development plan to catch up with the leading aviation nations within the next 15 years, because it had been recognised that China's current industrial base and standard in research was outdated. During an aviation industry convention held on 25 March 1958 the Air Force Commander Liu Yalou presented an important speech which demanded that the PLAAF should support the aviation industry as much as possible, starting with the necessary technological research that would provide the opportunity to produce indigenous designs. He ordered the country's leading aviation experts to make use of in particular the 'spirit and imaginative forces of youth to close the gap on the other leading aviation nations', and to do this within the next 15 years. On 7 May 1958 the industry presented its report to the CMC which described in detail the current weaknesses and declared that at this time there was a big variation between industrial production, the design effort and industrial research; in fact that Yalou's statement more than just an illusion. This occurred only just before the Shenyang JJ-1 trainer prototype took off for its maiden flight on 26 July, which was heralded by many politicians as a great success. At another conference held in Shenyang between 6 and 15 August it was decided to work towards the goal of independent design using self-mobilisation – in line with the then ongoing Great Leap Forward campaign. At first, however, this had the opposite effect of stopping nearly all industrial work and scientific and military research by the end of 1958.

In this context it is perhaps difficult to take the Dong Feng series seriously as 'real' or at least realistic projects, but one has to understand the political background as well. First of all, 1958 was a revolutionary time, when a wave of national enthusiasm saw everyone wanting to participate in, and contribute to, China's advance in the world. The air force in particular wished to play its part and so, besides the factories

This image shows the JJ-1 prototype during its roll-out ceremony in 1958, together with the development team. (via CDF)

and design institutes, many aviation schools would propose new aircraft. Indeed, several designs (sadly mostly still unknown 'paper-planes') were submitted not by the institutes but by students and their teachers, and the Party Committee supported this process. In order to assess these proposals another conference was held (possibly led by Tang Duo) which had the directors of several faculties and institutes present as well as secretaries from the political and military departments for education, and their objective was to decide whether to accept these new designs or not. These efforts were further stimulated by two emerging treats from America, the Republic F-105 and Convair B-58, which were seen by the CMC's Vice Chairman, Vice Premier and Minister of Defence, Marshal Peng Dehuai, as the main opponents for any new Chinese fighter types. When Peng Dehuai was inspecting one of the design institutes the design team reportedly asked him if they could consult with the Soviet Union, but he ordered that any new design and development work should be done independently, and under strict security.

In the end the Great Leap Forward did not bring the promised success or progress; instead it brought big setbacks to the aviation industry's initially flourishing development and the loss of time, money and also a lot of lives. Many of the goals were set by politicians and these proved to be over-ambitious and just too unrealistic, but their creators were too arrogant to admit it. Up to 1960, new aircraft and engine factories had been built both in Chengdu and Xi'an, and many older facilities had been updated, reconstructed and expanded, including both the Harbin Aircraft and Harbin Aero Engine factories. After that the plans for the future moved towards establishing some new factories and industrial bases in the inland areas of China's southwest and northwest, thereby starting a shift away from the older coastal areas. In addition, the initial success of the first five-year programme could not be doubled over the next five-year period (as planned) because there were still laws and rules for successful engineering that needed to be respected. One common phrase from these times was 'trial production at a fast pace', rather than working to a sensible programme of research, testing, quality management and production standards. As a result, there was a serious loss of quality caused by large-scale changes in organisation, production and manufacturing processes, and not a single aircraft or engine of the J-6 fighter was delivered between 1958 and 1960.

In fact, up to 1962, no new factories were completed to the required standards, while more than 70 per cent of the country's entire constructed facility area – about 1.02 million m^2 (10.97 million sq ft) – had to be repaired or rebuilt during 1958 to 1966. To make matters worse, owing to several disagreements, from the second half of the 1950s the secure relationship with the Soviet Union began to decline rapidly which eventually led to China braking away from the Soviet model of Communism and in particular its method of economic development. As a result, the Soviet Union ended the previous brief but flourishing period of technical assistance and cooperation by withdrawing all technical advisers (including aviation personnel), stopping deliveries of aircraft and spare parts to China, and taking back or spoiling a lot of technical drawings and documents used for manufacturing procedures. This is of course according to the Chinese version of the story – it is quite likely that a lot of documents were lost because of the political chaos in China itself – either deliberately or by accident.

The biggest problem was the fact that the engineers completely underestimated the development task while progress was constantly influenced by the politics of the

Great Leap Forward. During this period, and through national pride, arrogance and political ignorance, all the laws of science and the rules of good manufacturing with quality control were usually put to one side, with the result that the production standard for the early DF-102s was at best very poor. Again these efforts fell into the period when the nation had become far too over enthusiastic, over ambitious and in the end blinded by the success of its first aircraft projects and so, as before, most of the rules for proper engineering, careful testing and solid research were neglected just to get the aircraft flying. Because it was classified by the political leaders as a high-priority project the work was again rushed ahead without the necessary care. Not only was there the problem of mastering the new manufacturing techniques (which resulted in severe quality of manufacture problems for both airframe and engine) but the lack of certain critical materials was also an issue. This reportedly led to bad decisions to replace these materials in certain areas with parts made in materials offering lower strength and/or less heat-resistance, and these were manufactured without the necessary additional testing.

In retrospect, during the late 1950s and early 1960s China realised what a long and difficult task the development of an indigenous fighter would be. After holding several meetings to analyse the situation the Chinese Aeronautical Establishment came to two important conclusions: the first statement clearly admitted, that no suitable professional scientific research facilities were available in China and well organised design offices and experimental facilities were in short supply all over the country. And second, that the design teams, even if politically motivated and theoretically well prepared for their tasks, lacked sufficient reserves of manpower and resources and the necessary level of design experience. In addition, it was accepted that setbacks and twists and turns within the development process of a new aircraft were inevitable and normal and not a sign of political counter-revolutionary attitudes on behalf of engineers and workers; a statement which, however, was soon forgotten during the Cul-

In most photographs the serial numbers were deleted to hide the operational unit, as evidenced by these very early J-6 fighters.
(via CDF)

tural Revolution. In order to address these issues a tremendous effort was made during the late 1950s and early 1960s to establish several research and design institutes, such as the Aviation Research Institute founded in 1961, with the objective of having specialist establishments in the fields of aerodynamics, structural strength, materials and manufacturing, airframes, engines, instruments, accessories and weapon design. For example, the Shenyang Aircraft No. 601 Institute focused at first on a wide range of aircraft design, starting in May 1962 with an analysis of the Soviet MiG-21 under the term 'grasp of technology'. The significance of this slogan was often expressed by Tang Yanjie because he knew that scientific research was a solid foundation for advanced fighter design. First and foremost, it was not only necessary to 'know facts' but also to 'know why'. Anyway, with so many important projects right in their infancy and the aviation industry not capable enough to take over the development, self-reliance, independence and efforts to establish an indigenous industry with indigenous projects became an imperative.

In order to gain industrial knowledge and even more to compensate for the loss of the Soviet Union, in 1962, Chinese representatives from the 2nd Ministry of Machine Building, which was responsible for licenced aircraft production, visited aircraft production plants in Sweden and Switzerland in order to make arrangements for Chinese production of advanced designs under development in both European countries[11]. One of the top priorities was assigned to obtaining rights and assistance to produce an export version of the Swedish SAAB J 35 Draken including its highly sophisticated electronic fire-control system as well as a version of the Swiss FFA P-16 Mk III strike fighter. Overall, these negotiations fell through before any positive steps were to be taken and nothing came of the connection.

Also, even as the break between the Soviet Union and China occurred, there was still some cooperation in certain respects. For example, on the Dong Feng projects but how far this actually went is still an open discussion. Some say the Soviet part was only consultation, as for example the visit to TsAGI, while others argue a total dependence on Soviet assistance during these times. A hint may be a note from designer Wong Nanso, who said in an interview regarding Soviet influence on Chinese aviation, 'We wouldn't have anything without hand-in-hand tutelage from the Soviets. Even the Dong Feng 107 design team included Soviet experts'. In contrast, there are reports that the DF-113's development was ordered to be done in complete secrecy without any Soviet assistance.

The first supersonic fighter in PLAAF service was the J-6, which evolved from a licence-manufactured MiG-19 into several indigenous variants including the JJ-6 trainer seen here alongside a J-6Bing from the 2nd Division.
(via Top81.cn)

Another example was, why a licence for the MiG-21F-13 version was granted despite a growing deterioration in Sino-Soviet relations in 1960. The negotiations were certainly influenced by the cooling down but following the sudden (and for China surprising) breakdown in 1960 with the withdrawal of all Soviet advisers and engineers, there was not the complete end of relations that it might have seemed. In fact, the split clearly visible by the end of the 1950s, due largely to personal animosity between Nikita Khrushchev and Mao, but the events of 1960 were only one peak in their differences, before the rift became irreparable after the 1969 Zhenbao Island (Damansky Island) border conflict. In consequence almost during most of the 1960s both nations continued to collaborate on keeping American influence out of Southeast Asia. In exactly this short-lived warming springtime, the transfer of MiG-21 technology was discussed and the Soviets considered the release of a rather basic MiG-21 variant only a minor threat to its own security compared to the profits they could make out of the deal. A strange side effect was in fact, that this deal had a huge but mixed effect on China's aviation industry since immense resources were allocated to the resulting J-7 and all efforts to develop indigenous fighters were scrapped.

Two years later the recognition of the People's Republic of China by France in January 1964 seemed to offer another chance to acquire modern foreign aircraft and discussions at the French trade fair at Peking in April 1964 were said to include negotiations on sales of Dassault Mirage fighters as well as nuclear bombers. Even if these contacts again led to nothing, they at least showed the will to find another major supplier of technology as well as to shift the political ties. As a result, the overall industry output declined markedly through 1963, which was further hindered by a shift in priorities to the competing missile and nuclear weapons programme. Overall, the aviation industry began to recover only by about 1965, in parallel to the first deliveries of equipment to North Vietnam prior to the Vietnam War.

During this period also, several first indigenous Chinese designs like the J-8 were initiated and – even only briefly – Chinese representatives went out for shopping with quite mixed results. As noted by Kenneth Alan, 'perhaps only briefly between 1963 and 1966 – before the chaos of the Cultural Revolution begun – did the PLAAF feel it was finally on the threshold of recovering from the setbacks caused by the break with Moscow.' This however was only a brief spring and was completely reversed during the Cultural Revolution, which started in May 1966 and led China to a long and frosty politically isolated winter.

To understand the later part of creation of the PLAAF's divisions one has not only to look onto the political background and operational needs, but also – and maybe even more important – to the process of aircraft deliveries from the Soviet Union, since the usual procedure was not merely to upgraded an already established unit to new combat types, but simply by establishing additional units, when a new aircraft was introduced.
As such, between 1954 to 1971 the PLAAF created the final 22 divisions throughout China mostly related to the delivery of new aircraft types. Typical for this was the fielding of the 'modern' types like the H-5, H-6, J-6 and Q-5. For example, the PLAAF began receiving the indigenous H-5 in 1967 – even though other units were already operating Soviet-built Il-28s – the Q-5 in December 1969 and the H-6 in 1976.

Units re-established/newly established after March 1960

Date	Base/location	Unit	Sub-units	Aircraft types	Notes
1960 May	Donggou, Liaoning	30th Fighter Division	88th Regiment 89th Regiment 90th Regiment	MiG-15bis	Later Dandong
1960 March	Yangcheng, Jiangsu	31st Fighter Division	91st Regiment 92nd Regiment 93rd Regiment	MiG-15bis	Later Wengdeng
1960 April	Jinghai, Hubei	32nd Fighter Division	94th Regiment 95th Regiment 96th Regiment	MiG-15bis	Later Rugao
1960 April	Shanpo, Hebei	33rd Fighter Division	97th Regiment 98th Regiment 99th Regiment	MiG-15bis	Later Chongqing
1963 September	Beijing Nanyuan, Hebei	34th Fighter Division	100th Regiment 101st Regiment 102nd Regiment	Il-12?	Changed its status to independent transport regiment in September 1980; changed its status back to 34th Div, subordinated directly to HQ AF in March 1988
1965 March	Xingning, Guangdong	35th Fighter Division	103rd Regiment 104th Regiment 105th Regiment	J-5	
1965 March	Wugong, Shaanxi	36th Bomber Division	106th Regiment 107th Regiment 108th Regiment	Tu-16, later H-6	Later Lanzhou Lintong

Aircraft types

Shenyang Dong Feng-102/J-6 (ASCC 'Farmer')

The DF-102 was planned to be the first MiG-19 variant to become operational but in fact, it was not the first to fly since the DF-103 actually flew first and also received the 'later' designation J-6A. One reason for this was that the production licence at this stage only covered the MiG-19P all-weather interceptor and the Tumanskiy RD-9B turbojet to be manufactured at Liming as the WP-6 and not the MiG-19S. This type however was the PLAAF's preferred variant to enter service first and to make matters even worse, it was decided in May 1958 to complete all further development, testing and later series production without Soviet assistance, which proved to be a very bad decision.

Consequently, the requested day fighter version DF-102 was initiated by late 1958 based on the 'simple' plan to re-modify the MiG-19P back to MiG-19S standard. In the end a wrong decision since this proved to be much more difficult than predicted, particularly since no structural strength calculations were available and it was decided to omit a static test specimen. Shenyang began to build a prototype in February 1959, which made the first flight in late September 1950 and testing was finished already in December. Quite understandable, that type failed completely and did not even met the performance of the original MiG-19. Only 33 or 36 were built and Shenyang was ordered to go back to the drawing board. Again, however, this work was affected by the political situation, including the partial breakdown in relations between China and the Soviet Union but got going again in 1961 when more help was forthcoming from Moscow. After a first flight made in September 1963, the first examples now called J-6 were supplied to regular units in 1964.

The DF-102 was planned as a fully indigenous-developed MiG-19 derivative and as such had a unique intake configuration. Only a few were built, including this example in the China Aviation Museum. (via Top81.cn)

Shenyang Dong Feng 103/J-6Jia/J-6A (ASCC 'Farmer')

In parallel to the decision to reverse engineer the MiG-19S, it was decided to manufacture the MiG-19P as the Dong Feng-103. At least for this type, the Soviet Union had supplied all technical documents and parts for five prototype aircraft which were delivered by early 1958. Final assembly began in March 1958 and the maiden flight was performed in December 1958. The first true Chinese DF-103 was finished in January 1959 and the initial flight test programme was concluded in April. Again, just like the DF-102 the early DF-103s suffered from issues with manufacturing and quality, so that production was suspended until December 1960 and all 83 aircraft built so far had to be extensively reworked. Regardless all issues, production continued and several reports state that by late 1960 the factory tarmac was overcrowded by 'undeliverable' DF-102s and DF-103s. Nevertheless, a few were delivered until January 1961 when production was finally discontinued.

In November 1964 that type received the new designation J-6A (or J-6Jia), and the break in production lasted eventually until 1964. Some say from the original 83 airframes only 69 were delivered to operational units between 1962 and 1964, 12 were

One of the very few images known showing both an operational J-6A – here updated to XinA standard – and an aircraft from the 38th Fighter Division. (via CDF)

used as ground-instruction trainers and two acted as additional static test airframes. In all, the J-6As never played an operational role within the PLAAF.

Quite ironic, in August 1958 it was decided to transfer production of the DF-103 to the Aircraft Manufacturing Plant No. 320 in Nanchang and unfortunately only confusing information about the build-up at Nanchang is available. At least it seems, that Nanchang only build a few J-6A before it was decided to switch to the MiG-19PM missile-armed interceptor.

Shenyang/Nanchang Dong Feng 105/J-6Yi/J-6B (ASCC 'Farmer')

While the Shenyang Aircraft Factory was working on the DF-102 and DF-103 it was also decided to reverse engineer the missile armed MiG-19PM all-weather, day-and-night interceptor as the DF-105 and from 1964 on as the J-6Yi or J-6B. Quite similar to the J-6A, the main differences were the radar and it was able to carry four PL-1 AAMs instead of the standard cannon armament. After the PL-1 had been withdrawn from service, however, the guns were retrofitted during overhaul and maintenance work. Chinese sources state that production was to start at Nanchang with the objective to produce it later in parallel also at Shenyang. At least China received MiG-19PM manufacturing documents assembly got going during September 1960, however yet again, it suffered delays. Flight tests started only in 1963 and by 1966 Nanchang had managed to build only 19 aircraft plus another five from Mikoyan-supplied parts. In June 1967, it was decided, to cancel any further production at Nanchang's since it should concentrate on the development of the Q-5.

First Indigenous Proposals: Dong Feng East Wind Series

Even if China's current fighter types are quite well known, very few are aware, that since the late 1950s China has been developing fighters to its own designs, which unfortunately all remained on the drawing board. Originally initiated in March 1958 the Bureau of Aviation Industry (then called the Fourth Bureau) proposed a development plan to catch up with the leading aviation nations within the next 15 years. Conse-

Another rare image of operational J-6Bs with 11x5x serial numbers, which correspond to the original 4th Fighter Division.
(via CDF)

quently, and in line with the then ongoing Great Leap Forward campaign, it is perhaps difficult to take the Dong Feng series seriously as 'real' or at least 'realistic' projects, since the first result of this campaign was the exact opposite effect: by the end of 1958 nearly all industrial work and scientific and military research stopped.

Shenyang Dong Feng 104, 107 and 107A

The first indigenous fighter was the second Dong Feng 104 project, which seems to have entered the design stage in the time period between the DF-103 and DF-105 MiG-19 derivatives. Unfortunately not much is known about it, but it is understood that work began around the end of 1957 or early 1958 with the objective to produce an aircraft not based on any Soviet type but with comparable features displayed by the latest Western fighters. The DF-104 seems to have been a fighter quite similar in external appearance to the American F-5 and some say, it was to be powered by one WP-6. Despite being a promising design, it was soon abandoned in favour of a larger and much refined version called DF-107, which's design phase was to begin in early 1958.

In appearance the DF-107, has been often described as being similar but smaller than the American F8U Crusader including a unique sharply swept variable-incident wing, albeit with a solid nose housing a radar and two lateral air-intakes with separator plates. The two engines were apparently improved and up-rated derivatives of the WP-6, called Hong Qui-2. However, until mid-1958 severe technical problems still hampered and delayed the DF-107 programme.

In September 1958, the situation became more difficult for Shenyang when a competitor appeared in form of the DF-113, which it was said would be ready for a first flight in January 1959. As a result, in November the authorities decided to stop all development work on both the Hong Qui-2 and the DF-107, which was rejected and led to 'violent protests' because a successful development of a competitor within just three months was considered to be practically impossible.

Thanks to the influence of air force C-in-C Liu Yalou, the decision was reversed and a delegation travelled to Moscow in February 1959, to permit the TsAGI to examine the DF-107. The resulting report dealt a severe blow to the team because several structural faults were discovered. As a result, it was proposed to completely revise to design to the DF-107A, which featured a simplified structure and a fixed, high mounted delta wing. A full-scale wooden mock-up was built during this period and despite some progress, the whole project was cancelled in autumn 1959 after the political leaders had declared that the DF-107A had to be given up in favour of the competing DF-113 and the whole Shenyang design team was merged with the team at Harbin. Besides that, there was a yet another with the proposal of a 'nuclear powered' Mach 3.5 fighter called DF-109, which also only remained a paper project.

Harbin Dong Feng 113

The DF-113 was in fact not proposed by the Harbin Aircraft factory, but rather unusually by the Military Engineering Academy in Harbin in September 1958. In contrast to the DF-107, it received all of the necessary funding and political support since in mind of the political ambitions, it promised to be a true high attitude and high speed heavy

Due to the at-best vague project status of the Don Feng series, images related to these aircraft are extremely scarce. The top image shows models representing the DF-113 (left) and the DF-107 (right) at the China Aviation Museum. The centre image shows the only known picture of the DF-104 as a desk-top model, while the bottom photo is the only known image of the full-size mock-up of the DF-104.
(All images via CDF)

Among all the indigenious Dong Feng projects, it was probably the DF-113 that progressed furthest. Seen here is a wind-tunnel model.
(via Bai Wei)

all-weather fighter comparable to the best opponents. Work had actually started in March 1958 and even if several senior experts raised concerns in regard to the effects of the thermal barrier at high speeds and limitations in metallurgy these all were turned down. Not much surprisingly, to accomplish the task within the scheduled time of only 10 months and reach a first flight in January 1959, was beyond China's abilities. Design wise, the DF-113 had elements taken from the latest US fighters and bombers like the Lockheed F-104, Republic F-105 and Convair B-58 but otherwise not much information is available beyond a sketchy three-view drawing, a wind-tunnel model and some provisional equipment data. It was to be powered by one Type 814 turbojet even if there's no information on how Harbin's design team was to achieve the required performance and so most of this has to be regarded as politically motivated dreams.

After several conferences, the designer had to admit in autumn 1959 that this type was impossible to realise: a decision not accepted by the political leaders, which decided that these problems had to be solved by the middle of the following year. As noted, to speed up development, the DF-107A was abandoned and both design teams were merged so that the fighter was to be ready as a gift for the PRC and CCP's 40th anniversary on 1 July 1961. That date also passed by without a result and in due course it was accepted that it would be better to complete the J-6, begin with the J-7 development and most of all to learn more about the development and manufacturing methods of modern military aircraft, especially their powerplants. After Defence Minister Lin Biao crashed in September 1971, this political pet project was abandoned.

Harbin H-5 (ASCC 'Beagle')

Following the first operational use of the Il-28 during the First Taiwan Strait Crisis in January 1955, local production was planned but delayed until the Sino-Soviet relations had so much deteriorated in 1959 that a licence was never granted. As a consequence, it was decided to reverse engineer it as an improved domestic version under the designation H-5 at Harbin. Interestingly, even if the H-6 flew earlier, it received the later number. Development of the H-5 began in January 1963 and about 40 per cent of the airframe was modified.

A very early H-5 assigned to the 48th Bomber Division during a bombing raid.
(via CDF)

In addition, several systems from the H-6 were used to make the aircraft easier to operate and maintain, like the most visible changes a redesigned glazed nose and the H-6's rear gun position. The original VK-1 engines were manufactured by the Shenyang Aero-Engine Factory as the WP-5A. Construction of the prototypes started in early 1964 but once the Cultural Revolution slowed things down again, a successful first flight was only done in June 1966 (others give a date of September).

The H-5 was put into production in April 1967 and the first examples were delivered in December of that year. It is not clear how many H-5s were actually built, but several hundred were delivered until production ended in the 1980s.

China also developed a trainer version called the HJ-5, which flew for the first time in December 1970 and entered service in 1972. Altogether 187 examples were built.

During its service career the H-5 was used by both services mainly as a light bomber but it was also modified into other specialised versions like a nuclear bomber (H-5A), target-towing aircraft, and as a torpedo bomber (H-5B). The last bomber were retired from PLAAF service in 1986, but a small number were retained for training, reconnaissance (HZ-5) and especially for electronic warfare (HD-5) until the late 1990s, when they were finally replaced by the JH-7.

Tupolev Tu-16 and Harbin H-6 (ASCC 'Badger')

The successors to the Tu-4 as the PLAAF's long range bomber was the Tupolev Tu-16. In early 1956 the Soviet government agreed to help China create a medium bomber fleet and this decision was influenced (especially for the Soviets) by the idea of building a united Sino-Soviet nuclear force led by the Soviet Union. Although this arrangement would later become unacceptable to China, it led to an agreement in September 1957 to construct a Tu-16 assembly line at Harbin plus the delivery of all the necessary technical documentation. In China the type was initially designated Fei Long 201 (Flying Dragon 201) but later was renamed H-6.

The first two Soviet Tu-16s arrived in January 1959 and were to act as pattern aircraft together with a third Tu-16 in kit form delivered in May. Assembly started almost immediately with the help of specialists from the Kazan Factory and nearly 200 additional qualified workers from Shenyang in order to jointly manufacture at two factories in Harbin and Xi'an. In parallel, the Mikulin RD-3M-500 turbojet was to be manufactured under licence at the Xi'an Engine Factory as the WP-8. The first Chinese-built airframe, a Tu-16T/Tu-16A hybrid, flew first in September 1959 and a second aircraft shortly afterwards. At this point, the programme had been relatively trouble free; which was quite an impressive task, since the H-6 was by far the heaviest and most complex aircraft China had so far produced and required an enormous amount of modifications and rebuilding at both factories.

Allegedly an image of the famous H-6A '50671' after releasing China's first hydrogen bomb (as test no. 6) over the Lop Nor range on 17 June 1967. (via CDF)

Shenyang J-6 'Basic' (ASCC 'Farmer')

After the early failure of the first reverse-engineered MiG-19 as the Dong-Feng 102, 103 and 105, yet another attempt was made to copy the MiG-19S under the slogan 'back to the drawing board'. Prototype manufacture begun in December 1961, and the first static test airframe was built until October 1963. The first flight of prototype J-6 'Basic' – meaning there was no additional Roman number or Arabic letter – was performed in September. After again a brief flight testing phase (16 flights for a total flying time of 21 hours) production was approved in December 1963 with deliveries from 1964 on.

Shenyang J-6I (ASCC 'Farmer')

During the early 1960s the PRC was regularly overflown by US high-altitude reconnaissance or surveillance aircraft which were a deep annoyance to Beijing. Consequently, the PLAAF issued a RFP for a high-altitude interceptor version capable of reaching the heights flown by the American intruders and in 1965 development begun on a 'lightweight' version of the standard J-6 powered by an up-rated engine. This interceptor was named J-6I and featured some changes to the intake, a slightly larger wing area and especially a much lighter fuselage. The first modified aircraft performed its maiden flight in August 1966 and was soon delivered to an operational trials unit in early 1967.

However, even being certified for serial production it proved difficult for Shenyang to manufacture both the J-6I and regular J-6s side by side, so that the J-6I was discontinued only after 12 aircraft had been completed and its service career was only brief.

Shenyang JJ-1

In September 1956 the Shenyang Aircraft Development Department or Shenyang Aero Institute was founded, and its first project was a light jet trainer called Hongzhuan-503 (Red Craftsman). It was powered by single PF-1A turbojet; an indigenous version of the Klimov RD-500 centrifugal turbojet developed by the SADO (Shenyang Aeroengine Design Office) – before being renamed to JJ-1. Development begun in October 1956 and after an extraordinarily short period of development it performed its maiden flight in July 1958. Even if three prototypes were tested and the aircraft allegedly reached all objectives, at the end of 1958 the PLAAF changed its then three-part flight training system in favour of a new two-part course, which meant the JJ-1 was no longer required and therefore abandoned.

Mikoyan MiG-17, Shenyang J-5, Chengdu J-5A (ASCC 'Fresco') and JJ-5 trainer

The next jet fighter in PLAAF service was the MiG-17 day fighter version fitted with the non-afterburning VK-1A engine. Plans for setting up a local production line were started in October 1954 and in early 1955 the Soviet Union supplied a full set of technical documents, most of the tooling for the production of the improved MiG-17F and its Klimov WK-1F engine. Prototype construction began in April 1955 and was completed in mid-July. The type was briefly designated Dong Feng-101 or East Wind-101 and made a successful first flight in July 1956. The final and much better-known J-5 designation was allocated only in 1964.

Following a brief flight test programme, it was certified and declared it ready for serial production in September to replace the older MiG-15 and MiG-15bis. However, already then, the PLAAF was keen to switch production to the improved radar-equipped MiG-17PF. Design documents were received in early 1961 and production was allocated to the new Chengdu Aircraft Factory, since Shenyang was ordered to prepare production of the MiG-19.

Officially preparations were completed in September 1962 and fabrication of the J-5A begun in March 1963, however due to the growing political instability, it was much delayed. The prototype flew for the first time in November 1964 but by this time the fighter was already out of date, so that even after the type received its certification in December 1965, production was severely scaled down. In all only 767 J-5s and J-5As were manufactured until 1969. The J-5A is sometimes also called the J-5Jia or Dong Feng 104 (the second time DF-104 was used). Following the J-5's withdrawal from active service several hundred were converted into remotely-controlled Ba-5 target drones.

After the MiG-15UTI no longer provided sufficient capability to fully prepare pilots for operating the new types, in 1964 the PLAAF issued a RfP for a trainer variant. Development was assigned to the Chengdu Aircraft Factory and the JJ-5 became China's second indigenous jet trainer after the JJ-1. It was something of a hybrid using

The JJ-1 was an interesting design, since it was not based on any Soviet type. It was remarkably succesful given the circumstances of its gestation. (via CDF)

The MiG-17F was the first jet fighter in PLAAF service that saw not only widespread operational use, but was also succesfully built under licence as the J-5. (via CDF)

elements of the J-5 and J-5A's fuselage combined with a tandem cockpit and it was powered by an up-rated non-afterburning WP-5D engine. A first flight took place in May 1966 and 1,061 JJ-5s were built up to 1986.

Mikoyan MiG-19 and Shenyang J-6 (ASCC 'Farmer')

The driving aim for the introduction of the MiG-19 were hostilities, which began over the Taiwan Strait in August 1958, especially since the USAF's units transitioned to the new supersonic North American F-100. However, already during the early 1950s cracks had started to appear in the Sino-Soviet relationship, and in particular Joseph Stalin was reluctant to deliver the new MiG-19 to China before his Eastern-bloc allies had received the type. Only after his death in 1953, the situation improved a bit in 1957 when Nikita Khrushchev agreed in principle to transfer military technology again to the PRC. Negotiations on a licence manufacture begun in September 1957 and soon afterwards an agreement signed in October 1957. This included the transfer of full technical documentation, manufacturing technology, pre-manufactured parts and other related equipment.

Another line-up of very early J-6 fighters assigned to an unknown fighter division. (via CDF)

In due course all three basic versions of the MiG-19 were manufactured in China under the same agreement – the MiG-19P all-weather interceptor, the MiG-19PM missile-armed interceptor and from late 1959 on the basic MiG-19S day fighter. Design work began in December 1958 as the Dong Feng 102 in parallel to several more indigenous fighter projects under the same series.

Frustratingly there are still contradictory reports about the versions of the J-6 that were developed, especially regarding the accuracy covering the different sub-variants. In fact two separate lines of development need to be described, the first covering basic day fighters and the second the radar-equipped all-weather interceptors, which both ran pretty well concurrently and were later modernised several times or superseded by more capable versions.

Mikoyan MiG-21 and Shenyang J-7 (ASCC 'Fishbed')

Following the mixed success of the early J-6 licence production and failed Dong Feng series, it was only natural for China to turn back to the Soviet Union for its next fighter. First approaches for the MiG-21 were actually made already when the relationship was worsening. However, during a short-lived attempt to solve the issue, the Soviet Union agreed for a licence manufacturing in 1961, which covered only the rather basic MiG-21F-13 and its Tumanskiy R-11F-300 turbojet engine. A full set of technical documents, three complete MiG-21F-13s and 20 pre-manufactured airframes in kit form were delivered. However, the ongoing rift between the two states became worse and, as a result, the delivery of these items was stopped prior to completion, which left the Chinese with incomplete paperwork and Shenyang had to reverse engineer the MiG-21 from 1962 on. After long delays, construction of a prototype J-7 and its WP-7 engine was started in early 1964 and first Chinese-built MiG-21 – most likely a Soviet supplied one – made its maiden flight in January 1966 but again the programmeme lagged behind schedule.

An interesting line-up of several different fighters including the third J-7 prototype '043'. Further behind is a J-7III and three very early J-8IIs. This image must have been taken sometime after 1985-86. (via AFWing)

Again, as with the J-6, certification for production being granted much too early in June 1967 and regardless countless technical, which was even more worsened by the Cultural Revolution. Consequently, the first batch of J-7s were a disappointment and suffered by a poor reliability and these J-7s were not accepted by the PLAAF with production halted in 1970.

1   See *China's Air Force enters the 21st Century*, p 58ff and drawn by material from 'China Today' 1989a pp 319–328

2   See http://www.mongabay.com/history/china/china-the_great_leap_forward,_1958-60.html

3   See Xiaoming Zhang, p 269, according to Xu Yan, *Mao Zedong: A Military Strategist*, (Beijing: Party Central Historical Materials Press, 1995).

4   For a report with greater detail see *China's Air Force enters the 21st Century*, p 61ff and drawn by material from 'China Today' 1989a pp 333–351.

5   According to PRC documents, during the first aerial combat (on 29 July) at around 1103hrs four MiG-17s assigned to the 54th AR/18th Division, led by Zhao De-An intercepted three F-84Gs over Shantou. The fight lasted only about three minutes and Squadron Leader Gao Chang-Ji and pilot Zhang Yi-Lin each downed down one F-84G, while Zhao De-An damaged a third one. Also still in Phase One, eight J-5s (Chinese licenced copy of the MiG-17), of the 46th Regiment/16th Air Division, engaged on 7 August eight RCAF F-86s led by Col Wang Meng-Qan. Allegedly this fight lasted for five minutes during which Col Wang Meng-Qan's Sabre was damaged. No other fighters from either side should have been downed. The third air battle involved the 4th NAD, 10th AR.

6   Quite a surprise and luck for the Soviets – one AIM-9B hit a MiG-17 but did not expolode and this recovered missile led to the reverse engineered K-13 (AA-2 Atoll) and licenced PL-2.

7   For a report with greater detail see: *China's Air Force enters the 21st Century*, p 67ff and drawn by material from '*China Today: The Air Force*' (1989a) pp 333–351 and USAF Historical Division, 1962, p 39.

8   http://www.bharat-rakshak.com/IAF/History/1962War.html

9   Compiled from *China's Air Force enters the 21st Century*, p 18ff and p 71ff and for further information http://countrystudies.us/china/128.htm

10 Following Bueschel, R. M., *Communist Chinese Air Power* (Frederick A. Praeger, 1968), p 68, the Soviets withdraw 1,390 experts, cancelled 343 contracts and left 257 scientific and technical projects.

11 See Bueschel, R. M. (1968), pp 68–69.

CULTURAL REVOLUTION: MAY 1966 TO OCTOBER 1976

Interestingly, the official PLAAF histories provide a lot detailed information about the early years and especially for the gestation of the first 28 divisions but characteristically for the changing political climate through this following period virtually nothing is known especially about the remaining 22 divisions and this counts the same for their associated six air corps and two command posts. Overall this decade through the Cultural Revolution and the self-defined isolation can be regarded as a phase of politicisation of the PLA in general, a complete halt in all efforts of developments and even a harsh backward-turn in several aspects. However, it became an immense increase in size of the PLAAF in special, which was achieved on the cost of overall development, quality and most of all on training. Additionally, even if several new aircraft projects were initiated, most of them finally failed or were lumbering in a much too long development process with consequences recognisable even today. In the end – as K. W. Allen described – these 'cumulative effects of the 1960s devastated the air force organisationally and operationally, leaving it merely a shell of what it had been at the outset of the decade.'[1]

May 1966 to October 1976: Cultural Revolution[2]

Following the disastrous consequences, the Great Leap Forward brought and the resulting decline in political standing during the early 1960s, Mao Zedong initiated in 1962 an offensive and primarily political upheaval to purify the CCP from the – in his opinion – creeping capitalistic and anti-communistic tendencies within China. Additionally for him it opened the opportunity to clean the party from all who had opposed his Great Leap Forward policies especially Liu Shaoqi and Deng Xiaoping.

This Socialist Education Movement with the aim to produce major changes in official economic policies or the basic economic model was closely related to the new Minister of Defence Lin Biao. What started at first by sending students, intellectuals and bureaucrats to factories and communes in the countryside to 'restore the ideological purity' following the political slogan 'to learn from the People's Liberation Army', cumulated in a rage of Red Guards through the country blinded by revolutionary fervour. By around mid-1965 Mao Zedong had regained control of the CCP and finally initiated the Cultural Revolution in 1966. Quite consequently his most eager supporters were first of all the PLA and second millions of students. These were sent out as Red Guards, which again questioned everyone's loyalty and the whole movement brought chaos, with nearly all social norms largely evaporating. Nonetheless the influence of

this atmosphere of radical leftism was felt throughout the urban society – the countryside was not as much affected – it most of all led to the disintegration of the previously established political institutions at all levels of government. During the most violent years millions of people were persecuted in the violent factional struggles that ensued across the country, they suffered a wide range of abuses including torture, rape, imprisonment, sustained harassment and the seizure of their property. In the same way it profoundly affected the modern sector of the economy. However, the most direct effect was the near halt of industrial production because of the political activity of students and workers in the mines and factories. That alone would have been worse enough but in consequence virtually all intellectuals and – most of all important for the industry – engineers, managers, scientists, technicians and other professional personnel were criticised, demoted and 'sent down' to the countryside to 'participate in labour'.

Often they were even jailed or killed, which resulted in their knowledge and skills being lost for the factories and companies. Even worsening, to replace these 'suspect' persons, the leadership of factories was placed in the hands of so-called Revolutionary Committees, consisting of representatives from the CCP, political activists, and trusted cadres of workers and most importantly commanders of the People's Liberation Army. However, these members often had little knowledge of either management or the enterprise they were supposed to run. Aided by a near complete collapse of the of transportation – since Red Guards had to be distributed by requisitioned trains and trucks all around the country – a shortage of supplies, materials and especially rare ones led to near collapse of productivity within the high technology industries like the aviation industry. Overall the output of many factories suffered and the effect was a 14 per cent decline in overall industrial production in 1967. Even if in general the rural areas experienced less turmoil than the cities, agricultural production stagnated in a similar way.

Surprisingly, although the PLA in general was in favour of this 'support to the left', most regional PLA commanders ordered their forces to restrain the leftist radicals. By late 1967 or early 1968 ultimately a common degree of order was restored by the PLA throughout most parts of China and led to a new form of local administration in the form of the mentioned Revolutionary Committees, which were replacing the former local Party Committees. By late 1967 the most radical activist phase tided a bit and came to a halt in 1968, when Mao realised that all further revolutionary violence would bring no further use especially after his power had been fully restored and all 'revisionists' were purged from public live. Overall however the atmosphere of radical leftism persisted until Mao's death and the fall of the Gang of Four in 1976.

With the ultimate restoration of order throughout China the Cultural Revolution ended – at least officially declared by Mao himself – in April 1969 with the Ninth Party Congress. There not only Mao was again restored and confirmed as the supreme leader but also Lin Biao was declared to be Mao's political successor with being promoted to CCP Vice Chairman. However, in reality the active phase lasted until the death of Lin Biao in 1971. As a result the political instability between 1971 until the arrest of the Gang of Four in 1976 are commonly also accepted as part of the Cultural Revolution.

Overall the main emphasis was laid on a transition with an organisational rebuild and economic stabilisation – at least the industrial sector returned to a fairly high rate of growth in 1969 – to be followed by a greater attention to foreign affairs in the near

future. However, with the promotion of the highest military leader to the highest political position not few expected China to head towards a military rule, since the PLA was left as the only institution of power. On the other side – again as K. W. Allen states – 'an active role of the military in politics also meant that politics entered the military.'

Vietnam War

Slightly preceding the events described above, already by April 1964 the Chinese Communist leadership had become increasingly concerned about a possible all-out war with the USSR on one side, and a possible war with the US over Vietnam on the other. At one point at least, Lin Biao's paranoia about China facing an imminent war, was almost confirmed in his view by the Vietnam War, when both the PLAAF and PLAN Naval Aviation became involved in the conflict. Interestingly – and in a certain contrast to the Korea War and the Yijiangshan Campaign, were much more covered in detail than the Vietnam War. The most important reason for this neglect is surely, that no true PLAAF units were involved in Vietnam between 1965 and 1969 or Laos between 1970 to 1973. Anyway, the PLAAF deployed their air defence assets in the north of that country and also intercepted US combat and reconnaissance aircraft that penetrated the airspace over southeast China. The first units were deployed to Guangxi and Yunnan in August 1964 and later in August also AAA units from seven divisions, plus searchlight and radar battalions to Vietnam. Concerned about a possible escalation, Chinese pilots were initially ordered only to monitor the US aircraft that penetrated their airspace. However, when the number of such violations increased, in 1965 Beijing felt forced to make public an air defence demarcation line at the border. In this way it was hoped to deprive the Americans of any excuse for what were seen as provocative over-flights. Chinese fighter pilots deployed at air bases in Guangxi, Hainan Island, the Leizhou Peninsula and Yunnan received permission to open fire. Over the following year, they claimed to have shot down 12 and damaged four US aircraft. Additionally, the PLAAF and Naval Aviation established a number of special units organised and equipped to intercept US unmanned aerial vehicles (UAVs) that were deployed against China. By the end of 1965, no fewer than 20 such drones were reported as shot down.

Throughout 1966, the US administration expanded the list of targets within North Vietnam that could be attacked by its air power. Beijing thus felt forced to bolster its southern and southeastern frontiers. Nevertheless, the PLAAF never openly intervened on the Vietnamese side during the war: indeed, PLAAF and Naval Aviation pilots received very strict rules of engagement (RoEs) that prohibited any kind of operations over Vietnam. Therefore, related Chinese air operations remained strictly limited to the protection of the PRC's airspace during 1967 and beyond. Subsequently, the CCP leadership introduced measures intended to permit an approach to Washington in order to win the US as an ally in its own struggle against the USSR. Throughout this period, small-scale aerial confrontations with the Nationalist air arm occurred time and again, and several Nationalist reconnaissance aircraft were shot down, some of them while flying deep over mainland China. Overall – and again in contrast to USAF reports – the PLAAF by official account claimed to have shot down 597 US aircraft and damaging 479 more in 558 aerial battles. At the same time, they lost 15 AAA batteries, four radars and 280 troops while 1,166 more soldiers were wounded. Overall these sta-

tistics must be taken with a certain grain of salt – they appear highly exaggerated – but must be seen in the light of the political situation.

The final PLAAF troops left Vietnam on 14 March 1969, even more surprising however is the fact, that no official reason for the depart is given and even more, that by official account, no lessons were drawn from the Vietnam War. This is even more surprising since it would have been a perfect chance to study the way US forces fought, how they used their assets effectively, what new systems they used for the first time, where their own forces showed weakness and what conclusions could be learned. And – in this case not surprisingly – not even the bad influence of political intervention was admitted. In the end, 'although China acquired some of these weapon systems from downed aircraft and from the Vietnamese after the war, the country's preoccupation with the Cultural Revolution and the virtual non-involvement of aviation troops apparently led the PLAAF and aviation ministry to miss these changes in air warfare and fall even further behind.' In the aftermath of the Vietnam War, the PLAAF deployed AAA units to Laos between December 1970 and November 1973, altogether claiming the kills of 17 aircraft while damaging three more.

As noted, for the PLAAF the overall situation proved disastrous, with no clear concept and often enough contradicting decisions. In reality however, it was a complete failure, a true disaster, as noted flying hours dropped considerably, schools were closed and the quality of nearly everything dropped. Additionally, any imports of equipment not 'made in China' and so much eagerly required for any technological advancement, were curtailed by rampant xenophobia. The most important and in the end even more far-reaching negative effect of the Cultural Revolution – which in the end had catastrophic consequences for the industry and economy – was the dire shortage of highly qualified and educated personnel caused by the closing of regular schools and universities and the 'revolutionary fever'.

China's ability to develop any new technology and to absorb imported technologies was therefore severely hampered for years. But not alone in the industry, also the PLA lost nearly all people with any education – especially with a higher degree of specialisation – which was like a chain reaction for the standard of maintenance, serviceability and operation readiness. To ignore any scientific standards, disrespect the laws of design, manufacturing and even nature science led to an overall drop of aircraft quality levels to sub-zero standards and production of aircraft became out of the question. This probably most serious and long-lasting effect proved lengthy and tortuous and was eventually the most dramatic achievement of the Cultural Revolution.

The PLAAF during the Cultural Revolution

If not the break with the Soviet Union was a hard blow since it held back any further progress in the development of new types as well as a steady delivery of aircraft to the newly established units, the following years were a true disaster. Kenneth Alan noted: 'Although the PLAAF matured rapidly during its first fifteen years, it has spent the past twenty-five years recovering from the disastrous effects of the Cultural Revolution.'

By instigating a process of 'controlled anarchy' to remove his inner-party opponents, Mao's new movement had led to widespread chaos and the disintegration of all levels of government, together with the evaporation of any social norms. The Cultural

Revolution badly damaged China in economic and social terms, and also involved the PLAAF. One of the most severe consequences – and immediate ones – was related to flight safety, training and education as well as strategy and tactics and not only since military installations were occupied by revolutional guards with the equipment not being returned. In several cases, the installations were destroyed in political fever, books, teaching materials burned and equipment got lost and even worse, often also the instructors and teachers were killed.

Until 1959, the PLAAF had created 17 aviation schools as well as several more schools not strictly related for flight training. This however, changed completely in the aftermath of the Cultural Revolution when ironically even two contradicting ideas crashed together and competed simultaneously: the first idea – by Lin Biao and the leftists – were advocating the complete closing of all non-pilot training schools. They canceled all theory classes for pilots, and reduced the flight training time dramatically. Main slogan during that time was 'stop classes, make revolution'.

The contra pole to this concept was the 1960s war in Vietnam, plus Lin Biao's paranoia about China facing an imminent large war, led to an intended increase in flying hours at the flying schools and the aim to improve flight training based on the own lessons learnt and an increase in flying hours. Also, for the first time the training and educational systems was set to be reformed following the withdrawal of the Soviets and based on the lessons from the Taiwan campaign and included and the plan to compile all regulations, flight manuals, rules and guidance based on the own needs.

In retrospect, in August 1966, all non-flying schools suspended classes for nearly six years with virtually no non-flying and ground training. Consequently, the expected training goal for all 13 non-flying schools during this period was 21,900 students, but only 5,650 graduated.[3] The consequence was, that this lack of education was even more worse for the PLAAF than for the society in general, since the few graduates were barely useable in the units they were later assigned to. And if this was not bad enough, Lin Biao's advocacy of an imminent war doctrine – the above mentioned contradiction – led to even worse situations. In mind of the urgency, pilot training time was reduced while at the same time flight hours were increased. When flight training took previously 30 months, this was now reduced to 12 months only in 1967.

In parallel the number of flying hours however was increased dramatically: 180,000 in 1966; 260,000 in 1968; 310,000 in 1970; and 400,000 in 1972. But to let unqualified graduates fly even more in less time on poorly maintained aircraft, will surely not improve the training qualities even more when de facto the pilot's flight training was reduced significantly. When in 1964 an average pilot flew around 122 hours, this dropped to 23 hours and 45 minute in 1968, and 55 hours in 1970.

The Naval Aviation logged comparable hours with even slightly less flight time: flying an average of 26 hours between 1965 and 1971, this dropped to only 12.5 hours in 1968. But not only the lack of flight time, also maintenance was so poor that by 1969 the officially admitted 'serious accident rate' – meaning the loss of aircraft and pilot – rose from 2.49 in 1964 per 100,000 flight hours to a shocking rate of 6.0 in 1969. The comparable data for the Naval Aviation is even worse: 11.2 per 100,000 hours and it is known that between 1969 and 1978 more than 70 serious accidents resulted in total loss of the aircraft and 62 pilot deaths.

Impact for the developing aviation industry

As noted in the previous chapter, the Great Leap Forward (1958–61) and especially the break with the Soviet Union had severe implications for the developing aviation industry, the cautious approaches to recovery by around 1965 made completely smashed during the Cultural Revolution (1967–77). Not only the lack of industrial base or available technology, and the unwell to accept the laws of manufacturing were the most hindering issues, but the political interference. More than once, the PLAAF directly blamed politicians blinded by 'revolutionary fever' – especially the PLAAF commander Wu Faxian – for damaging more than assisting the projects.

For example, in 1971 alone, 27 different aircraft types – ranging from modern fighters to strategic bombers – were authorised for development at the same time. However, the clear political given goal was, each of them had to be completed within one year, and for only a long range bomber project (the H-7), a civil airliner (the Y-10) and a V/STOL fighter were longer development times lasting two to three years accepted, and all this even if factories were not ready, blue-prints were non-existent, materials were neither developed nor even components tested. In the end, the aim for more and more (performance) led to the constant delay of decisions by the leadership, the repeated revision of specifications or even the successive replacement of one project by another. According to official documents[1] 46 projects were started – 36 of them not even officially approved – and actually underwent production between 1969 and 1971. Not surprisingly, the development time – even for dated types by Western standards – was delayed sometimes for 10 or even 15 years as demonstrated by the most important types, which in the end reached operational status: the final variant of the J-6, named J-6III conducted its maiden flight in 1969, but during the Cultural Revolution it was neither tested or certified throughoutly, but instead it was put into serial production with defective parts and design faults with the result, that several hundred aircraft hat to be completely refurbished during overhaul in 1975. Similar, the only in

Only two J-6IIIGai aircraft remain and this one is preserved at the famous Datangshan museum, today known as the Chinese Aviation Museum. This fighter was the first in China to carry missiles on wingtip pylons. (via Top81.cn)

the end successful project during the 1960s, the Nanchang Q-5 was initiated in 1958, had its maiden flight only in 1965 and in 1975, the CMC ordered, that all aircraft built so far had to be withdrawn from service and to be returned to the factory for overhaul due to design failures and the lack of manufacturing quality control. How under these circumstances anyone could expect that comparable modern and competitive design could ever be fielded is a question, none of these politicians were able to answer nor that such a question would be tolerated.

September 1971: Lin Biao's mysterious death

One prime example on how political interactions severely inflicted the PLAAF's overall development was yet another event: Wu Faxian, who had been the PLAAF political commissar from 1957 to 1965, became the PLAAF commander in May 1965. He was concurrently a deputy chief of the general staff and a deputy director of the General Office in the CMC. While in these positions, he became a member of Defence Minister Lin Biao's circle, who in September 1971 was involved in an alleged coup attempt against Mao Zedong. Officially, the circumstances surrounding this episode remain still classified.

Known is that Lin Biao was promoted China's second-in-charge on 1 April 1969 and therefore legitimate successor in the event of Mao's death. However, he advocated the restoration of the position of state president – in fact a position, previously held by Liu Shaoqi until his demotion. Liu Shaoqi was actually the First Vice Chairman of the Communist Party of China between 1956 and 1966 and Chairman (President) of the PRC, China's *de jure* head of state, from 1959 to 1968. For this period, he was the third most powerful man in China, behind Mao Zedong and Premier Zhou Enlai and, originally, he was to become Mao's successor. However, in the early 1960s shortly before the Cultural Revolution Liu antagonised Mao – he implemented policies of economic reconstruction in China – and from 1966 onward more and more criticised by Mao. Liu was purged and even labelled a 'traitor to the revolution'. He died under harsh treatment and torture during the Cultural Revolution and was only posthumously rehabilitated by Deng Xiaoping's government in 1980.

Lin Biao's aim to restore the presidency was to ensure an orderly transition of power after Mao's death. On 23 August 1970, the CPC held the second plenum of its Ninth Congress in Lushan, where Lin would speak for restoration of the position of president along with his supporter Chen Boda. However, it seems as Mao had become uncomfortable with Lin's power and had planned to purge him. Some scholars – including Professor Hu Xingdou – noted that Lin Biao steadily opposed in private against Mao: so he became alarmed by Mao's excesses and cult of personality, he allegedly opposed Chinese entrance into the Korean War, the purging of Liu Shaoqi during the Cultural Revolution, as well as the disastrous Great Leap Forward campaign and he even refused to become Mao's successor. Officially, the standpoint of the Chinese government was that Lin and his son, Lin Liguo, were accused of planning a pre-emptive coup and even had planned to assassinate Mao sometime in early September 1971.

Following this, after the planned coup was uncovered, Lin Biao, his family and several personal aides attempted to flee to the Soviet Union. Unfortunately, the prearranged Hawker Siddeley Trident airliner (CAAC B-256 piloted by Pan Jingyin, deputy

commander of the PLAAF's 34th Division) crashed near the town Öndörkhaan in Mongolia – today known as Chinggis City – on 13 September 1971, killing all on board. The true circumstances are still unclear and there are several contradictory theories as to the reason: while the official report claimed the airliner was not fully fuelled before taking off and crashed after running out of fuel, the official Mongolian report points out that there was still plenty of fuel left at the time of the crash and the aircraft crashed due to pilot error or due to an engine failure. Regardless of the facts, Lin was never politically rehabilitated and therefore all charges against him stand until today. However, in recent years, the attitude towards him has slowly changed and – since Lin is still regarded as one of the best Chinese military strategists – since 2007 his image has again been shown at the Chinese Military Museum in Beijing in a display of the 'Ten Marshals', the group of military leaders considered the founders of the PLA.

Aftermath – disaster for the PLAAF and reorganisation again

Lin Biao's death put severe pressure on the Chinese government and even if the Politburo met in an emergency session on the same day to discuss matters Lin's death was confirmed by Beijing only on 30 September. Even more the Central Committee kept information a heavily guarded secret and the public was informed only two months following the incident. Anyway, the National Day celebrations on 1 October 1971 were cancelled. For the PLA this even had even more severe consequences:

A massive purge within of the armed forces – and most of all the high military command – followed and military officials identified as being close to Lin or his family (in fact most of the PLAAF's high command) were within weeks either dead or arrested. This especially included Wu Faxian, who was accused of complicity and immediately arrested. He was tried 10 years later and sentenced to 17 years in prison. This had devastating effects for the PLAAF, even more far reaching than the Great Leap Forward and the Cultural Revolution, because within the PLA hierarchy Mao downgraded the air force to a minimal level of importance, and for nearly a decade the PLAAF had no C-in-C because Mao never again trusted high ranking air force officers. The Department of the air dorce also stopped all projects associated with Lin Biao or his supporters. Under the chaotic conditions that prevailed in China in those days, the PLAAF's development however suffered the most, since the PLAAF did not get a new commander until May 1973, when the CMC appointed Ma Ning, who was a Lanzhou MRAF deputy commander. Ma remained as the commander until March 1977.

Although the PLAAF reached its historical peak in terms of personnel strength – estimated at 760,000 by 1972 – the lack of guidance from Beijing, diminishing political trust, shortages of fuel and spare parts, and maintenance problems related to the widespread chaos, combined to result in serious setbacks. These manifested themselves in particular within training institutions, while pilots and ground personnel had their flight training and exercises significantly reduced, so that its educational departments suffered serious setbacks. For example, prior to the Cultural Revolution, there were 29 schools active of which in 1969, 12 of them were shut down. According to the PLAAF, the number of hours its fighter pilots flew annually during this decade hit

record lows. Although regulations required about 123 flight hours annually, the actual number flown in 1970 was as low as 30 to 40 hours. By 1977, however, flight hours had increased to an average of about 80 hours. The driving factors for the reduction in flight hours were the lack of training guidance from Beijing, lack of fuel and spare parts, and maintenance problems. In addition, the lack of political trust in the PLAAF during the Cultural Revolution negatively affected flight training.

On the other side, the PLAAF at least numerically on paper expanded its force during the early 1960s with the introduction of new AAA, more modern SAMs and also additional radar units were formed. This bolster of the PLAAF's air defence force occurred mostly between mid-1966 to 1971. And – quite surprisingly in mind of the low production and quality of aircraft delivered – the PLAAF formed 21 additional air divisions throughout China, for a total of 50; the highest number in its overall history. But not only the number of units was increased but also new types introduced – namely the advanced J-6 variants and the J-7 – and several projects – like the J-8, H-6 and JH-7 – initiated. Subsequently, the PLAAF was gradually decreased in capabilities and size. Concerning the mentioned reduction in force, an analysis of available data indicates – even if the PLAAF did not provide any specific official numbers for its personnel for any given period – the implemented reduction, concerned about a 190,000-man, bringing it down from 760,000 in 1972 to around 570,000 by the end of the year 1976. This situation began only to change in the early 1970s when schools were reopened and technical and theory training was reintroduced. Since then, the PLAAF's overall organisational structure has remained fairly constant and even while different administrative departments have combined and split several times and new operational commands have appeared and been disbanded, their basic responsibilities have not changed appreciably.

Following the 1969 reduction in force, the PLAAF's HQ followed suit by reducing its organisation to the three core first-level departments: Headquarters Department (siling bu), Political Department (zhengzhi bu) and Logistics Department (houqin bu). Because of this consolidation, the PLAAF changed the status of the following departments by merging the Training and Schools Departments into the Training Department, reducing and resubordinating the AAA Command Department, the 2nd AAA Command Department, the Radar Department and the Scientific Research Department to the Headquarters Department, the abolishment of the Engineering and Directly Subordinate Political Departments. In addition, the Engineering Department's administrative and field maintenance work came under the Headquarters Department's responsibility and finally the Engineering Department's repair and procurement work was reassigned under the Logistics Department's responsibility. Especially this caused even more problems for maintaining not only the established but also the newly formed units which even more problematic gained often enough sub-standard manufactured new types which caused even more problems, typically with the introduction of new equipment. Consequently, the Engineering Department was reactivated as the Aeronautical Engineering Department (hangkong gongcheng bu) in May 1976 as the fourth first level administrative department.

In parallel, the consequences for the command structure – especially after Lin Biao's mysterious death – were dramatic: of the 13 air corps and several command posts created during the 1950s and 1960s, with the aim to control aviation and air defence units within certain geographical areas, many command organisations ceased

Images of early J-6Bing aircraft in service are very rare and seldom of good quality. This is an example from an unknown fighter division.
(via Top81.cn)

to exist during the Cultural Revolution, and were only re-established in the late 1970s. In parallel to the expansion and realignment of operational areas with those of the PLA Ground Forces, several of the established air corps replaced MRAF headquarters, were disbanded, or were downgraded to a command post. When they moved, they did not necessarily have organic aviation and air defence units that moved with them. This sometimes led to such absurd situations, where a new command organisation was moved around to replace an existing one – or to establish a new command organisations – only to take over control of aviation and air defence units that already existed in the given command area. And finally in order to tighten political control over important units and the command structure in general, it must be reminded, that while most of the regular aviation and air defence units are subordinate to their MRAF, all air corps, command posts or bases and a few dedicated aviation and air defence units are directly subordinate (zhishu budui) to the PLAAF's headquarters.

Cultural Revolution: May 1966 to October 1976

To better understand the later phase of the creation of the PLAAF's divisions, one has not only to look at the political background and operational needs, but also – and perhaps even more importantly – to the process of aircraft deliveries from the Soviet Union. In this sense, the usual procedure was not just to upgrade an already established unit to new combat types, but simply establish additional units when a new aircraft was introduced.

As such, between 1954 and 1971 the PLAAF created the final 22 divisions throughout China, most of which related to the delivery of new aircraft types. Typical for this was the fielding of 'modern' types like the H-5, H-6H, J-6 and Q-5, regardless of the previously outlined quality issues. For example, the PLAAF began receiving the indigenous H-5 in 1967 – even though other units were already operating Soviet-built Il-28s – the Q-5 in December 1969, and the H-6 in 1976.[5]

Units re-established/newly established after May 1966

Date	Base / location	Unit	Sub–units	Aircraft types	Notes
1966 August	Dandong Langtou, Liaoning	37th Fighter Division	109th Regiment 110th Regiment 111th Regiment	MiG-15bis	Later Kuerle
1967 June	Jinghai, Hebei	38th Fighter Division	112th Regiment 113th Regiment 114th Regiment	MiG-15/ MiG-15UTI	Formerly 1st Training Base
1697 June	Liuhe, Jilin	39th Fighter Division	115th Regiment 116th Regiment 117th Regiment	MiG-15bis	Formerly 2nd Training Base, Lihue confirmed
1969 July	Liaoning Langtou	40th Fighter Division	118th Regiment 119th Regiment 120th Regiment	J-5, MiG-15bis	
1969 August	Gongmiaozi, Inner Mongolia	41st Fighter Division	121st Regiment 122nd Regiment 123rd Regiment	J-6, MiG-15	

1969 August	Guilin, Guangxi.	42nd Fighter Division	124th Regiment 125th Regiment 126th Regiment	J-5	Later Nanning Wuxu
1969 September	Dongfeng, Jilin	43rd Fighter Division	127th Regiment 128th Regiment 129th Regiment	MiG-15bis	
1969 November	Hubei	44th Fighter Division	130th Regiment 131st Regiment 132nd Regiment	J-5, MiG-15	Kunming Wujiaba
1969 November	Anhui	45th Fighter Division	133rd Regiment 134th Regiment 135th Regiment	J-5	
1969 October	Gansu Dingxin	46th Fighter Division	136th Regiment 137th Regiment 138th Regiment	J-6	
1970 February	Yinchuan, Ningxia	47th Fighter Division	139th Regiment 140th Regiment 141st Regiment	J-5, J-5A, MiG-15bis	
1970 August	Fuyang, Hunan	48th Fighter Division	142nd Regiment 143rd Regiment 144th Regiment	H-5	
1971 July	Zhangshu City, Jiangxi	49th Fighter Division	145th Regiment 146th Regiment 147th Regiment	J-6, MiG-15bis	
1971 August	Leizhuang, Guiyang	50th Fighter Division	148th Regiment 149th Regiment 150th Regiment	Tu-2?	

Aircraft types

Xi'an H-6A (ASCC 'Badger')

The first two airframes were delivered to the PLAAF in December 1959 for service testing, but at this point the political influences made their mark and delayed this promising and important programme for years. The first was the decision in 1961 to transfer all H-6 production to the Xi'an Aircraft Factory, while Harbin was ordered to reverse-engineer the Ilyushin Il-28. This transfer started in 1962, but moving the entire H-6 production line over a distance of 2,280km (1,420 miles) was not an easy task. This took until 1964 to complete and during the process it was realised that a large amount of technical and manufacturing papers had been lost. The true reason behind this is unknown, but China putting the blame on the Soviets did not improve the already cool relationship between the two countries. What followed was a huge effort to retrieve the missing materials, which included dismantling the two Soviet-built Tu-16s in order to reverse-engineer the aircraft. The first Xi'an built test airframe was completed in October 1966 made its maiden flight in December 1968. In order to distinguish these airframes from the first ones at Harbin they were designated H-6A.

Operational wise, the H-6 was to be part of China's nuclear deterrent force and already one of the two H-6s assembled from Soviet-supplied parts featured a specialised bomb-bay to carry nuclear stores. The first true conversion was completed in September 1964 and in May 1965 this H-6A dropped a 25-kiloton yield nuclear device at the Lop Nor nuclear test site in Malan/Xinjiang. In June 1967 the same aircraft was also used to test China's first thermonuclear hydrogen bomb. H-6As were delivered to the PLAAF from 1970 onwards with full rate production since 1971 so that by 1986 about 140 examples had been delivered. Despite being built to slightly varying standards, all were all usually called H-6As. However, two minor updated versions were also produced: the first is a mysterious H-6B certified in 1979, most likely for reconnaissance fitted with optical cameras and a HD-42 infrared camera.

The second subtype is the H-6C, which was an improved conventional bomber fitted with an additional electronic warfare suite comprising an ECM jammer, ELINT equipment, radar warning receivers and chaff/flare dispensers. Development reportedly began in 1977, a maiden flight was made in 1980 and the type entered PLAAF service in 1983.

Even more secretive is an often-mentioned ECM/ELINT version designated HD-6, which is understood to be flown in three subtypes, known as the HD-6I, HD-6II and HD-6III. Otherwise, several H-6 airframes were used for test purposes like an engine testbed, a drone carrier for the high attitude supersonic target drone called the Ba-6 which entered service in 1971.

Failed projects: H-6I, H-7 and H-8

Due to some shortcomings, the PLAAF suggested several developments in order to improve the H-6's range and weapons load capacity. The first one was initiated in June 1970 by replacing the two WP-8 engines with four more modern and more fuel-efficient

Top: The H-6I powered by four Rolls-Royce Spey turbofans was a unique concept that failed since the engines were no longer available.
(via CDF)

Bottom: Only a few images of factory models of the H-7 are known. This one shows the enlarged H-6 airframe with four airliner-style engines under the wings.
(via CDF)

The H-6A was flown for quite some time before being replaced by the H-6E/F in the late 1980s; even today some are still in use as trainers. This example is from the 10th Bomber Division. (FlyWing/0624 via CDF)

British Rolls-Royce Spey 512 turbofans. Little has been revealed to the public about this improved H-6I, but it appears that initial design took place during 1971 and led to a first flight in late 1977 or early 1978. The new engines were placed in each wing root nacelle and in slim underwing nacelles. Even if the single aircraft indeed showed improved performance, it was subsequently cancelled in early 1980; most likely being either too expensive or impossible to acquire the Spey engines.

The second development was proposed in March 1970 as a true long-range bomber called H-7 Yuanhong even before the H-6I programme had started. Altogether, there were three different designs called H-7, which – besides different powerplants and number of engines – were all based on an enlarged and aerodynamically refined H-6 fuselage. The H-7I was to be powered by four Type 910 (WS-6 derivate) turbofan engines or as a the H-7II backup proposal by six JT-3D-3B turbofans in airliner-style nacelles. Unfortunately, very little is known about these unbuilt heavy bomber projects, which allegedly even included a much larger design sometimes known as the H-8.

Ilyushin Il-10 re-engined (ASCC 'Beast')

Most unique, due to reliability and maintenance issues with the original Mikulin AM-42 liquid-cooled engine, at least two were re-equipped in the late 1960s with a much more powerful AI-20K turboprop engine as used by a few Tu-4 bombers. Noteworthy, some reports mention, that not the intended AI-20K was fitted but an engine based on the HS-8 radial engine, itself a locally produced ASh-82 as used by the La-11 and not a turboprop. In the end, this was not successful even if this programme was once an urgent stopgap solution due to the delayed development of the later Q-5. Following conversion, it was transferred to Hangzhou Xi'an air base to continue its trials, however, due to several issues it failed. Both modified aircraft were lost – the first crashed during a test flight in 1972 and the second was destroyed in 1978 when its engine caught fire during routine maintenance.

The sole image of the re-engined Il-10 showing an impressive array of stores. This type also failed and was later replaced by the Q-5. (via CDF)

Shenyang J-6Bing ('J-6C') (ASCC 'Farmer')

The 'basic' J-6s were de facto almost exact copies of the original MiG-19S, with only minor improvements introduced by other versions in production that time, so that after 1968 with a new drag chute located at the fin base as introduced with the J-6III (see later), these J-6 received the new designation J-6Bing. In addition, up-rated and more reliable WP-6As were fitted and these improvements led to a successful maiden flight in early August 1969. It must be pointed out that the J-6Bing was never designated J-6C in PLAAF service, despite several Eastern and Western publications usually describing this version as 'the standard Chinese fighter'.

Most likely the designation J-6C was based on an error in early translations of the original Миг-19C, which mixed the Cyrillic 'C' with the Latin 'S' (for MiG-19S). This type was mainly produced at the Shenyang Factory No. 112, but later also at an additional production line and maintenance centre at Guizhou.

The first serial J-6Bing performed its maiden flight in December 1974 and production continued until the second quarter of 1975 with 115 machines built at Guizhou. Altogether, a total of 3,562 aircraft were produced by the main facility at Shenyang between 1964 and 1984. After being withdrawn from frontline service, several were converted into J-6W UCAVs.

Shenyang J-6II (ASCC 'Farmer')

After the failure of the J-6I as a daytime high-altitude interceptor, a J-6II was proposed as a further development. It featured the increased area wing and added a redesigned intake with an adjustable central shock cone and presumably to compensate for the smaller intake there were now eight rather than four auxiliary intake (blow-in) doors placed around the intake lip. The first aircraft performed its maiden flight in March 1969 and even if the flight test programme was quite successful, only two prototypes were built and it was superseded by the improved J-6III.

One of two J-6II prototypes, now preserved at the China Aviation Museum. It wears a unique colour scheme and fictional serial numbers (via F. Käsmann)

A unique J-6Bing with an unusual three-digit serial number. It is likely an early prototype or an example assigned to a test unit. (via CDF)

Shenyang J-6III & J-6IIIXin or J-6IIIC (ASCC 'Farmer')

This specialised interceptor variant is often rated to be the most potent J-6 variant while opponents usually emphasise the limits of being based on a desperately dated design. Development of the J-6III started in 1968 to meet a RfP as a fall-back option in case the higher priority projects J-7 and J-8 would suffer delays. One outcome, which in particular took into account the expanding workload required to finish the J-8's design, was to transfer the entire J-7 programme to Chengdu in August 1968, where the first J-7I flew in June 1969. Similar, at the main facility in Shenyang the first J-8 prototype flew first in July 1969 and it already seemed likely that the J-6III could be cancelled. In the end this was not the case, since not surprisingly, both the J-7 and J-8 were delayed and the J-6III was available as an interim aircraft. Airframe wise, the J-6III was based an improved J-6II mated with elements from the standard J-6Bing. Most importantly, it used a modified intake as well as up-rated WP-6A turbojets. The most important improvement however, was a new wing with reduced span but extended chord. The first J-6III made its maiden flight in August 1969 and after a flight demonstration in October, it was directly afterwards ordered for production. Altogether 303 machines were built.

A rare image of an operational J-6III assigned to the 14th Fighter Division showing its unique intake design with the adjustable central shock-cone. (via CDF)

However again, this rush into production without full testing led to some quite serious quality issues so that between 1969 and 1970 nearly 50 per cent of the almost 700 J-6s of all variants built were defective in certain areas. Additionally most operational units (some sources say 50 per cent) lacked the necessary support infrastructure and equipment and, only few J-6s could be delivered. In the end the J-6III needed lengthy and expensive modifications, so in late 1971 the Third Ministry of Machine-Building ordered to modify the already built J-6III airframes to bring them into operational service. Consequently, all 303 J-6IIIs manufactured at SAC were 'repaired' between 1971 and 1973. Some accounts state that additional work was done at Guizhou.

First flight of a modified aircraft was accomplished in early 1977 and work was completed in May 1980 with the updated aircraft now redesignated J-6IIIA, J-6IIIC or even J-6IIIXin. The J-6III was finally retired in 2000.

Shenyang J-6IIIGai or J-6IIIG (ASCC 'Farmer')

Alongside the efforts to finally introduce the J-6III into service and ease the maintenance problems there was another improve programme in 1974. The first aircraft made its maiden flight in August and as the most prominent features this updated J-6III 'new' or J-6IIIGai had a lengthened front fuselage, again a new inlet configuration, for the first time wingtip pylons for PL-2 AAMs were added and it featured the new Type 225 ranging radar. However since this type was simply too old especially against any potential adversary, the PLAAF abandoned the J-6IIIGai in 1978 and only five aircraft were produced.

Shenyang/Guizhou J-6IV (ASCC 'Farmer')

In parallel, there were similar attempts to correct the issues of the J-6B and SAC began development based on the experiences gained from the J-6I to J-6III series. In March 1976, development was officially initiated and the J-6IV was to be equipped with a Type 645 radar. Therefore, the front fuselage and the intake area needed major modifications; the fuselage was made slimmer by a new front fuselage featuring a slightly relocated canopy as well as the J-6III's wings. Development was actually carried out at Guizhou and the first prototype made its maiden flight in September 1976, so that the new type was put into production in 1977. However, due to manufacturing issues, a poor performance and reliability of the radar, all further work was stopped after only seven (other sources say just two) aircraft had been built. It seems as if they were only used for ground training.

The J-6IV could have emerged as the most capable all-weather variant, but failed for several reasons and was only built in very limited numbers. This one wears serial numbers from the 14th Fighter Division and is now on display at the Chinese Aviation Museum.
(via CDF)

Shenyang/Guizhou J-6AXin/J-6XinA (ASCC 'Farmer')

In November 1973 the PLAAF issued an RFP which resulted in another attempt to modify the J-6A from 1974 on at Guizhou. This new type was called the J-6AXin or J-6XinA and performed its maiden flight in December 1975. With an alleged production from 1977 onwards it featured several changes made to the radar and armament; most of them taken oven from other versions at the time.

Another rare image, of an operational updated J-6XinA armed with PL-2 AAMs and assigned to the 2nd Fighter Division.
(via CDF)

Chengdu J-7I (ASCC 'Fishbed')

A second attempt on the MiG-21 was then initiated at Chengdu, where as decided in 1965 the J-7 production line was transferred. Chengdu took this as an opportunity to include several changes to the original design. Flight testing of the prototype was delayed until June 1969 and even if none of these early models became operational, they paved the way for the first serial variant, which flew in April 1970 as the J-7I or

J-7A. After again much delay, this day fighter variant received certification in June 1975. Its service career was rather limited due to several flaws and manufacturing quality issues but anyway, production continued until 1981 with 188 aircraft built.

Chengdu J-7II/J-7B (ASCC 'Fishbed')

Consequently, already in 1974 Chengdu begun to consider the next improvements, which resulted in the better-known J-7II or J-7B, which introduced a new ejection seat under a re-designed canopy and an improved WP-7B engine. Several minor improvements on the avionics were also added as well as the now characteristic braking chute container at the tail root. The first J-7II made its maiden flight in December 1978 and the type was certificated in September 1979. Full rate production was initiated one year later altogether two production lines at Chengdu and Guizhou delivered around 475 J-7Bs up to 1986. Even if heralded a great achievement, its biggest weakness simply was, that its development had taken so long and what finally arrived at frontline units was desperately outdated in comparison to other contemporary fighters.

During its career, the J-7B received several upgrades, formed the basis for the countless export variants[6] – and was produced in several more subtypes: worthy of mention are the J-7IIA MLU with some Western avionics (Type 226 Skyranger radar – 1982), the J-7IIH with four pylons and able to use the PL-8 AAM (221 built until 1993) and the J-7IIK MLU (58 delivered until 1999). Quite remarkable, even today several of these 'dinosaurs' are in use at second line units.

The J-7B also formed the basis of several projects – like the J-7CP, which later evolved through the Sabre II and Super-7 projects in cooperation with Grumman including a new front fuselage, a Western radar and eventually engine, into the FC-1/JF-17 Thunder.

Top: An old J-7I assigned to the 7th Fighter Division.
(via AFwing)

Bottom: The prototype of the J-7II clearly shows the most important change compared with the previous model – its new rearward-opening canopy.
(via Top81.cn)

Shenyang J-8 (ASCC 'Finback')

In parallel to the ongoing J-6 and J-7 development, the Chinese Academy of Engineering (CAE) initiated already in May 1964 the search for a fighter superior to the J-7. Consequently, Shenyang's No. 601 Institute began and considered two possible lines of development, which were to be pursued in parallel: the first was to use the J-7 design and to develop an advanced twin-engined fighter and high-altitude interceptor, which evolved into the J-8.

The second path was to develop and all new single-engined fighter powered by a new turbofan engine and this type resulted in the J-9. The operational requirements for the new fighter, later called J-8, were set around an ambitious set of target specifications, most of them – in retrospect – simply overambitious or even unrealistic, but nevertheless it was approved in May 1965. In configuration the J-8 proved to be a quite straightforward enlargement of the J-7 layout with large delta wings, an enlarged circular nose intake with a Type 204 fire-control radar, and a wider fuselage to accommodate two WP-7A turbojets. Although it resembled Mikoyan's experimental Ye-152A fighter prototype the J-8 was not based on that aircraft, despite this 'fact' being quoted repeatedly by several sources.

A J-8 prototype with serial numbers denoting it as operational with the FTTC.
(via Bai Wei)

A very rare image showing the first two J-8 prototypes, two early J-7Is and several J-6s in the background, presumably taken at the FTTC.
(via Top81.cn)

Unfortunately, the early phase of development was hampered by several tragic events, when several chief designers died, or were purged during the Cultural Revolution. As much by chance as anything else, final assembly of the first two J-8s was completed in July 1968 and the first flight was performed in July 1969. Despite this success, the Cultural Revolution took its toll, further development was slowed, and production was not authorised for another 10 years. At least by 1978 some political stability had been restored and the design was officially certified in March 1980. However, despite being regarded as a great achievement, it was already too dated, so work began on an improved version, the J-8I.

Shenyang/Chengdu J-9

As mentioned, in parallel to the initial J-8 studies, an alternative design, was considered. This type however after many several design changes and yet another overlong period of development failed in the end. As noted, it too started in spring 1964 as the J-9. The initial objective was to create an air superiority fighter with an operating altitude of 22,000m (72,180ft) and a maximum speed of Mach 2.2. This was step by step increased to 25,000m (82,020ft) and Mach 2.5, so that it was hoped, it would be able to match the performance of the F-4 Phantom II.

The most interesting part of the J-9's development is, that it mirrors the individual phases of the Chinese aviation industry influenced by politics par excellence: initiated during the pre-revolution, when 'only the sky was the limit' and China eagerly tried to catch up with the best in the world. It lead through the disastrous time of the Cultural Revolution, when politics decided to ignore the laws of manufacturing until its cancellation in the 1980, when it mysteriously formed the basis for the successful J-10.

In early 1965 Shenyang submitted four alternative designs each showing a slightly different aerodynamic layout named J-9I to J-9IV each with slightly different wing geometry – regular swept-back wing, delta wing, double-delta or cranked delta wing – and some with a canard configuration. In late 1965, one concept was selected, while

The J-9 – here in its final iteration - could have been a formidable fighter but its development came at a time of political instability with repeated changes as well as numerous technical issues.
(via Bai Wei)

in parallel development of the WS-6 turbofan continued. Unfortunately, by now the Cultural Revolution had reached its full intensity and the J-9 programme was brought to a standstill, so that now in configuration J-9V it was finally terminated in June 1968. What followed was the beginning of a long phase of struggle between research to overcome the fighter's technical problems and the political influencing background, which again changed the requirements. Additionally, to allow Shenyang to concentrate on the J-8's development it was decided in October 1969, to transfer the J-9's development to Factory No. 132 in Chengdu. Alongside all of this, the refinement of the J-9 continued through several more from a tailless delta wing configuration to a delta canard design quite similar to a SAAB AJ 37 Viggen. In addition, configurations with belly intake or two side intakes were wind tunnel tested between November 1970 until August 1971. After yet another break, the PLAAF at least began to accept more realistic requirements in 1974, so that in February 1975, under the personal direction of Deng Xiaoping, full development of the J-9 was installed again with the aim to perform a first flight around the turn of 1980/81. The final design was now called J-9VI-3 but even if development continued until 1978, the priority of the J-9 was downscaled yet again and in June 1978 it was finally terminated.

The J-9's design was revised on numerous occasions. This is one of the intermediate pure-delta configurations.
(via CDF)

Further miscellaneous unbuilt projects: China's teen-series

Most often, Chinese design are denounced as being only copies of stolen designs, however there are quite a few unbuilt projects, which give another image: worthy of mention is the Project 751 delta canard project, which was researched in 1974 as a potential successor to the Q-5 based on an operational requirement for a highly manoeuvrable fighter. This was – as well as a Project 701 Yanan four-engined STOL transport – formulated by group of officers working with the then Minister of National Defence, Lin Biao. Based on his paranoia, China had to prepare for an almost immediate next war, the PLAAF studied highly mobile, rapid deployable assets for both the army and the PLAAF. However, in 1971 this all ended after Biao's reported coup against Mao and his death in an aircraft crash. As such again, the fate of several interesting concepts – as so often before – was sealed by politics. Another hot topic was the development of variable geometry (VG) wing designs and although none ever came anywhere near flight status, there were at least several proposals.

The probably most enigmatic types under development were however a number of projects ranging under the designations J-10 to J-13: the rarely known Shenyang J-10 – not to confuse with the Chengdu J-10 – was a MiG-25-like twin-engined heavy interceptor fitted with a huge delta wing, twin fins canted outward and enormous boxy air intakes. If one considers the timescale of the Chengdu J-9 and the original Shenyang J-11 lightweight fighter, it seems as if this project was under consideration during the 1968 to 1970 time period.

The next two numbers are a pair of lightweight fighters based on a requirement issued in April 1967. This was to be STOL-capable and smaller, lighter and more agile than any other fighter in service. Two design teams responded with very different concepts: Shenyang proposed their J-11 project (again not to be confused with the later J-11 designation given to Chinese 'Flankers') and Nanchang with the ultra-lightweight J-12. The J-11 is often shown as a Dassault Mirage F1-style design powered by a sin-

gle Spey 512 engine, whereas the J-12 – which actually even flew first in December 1970 – was a MiG-21-like design with a highly swept wing and powered by one WP-6B afterburning turbojet. Following a brief test-phase, some changes were necessary and the first of three improved J-12A flew in July 1975. However, in due course the PLAAF reviewed its requirements again and decided that the J-12 was just too small and too light, to be useful in modern aerial warfare and the project was terminated in February 1978.

The final design, often called the Chinese F-16 analogue, was the Shenyang J-13. Initial studies were initiated at the end of 1971 and it was long thought to be the PLAAF's backbone fighter along with the Shenyang J-8B interceptor and Xi'an JH-7 fighter-bomber. A first preliminary concept was submitted in March 1972. However, politics interfered again as well as the lack of an engine badly delayed further work. Design wise, between November 1973 and April 1974 several different configurations were tested, before the two final configuration was chosen. The preliminary design was completed in the late 1970s but after initially a variant of the WS-6 engine was planned to power the J-13, later a reverse engineered variant of the MiG-23's Tumansky R-29 turbojet as the WP-15 failed, it was briefly considered with a WS-9. This again delayed this project until early 1979 up to a point, where it was no longer feasible, so that in March 1981 the J-13 programme was terminated. Interestingly, given this lineage, the current J-10 and J-11 fighters should have been named J-14 and J-15.

A rare image of the improved J-12I, showing at least part of its revised intake geometry with a centre shock-cone replacing the original one.
(via CDF)

Shenyang JJ-6 trainer

With the beginning of the 1960s and a considerably growing number of supersonic fighters entering service, a more modern trainer than the JJ-5 became an urgent need. Consequently, the best option was a design based on the J-6. Formal approval was issued in October 1966, and in March 1967 the manufacture of two prototypes began. Interestingly, even if there was actually never a MiG-19 trainer, even today some publications still claim that the JJ-6 was a copy of a MiG-19UTI trainer. With both aircraft being finished in 1970, a successful first flight was performed in November 1970. Similar to the JJ-5, the JJ-6 used a tandem arrangement; however, unlike the JJ-5 which saw the second cockpit installed in place of a fuel tank, the JJ-6 had an extension inserted into the forward fuselage ahead of the wings to make room for the additional seat. Otherwise, in order to increase directional stability, two large outward-canted fins were placed under the rear fuselage. The JJ-6 entered production in November 1973 and until 1986, a total of 634 had been built by two lines at Shenyang and Tianjin. Although the JJ-6 represented a huge improvement over the JJ-5, it was already outdated when it entered service.

◄ Three very different but typical projects for this overambitious period:
Top: The still secretive SAC J-10 heavy interceptor looks remarkably like a delta-winged MiG-25.
Centre: The SAC J-11 lightweight fighter was comparable but smaller than a Mirage F1.
Bottom: Probably the most promising project until the 1980s, the J-13 was planned as an equivalent to the F-16, In the end all failed.
(All via Bai Wei)

Shenyang JZ-6 reconnaissance aircraft

Based on an official RfP Factory No. 112 began to adapt an airframe as a prototype in 1966 and already in March 1967 the Third Ministry of Machine-Building ordered that series production of the new JZ-6 based on the current production J-6Bing. In all 49 machines were built up until 1972. Compared to the fighter versions, the recon-

The JJ-6 was for many years the standard supersonic jet trainer in PLAAF service, and was also available as the JZ-6 reconnaissance variant. The final examples served within Q-5 units.
(via Top81.cn)

One of the last remaining JZ-6s assigned to the 26th Division, before that unit gained JZ-8Fs. Today this division is the PLAAF's sole AEW unit.
(via Top81.cn)

naissance variant was structurally pretty identical. Its most noticeable difference was a semi-conformal camera compartment underneath the lower front fuselage which housed two Type 13-40 and three Type 11-10 cameras (other sources say four cameras only), which required the belly gun pack to be discarded and only the two wing root guns left. It seems as if in October 1969 the PLAAF considered the development of an improved version for high-altitude reconnaissance based on the J-6II with a different camera fit, comprising a new Type 15-60 high-altitude camera. Allegedly, one aircraft was modified in April 1971 but this type did not enter series production. In addition, other specialised high-altitude and low-level reconnaissance versions were proposed and even tested, in early 1975. However, none entered true serial production. In December 1976, the reconnaissance types were officially re-designated JZ-6 and the reconnaissance version was the last J-6 variant to be retired from PLAAF service some time after 2010.

Two typical images of Q-5IA or Q-5B aircraft operated during this period. They wore simple white colours with prominent red serial numbers and often carried unguided rocket pods. (**Left:** via F.C.Scan, **Right:** via CDF)

Nanchang Q-5 (ASCC 'Fantan')

The battle around the Yijiangshan Island in 1955 saw the PLAAF's first operational use of the Il-10, however even if quite successful, several lessons were learned from, which led to a requirement for the development of a supersonic ground attack aircraft.

In March 1958, the PLAAF requested an attack aircraft which could provide more speed, more range and could carry a greater load. In June a first preliminary layout for a supersonic fighter bomber was presented by the Shenyang Aircraft Design Department as the Dong Feng 106 based on the MiG-19 but with new front fuselage with a conical nose to take the necessary avionics, two side intakes replaced the conical MiG-19-style intake. It also got a re-designed fuselage and wings as well as provision for a bomb bay. Since Shenyang was responsible for other important projects, it was decided to transfer development to Nanchang, where a full-size mock-up was completed in October 1958. There the new attack aircraft was rechristened the XionYing 302 (Mighty Eagle) but again the biggest difficulty was the Great Leap Forward. Again, the design of structures and systems was done with too much haste with the manufacture of certain parts underway even before wind tunnel testing had been completed or a static test airframe was assembled. The worsening Chinese economic and political situation resulted even in the cancellation of the Q-5 programme in 1961 and a planned prototype was not built. The development team of over 300 staff was broken up and the production line was taken apart.

Anyway, in early 1964 the PLAAF was again interested in the Q-5 as it was now known, and as a result the project was revived, that a prototype even flew for the first time in June 1965. The flight testing revealed some shortcomings, so that several more changes were and additional prototypes were necessary. The first of them flew in October 1969 and after the subsequent flight test programme was completed, the Q-5 was officially approved for serial production in November 1969. It appears that following the type's hasty introduction into service, the original Q-5 was in production only until 1978 with about 400 Q-5s manufactured.

Interestingly, when the Q-5 was first recognised in the West it was thought to be another fighter variant of the J-6 and so was given an ASCC fighter codename and the wrong designations J-6bis or even J-9, before the correct designation became known in 1980.

Nanchang Q-5A and Q-5B (ASCC 'Fantan')

It is worth noting that, like the J-6 family, the designations for subsequent Q-5 variants are somewhat confusing, since two systems were in use before both were replaced by a sequential one using Roman letters. However, both systems were long used in parallel, adding to the confusion. Additionally, some designations were reused. Following the regular close air support and battlefield interdiction variant, the first such specialised version was the nuclear-capable Q-5A, which featured a modified weapon bay to carry a semi-recessed nuclear device. The Q-5A first flew in August 1970 and in January 1972 a Q-5A delivered a 20-kiloton nuclear bomb over the Lop Nor nuclear test site in Malan, Xinjiang. Allegedly, only a dozen such aircraft were modified.

The next variant – the first of at least three versions to carry the suffix 'B' – was a proposed naval torpedo-bomber. Three airframes were modified between 1968 and 1970 but the programme was later abandoned and replaced by another Q-5B missile-carrier. This one was to carry two YJ-8K anti-ship missiles and featured a Type 317A fire-control radar in a rounded nose; the cockpit was also raised. Allegedly only a very limited number entered naval service in the late 1970s, before this version was withdrawn from service in the late 1980s.

1   ALLEN, K. W., *China's Air Force enters the 21st Century*, p 71.

2   Compiled from *China's Air Force enters the 21st Century*, p 18ff and 71ff and for further information http://www.mongabay.com/history/china/china-events_during_the_cultural_revolution_dec-ade,_1966-76.html

3   *China Today: The Air Force* (1989a), pp 298–300, 524.

4   *China Today: The Air Force* (1989a), pp 83–84.

5   See YAO JUN, pp 260, 413, 415, 664.

6   The launch customer was Egypt, which signed a contract for 60. The US Air Force also acquired 15 between 1982 and 1983 (others say only 12 examples in 1987) for simulating MiG-21s in dissimilar air combat training.

It is quite difficult to differentiate the Q-5A and Q-5B, especially after both received updates in the later parts of their service careers. This particular aircraft is from the 5th Ground Attack Division. (via CDF)

MODERNISATION:
OCTOBER 1976 TO THE PRESENT

The previous phase following the Cultural Revolution and its overall disastrous consequences needed time of reconciliation, which however was only initiated after Mao's death in 1976 and implemented after Deng Xiaoping gained control of the CCP in 1978, when forces within the party that opposed the Cultural Revolution, gained prominence.

In the 1950, Deng Xiaoping was the CCP's Secretary General and presided over anti-rightist campaigns. However, his main focus through all his political career and the point, where he became the paramount figure of the 'second generation' of Chinese politicians, was China's economic reconstruction. He was already instrumental following the Great Leap Forward, but he gained even wider importance and foreign respect after the Cultural Revolution. Especially his economic policies – more than once against the revolutional spirit of Mao and the official party line – caused him to fall out of favour with Mao Zedong and he was purged twice during the Cultural Revolution. Anyway, he managed to politically survive and even was able to outmanoeuvre Mao's chosen successor Hua Guofeng in December 1978. What he earned after Mao Zedong's death in 1976, was a country beset with social conflict, disenchantment with the Communist Party and institutional disorder resulting from the chaotic policies. Concerning the PLAAF, this service – as Kenneth Allen noted – 'emerged from the Cultural Revolution – including the residual years of leftist influence in the early 1970s – as an organisational shell. The air force was intact, but their effectiveness had been severely degraded.'

Most often, the mid-1970s were mentioned as the true turning point: Mao Zedong died in 1976 as well as Zhou Enlai and Marshal Zhu De. Additionally, helpful was the subsequent arrest and purge of the Gang of Four, since – even if only singular events – they led to a redirection of the political orientation, to the reinstallment of social norms and tremendously helped to consolidate political and military power. During the following decade – until his retirement in 1989 – Deng Xiaoping became the paramount leader and most influencing Chinese politician for China's far-reaching market-economy reforms. Interestingly, Deng never held office as the head of state, head of government or General Secretary of the CCP, he managed to become the architect of China's new and then new brand of thinking of 'socialism with Chinese characteristics'; in fact a system combining socialist ideology and until today a very strict party rule with free enterprise and modern market-oriented economics, so that China developed not only into one of the fastest-growing economies in the world but also as an alternative way of leadership in contrast to the Soviet Communist system or the Western system.

In consequence, most of the Maoist reforms associated with the Cultural Revolution were abandoned by 1978 and even the Cultural Revolution has been treated officially as a negative phenomenon ever since. In 1981, the party assigned chief responsibility to Mao, but also laid significant blame on Lin Biao and the Gang of Four for causing its worst excesses. So that after decades of repression, violence and turmoil, the probably most important result of Deng's policy was the raising the standard of living of hundreds of millions.

Regeneration of the PLAAF

Again citing Kenneth Allen, 'Although the basic administrative infrastructure was still in place, the routine functions, operating procedures, training, education, tactical and strategic planning, and corporate identity of the air force were nearly moribund. Discipline had seriously eroded, and standards of competency (e.g. leadership, flying, technical support and administration) were also low.' Consequently, in parallel to the socio-economic reforms, the PLAAF – and PLA itself – prepared for an overhaul. This reform, however, had not only the intention to regain former capabilities and re-establish a functioning force, but also – since seen politically as a potentially dangerous service branch within the PLA hierarchy – to assert much tighter party authority and control over the PLAAF than other service branches. This can be clearly seen in the choice of future PLAAF commanders and deputy commanders concerning their individual political background.

A first step in this direction was the promotion of Ma Ning, a former deputy commander of the Lanzhou MRAF, who became commander of the PLAAF in 1973. Although only a transitional figure – he was in fact more a politically opportune person not related to the former Lin Biao clique than an aviation related skilled military leader – who not really initiated the addressing of the countless serious problems, he at least brought stability during the early 1970s. With the leadership finally in more profound hands, the PLAAF was only able to initiate a deeper reform in 1977. Starting point of this was the appointment of Zhang Tingfa, who had formerly been the PLAAF political commissar since 1975, deputy commander chief of staff and member of the CCP's Politburo, as the new PLAAF commander.

Preceding this change in leadership was already another major change: the PLA reduced the number of the 13 military regions established by 1955–56, to 11 in 1969–70. This was accomplished by the downgrading and incorporation of the Inner Mongolia and Tibet Military Regions into the Beijing and Chengdu Military Regions in 1967 and mostly related to concerns about a steady Soviet buildup along the northern sector and the aim to streamline its own command and administrative structure. In parallel, a broader administrative structure was reinstalled after it was accepted that the 1969 reform – to galvanise the former 11 major departments into only three – was too strict, since abolishing the Engineering Department created problems for maintenance support. As a consequence, and especially in order to improve the maintenance situation of the operational units, the Engineering Department was reactivated as the Aeronautical Engineering Department (hangkong gongchengbu) in May 1976 as the fourth first-level administrative department. With the exception of changing the Aeronautical Engineering Department to the Equipment-Technical Department in November 1992

● **Bases**

1. Changchun, Jilin
2. Andong, Liaoning
3. Dalian, Liaoning
4. Shanghai
5. Weifang, Shandong
6. Yangcun, Hebei
7. Shantou, Guangdong
8. Jinjiang, Fujian
9. Wulumuqi, Xinjiang
10. Datong, Shanxi
11. Hetian, Xinjiang
12. Xingning, Guandong
13. Shijiazhouang, Hebei
14. Kunming
15. Lhasa, Tibet
16. Xinjiang, Tibet
17. Zhangzhou, Fujian

● **Command Posts**

3a. Dalian CP (1985)
4a. Shanghai CP (1985)
5a. Kunming MRAF CP (1978)
6a. Tangshan CP (?)
7a. Shantou CP
8a. Fuzhou MRAF (1958)
8b. Fuzhou CP (1961)
8c. Chengdu MRAF CP (1978)
9a. Xinjiang MRAF CP (1979)
11a. Xi'an CP (1985)
12a. Shantou CP (1962)
12b. Xingning CP (1969)
14a. 5th Air Corps (1976)
Kunming MRAF CP (1978)

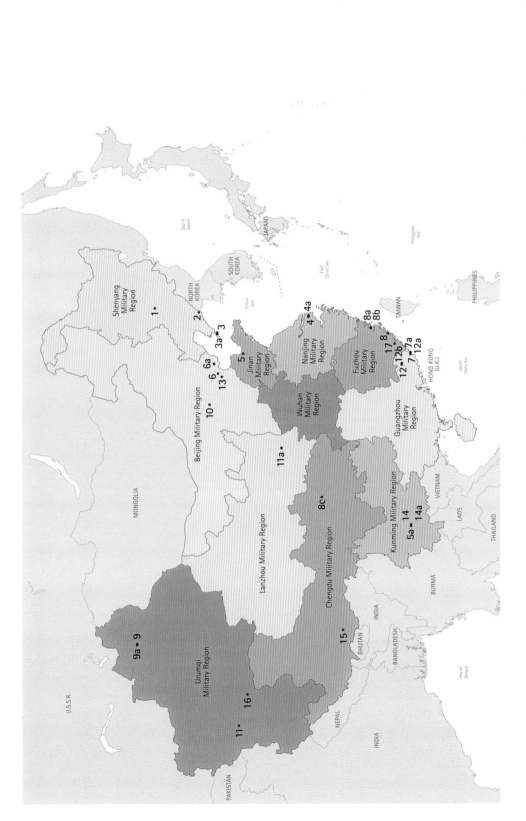

Map showing the organisational structure of the 11 military regions between 1970 and 1985.
(Map by James Lawrence)

and moving some of the second-level departments from within the Headquarters and Logistics Departments to the successor Equipment Department in 1998 to conform to the newly-established General Armament Department (GAD), the administrative organisational structure, has remained fairly stable since 1976 up until the mid-1990s. In 1977, the CMC began implementing a major readjustment of the PLAAF in the areas of leadership, regulations, training, combat readiness, political work, discipline, aircraft maintenance, logistics and headquarters staff work. The first step under Zhang Tingfa's leadership was to reestablish its training and education systems. The second aim was to overall rectify all organisational and operational standards and practices. Several conferences were held to address all issues and operational units were increasingly sent to joint-service exercises. This also – a first for the PLAAF leadership especially after the long self-proclaimed hiatus – included to travel abroad, the participation on international conferences, on goodwill visits, international exhibitions and technology trade shows to gain as much information on modern aerial warfare in order to direct these necessary reform into the right direction. And a positive side-effect was also, that the PLAAF gained a new perception of its own and standing as a military service.

1979: the Sino-Vietnam Border Conflict

Quite surprisingly, right in the middle of these ongoing reforms, the PLAAF became embroiled into a military conflict in 1979. The conflict itself is beyond the scope of this book, especially since the PLAAF was not directly involved in offensive missions. However, especially this lack of operational use, the overall rather unsatisfactory performance of the PLA and the conclusions drawn thereafter are relevant.

In short, the 1979 Sino-Vietnamese War – also known as the Third Indochina War – was only a brief border war fought between China and Vietnam in early 1979 (17 February to 16 March 1979) after China had launched an offensive in response to Vietnam's invasion and occupation of Cambodia in 1978, which de facto ended the rule of the Chinese-backed Khmer Rouge.

As such, this war was a typical proxy war with the aim to deter Vietnam from Cambodia – which in the end China was unable – but also to demonstrate its Cold War communist adversary, the Soviet Union, its limits, since Moscow was unable to protect its Vietnamese ally from Chinese intervention. Another side aspect of this war was constant repeated – and still ongoing – accusations from both sides against each other on spying, occupying potentially resources-rich islands in the South China Sea since 1974.

Quite remarkable, only a few official books ever discussed the PLAAF's role during the 1979 border conflict with Vietnam and if, most often it is stated, that '… based on the CMC's guidance, PLAAF units conducted patrols within China's territory.' This in fact is surprising, since the PLAAF reportedly deployed about 1,000 aircraft to the border area and even more surprising, neither the PLAAF nor the Vietnamese Air Force flew any actual combat missions in direct support of their ground troops. On the PLAAF, the most modern type in use were a few J-7s operated off air bases in Yunnan and Guangxi to deter the limited number of Vietnamese People's Air Force MiG-21bis, however that type was so much in trouble during these days and on the edge of being abandoned.

In addition, the PLAAF's air defence forces did not engage any Vietnamese Air Force aircraft operating along or across the border. In one PLAAF history book it is mentioned, that between '...17 February to 16 March 1979, the PLAAF dispatched 3,131 groups of aircraft and flew 8,500 sorties on the Chinese side of the border.' A bit more in detail, the *China Air Force Encyclopedia* mentioned that 'transport aircraft performed a very crucial logistics support function, flying 228 sorties, carrying 1,465 troops and 151 tons of material. Another source mentioned that there were 948 aircraft deployed from different areas in China and based at 15 air bases altogether in the Guangdong, Guangxi and Yunnan provinces and Hainan Island. The number of sorties also included a large number of helicopter sorties, including those used to transport over 600 wounded soldiers from frontline hospitals to Nanning.' In consequence, it is difficult to assume, why the PLAAF did not actively intervene other by the lack of capability or due to a political decision, not to further escalate the war. Another possible explanation might be that the PLA was long undecided upon an approved history of the event and in the end felt more comfortable to ignore or downplay it. For example, in the former PLAAF Commander Wang Hai's autobiography – he succeeded Zhang Tingfa in 1985 – not a single reference to the conflict is mentioned, even though he was the Guangzhou MRAF commander at the time.

The best-known facts are that the relevant Guangzhou MRAF Headquarters established a dedicated forward command post (qianzhi) in order to cooperate with the 7th Air Corps at Nanning. This should have acted as the unified authority for any PLAAF's participation, which was identified as to prepare the airfields in Guangxi for the transfer of more than 20,000 PLAAF aviation, SAM, and AAA troops. On the opposing side and according to PLA reports, 'the Vietnamese Air Force did not dare start anything during the border conflict, which the Chinese limited to a certain area, time frame, and goals, because the PLAAF was able to maintain air superiority.' In consequence, the PLAAF's missions were restricted to regular supply and transport, reconnaissance and early warning missions along the border, rescue missions – most often by helicopters – to pick up wounded soldiers, and air transport missions. As noted, the PLAAF did not use any ground attack aircraft or even bombers.

At first sight, the numbers of sorties and aircraft probably sound impressive and the calm reaction of the PLAAF can be rated a diplomatic wise decision, but in detail it was most likely another reason: the PLAAF simply lacked any decent offensive capabilities and knew that quite well. Even more – Kenneth Alan again analysed that the mission rate per aircraft given even a lower estimation of roughly 700 aircraft in the close border area, equals to only about 12 sorties per aircraft over the period of this two-month conflict. In the end that is about one mission every five days and represents in no way an improvement over the already low mission rate in the 1958 Taiwan conflict. In conclusion, this conflict and the rather poor performances resulted in a wake-up call for the PLAAF that was even more a reason to justify a profound modernisation and reform process.

The brief Sino-US honeymoon

Similar to Sino-Russian relations, the diplomatic connections to the US have and had a very turbulent history and often enough, were not friendly leading into the current situ-

ation of a strong, complex and extremely extensive economic partnership based on the great amount of trade between the two countries, spiced by yet significant issues especially their hegemonic rivalry in the Pacific. In contrast to an overall more conflicting relationship – especially related to the Taiwan issue – the end of the 1960s brought a period of transformation one major reason for this was the US decision no longer expand its sphere of influence in Asia while at the same time the Soviet Union was rated a more serious threat. The brief but still unforgotten Sino-Soviet border conflict in 1969 clearly demonstrated this. Also for long, the PRC was diplomatically isolated – mostly a self-proclaimed fate – but the Chinese government became slowly aware, that improved relations with the United States could be a useful counterbalance to the Soviet Union. These aspirations were indeed initiated via the Premier of China, Zhou Enlai and even officially backed by Chairman Mao Zedong, however this rapprochement was stalled at first by the Vietnam War. A good luck moment tremendously helping to ease the situation was the unexpectedly friendly encounter between the US and Chinese table-tennis players Glenn Cowan and Zhuang Zedong in Japan, which opened the so-called 'ping-pong diplomacy'. The first – then still top-secret – meeting occurred in July 1971, when Henry Kissinger met Zhou Enlai in Beijing.

This announcement was noticed with varying emotions, ranging from condemnation and opposition by hard-line anti-communists in the US and by left-wing elements in China – allegedly led by Lin Biao – to a pleased notice in the West but as expected Soviets concerns about a possible alliance of its two major enemies, which were trying to resolve their differences. Especially important for the PRC was, that – even if the US did not officially immediately recognised the People's Republic of China as the sole China – the US acknowledged the 'One China' position and that Taiwan is part of China, leaving at least the Taiwan issue open for the moment. What followed was the opening of the United States Liaison Office (USLO) in Beijing and a counterpart PRC office in Washington and several high-ranking visits, which all reaffirmed American interest in normalising relations with Beijing. Normal diplomatic relations between the People's Republic of China and the United States were establish on 1 January 1979. To go deeper into the political issues is well beyond the scope of this book, but the military connections are relevant[1]: especially both the threats of the Soviet invasion of Afghanistan and the Vietnamese invasion of Cambodia were two major reasons to align an even closer Sino-US military cooperation. These too were initiated in 1979 and first initial steps to establish at least some sort of dialogue between both military establishments occurred in 1980 with the visit of Secretary of Defence Harold Brown to Beijing in January 1980. Interestingly, already between 1978 and 1980 several studies were made to determine how the US could assist the PLA in order to make the PLA an effective deter against the Soviet Red Army. One year later in 1981, the willingness to directly sell arms to the PRC was first announced by Secretary of State Alexander Haig in June 1981, which successively lead to the first US Foreign Military Sales (FMS) contract to the PRC signed in June 1984. A negotiated framework not only lead to a high-level strategic dialogue between senior US and Chinese military leaders but also to military exchanges and a healthy and most influencing brief period of arms sales and technology transfer agreements. These contracts included modern antitank weaponry, artillery, air defence, and surface-ship antisubmarine warfare (Mark 46, Mod 2 lightweight ASW torpedo), but also the delivery of 24 S-70C Black Hawk helicopters, modern LM2500 gas turbine naval engines, coastal defence radars, and

The J-10 is often described as a 'Lavi clone'. Although it shares the same basic configuration, the Chinese fighter is a substantially larger, heavier and very different. However, there have been close connection between IAI and CAC and this image shows the J-10's 'father' Song Wencong in front of the Lavi prototype.
(via CDF)

communications equipment. Even further, it was agreed, to modernise the Shenyang J-8II fighter, to co-develop a modernisation project for the J-7 fleet under the Sabre-7 and Super-7 project and even on considerations to deliver or co-develop new military aircraft. These commercial contracts with the US lead to comparable contracts with other Western nations like France (helicopters), Israel (avionics, radar systems, missiles), Italy (missiles, radar systems) and the United Kingdom (engines, radar systems, avionics). Also well known in this regard are attempts to licence manufacture Western types like negotiations on the BAe Harrier, the delivery of British Spey Mk 202 engine or considerations to buy the Dassault Mirage 2000. Lesser known, however, are attempts to purchase the Swiss FFA P-16, the Swedish J 35 Draken and negotiations surrounding a huge Sino-French military cooperation project.

Interestingly, this close cooperation was – and even more interesting now is – not always seen as unquestioned positively. There were particular strong reservations on selling US high-end technology to a just newly gained ally – in case the political climate might change sooner than expected – due to continuing distrust of communism in general, the Chinese rather lax acceptance of intellectual properties or the fear, China might sell arms to countries that were openly hostile to American interests like Iran and North Korea. In addition, on the Chinese side – and here broadly comparable to the unrealistic high hopes in an all-around and unquestionable delivery of systems by the Soviet Union in the early days – not all demands for advanced technology from the US were met. For example, there are repeated reports about attempts to purchase the F-16 or other advanced systems like the AH-1 Cobra combat helicopter, modern tanks and so on. In addition – especially in retrospect – many in the US do not like to be reminded, that they were themselves responsible for a certain part of China's technological rise, the ability to redesign and improve certain US systems for their own needs and even for export. The latest Z-20 is a prime example. As feared by some, the Sino-US honeymoon only lasted for a brief period, since even if high-level exchanges continued to be a significant means for developing the US-PRC relations, that included also a growing number of social, cultural and educational exchanges, the Tiananmen Square protests of 1989 abruptly ended this all. The following arms embargo not only disrupted the Sino-US military cooperation but was also a severe blow in the bilateral trade relationship. Since then, US administrations increasingly denounced the repression of civil rights in China and suspended certain trade and investment programmes. And in mind of the latest changes – the US shift to the Asia-Pacific area, President Donald Trump's 'America first' policy and the overall rising rivalry on economic and political influence and most of all military capabilities, both countries are connected via a unique rivalry characterised by mutual suspicion over the other's intentions and a wary attitude regarding the other one as a potential adversary.

...and the Sino-Soviet relationship following the rift in 1960[2]

In contrast to the Sino-US relationship, which was most of the time more characterised by certain issues and difficulties, the Sino-Soviet one was quite complementary: whereas the former was only good for a brief period, the latter had only one phase

A chapter that many in the US would like to forget was that country's close cooperation with and influence on the Chinese aviation industry in the 1980s. For example, this is the single J-8II prototype, modified by Grumman. After being stripped of its avionics it is now on display at the China Aviation Museum.
(via Top81.cn)

of severe mistune. As noted, this relationship began to receive some cracks during the Cultural Revolution, when China's growing radicalism and xenophobia had severe repercussions for Sino-Soviet relationship. This resulted even in an event in 1967, when Chinese Revolution Red Guards besieged the Soviet embassy in Beijing and harassed Soviet diplomats. Beijing during this time was no longer in the mood to be the junior partner and began to interpret the Soviet dominance – also against other Eastern bloc states – as 'social imperialism.' After the break with the Soviet Union and the leaving of all advisers, military experts and the cancellation of nearly all major military cooperation projects in 1960, the Sino-Soviet dispute reached its highpoint in 1969 when a short but serious border conflict erupted into armed clashes at Zhenbao (or Damanskiy) Island on the northeast border. For good luck, both sides refrained from expanding this dispute, however the relationship became never the same since then. At least both sides found ways to relax the tension and during September 1969 Soviet Prime Minister Alexei Kosygin visited Beijing to begin border negotiations with his Chinese counterpart Zhou Enlai. This threat of war brought many political developments and at one stage confirmed Defence Minister Lin Biao as Mao's successor.

With the 1970s, policy in Beijing shifted to a slightly more moderate course and ended the most radical phase of the Cultural Revolution, which resulted in a rapprochement with the US in order to build a counterweight to the perceived threat from Moscow. Especially this threat was probably more a perceived than a real one, even if the Soviet Union's increased its military build-up in East Asia in the late 1970s, was without doubt some sort of encirclement, which could only heightened China's awareness; between 1969 and 1973, the Soviet garrisons were almost doubled in size and the invasion of Afghanistan in 1979 not really helped to ease this perception. So on the one side, it prevented a direct armed confrontation with the USSR, but did not really improve their diplomatic relations since even if the ideological rivalry between the USSR and the PRC diminished, it increased on geopolitics. The Sino-Vietnamese War from 1979 was another example for these increased tensions. After Deng Xiaoping has consolidated its power in the 1980s, China's approach toward the Soviet Union shifted once more. Beijing slowly adopted an independent foreign policy and gradually opened up its economic policy. On the other side, the quite quick successive changes Soviet leadership from Leonid Brezhnev, Yuriy Andropov and Konstantin Chernenko between 1982 and 1985, provided the change for a renewed diplomacy. In consequence, the Sino-Soviet relations steadily improved in trade, economic and technical exchanges – including certain projects initiated in the 1950s – and the intermediate climax was General Secretary Mikhail Gorbachev's July speech in 1986 at Vladivostok, which a bit later resulted in bilateral consultations on open issues including the reduction of Soviet Army concentrations at the Chinese border and in Mongolia, the resumption of trade and negotiations on the border issue. In addition, the PRC's government was doubtful about Gorbachev's reform programmes of perestroika and glasnost. Interestingly, the sale of US weapons to the PLA during Ronald Reagan's presidency was again a minor setback.

In the end, history went on very much differently: the Tiananmen riots ended the brief Sino-US honeymoon; Gorbachev's reforms ultimately ended the competitive communist government in the Soviet Union and resulted in the dissolution of the same in 1991. The resulting missing socio-economic reforms in Russia led to the current situation, whereas in China the economic reforms – a unique combination of a strictly

market-ruled economy but always under tight political control by the Chinese Communist Party – led to China's rise. Consequently, Russia was quick to step in again as China's most important ally and it major weapons provider.

Consequently it is relevant – especially in retrospect – to take a brief but deeper look onto the Sino-Soviet or now Chinese/Russian military cooperation: the surely most important point to note is, that China's aviation industry and its military, would not be where it is today without this cooperation and assistance. This relationship was not always an easy one, sometimes mixed with unwillingness to simply gift and share its most modern technologies but often explained with more important political reasons, the Soviet Union and thereafter Russia – as one famous blogger correctly summarised – 'has assisted China's military industry more than any other nation. In fact, I would say that this military relationship has yielded more benefit for China than any other military relationship has yielded for any nation.' Even if this most of the time very much uneven partnership has dramatically changed since China's economic rise and some might even already question, what interest can China still have in Russia's military technology today, there are several certain fields like metallurgy and engine technology, where China is behind or can still benefit from a cooperation. The fact, that this was different for most of this relationship, even a very much different one is still an issue, that is sometimes neglected: it honestly must be reminded, that in the very early phase, Chinese were more than thankful to follow the guidance of their 'bigger brother' eager to learn everything, since its own industry was very backward after being ravaged by a century of war.

Only in the 1950s, some sort of industrial revolution was initiated especially thanks to the USD300 million loan provided by the Soviet Union in order to establish some sort of modern industries in China. Again, as noted by Feng, there is probably not 'another example in the history where one country provided that much assistance in the industrialisation of another country'. This assistance not only included assistance and guidance, but also the 'delivery of complete blueprints, materials, production equipment and manuals on many of its latest aircraft and their subsystems like engines and missiles.' The strange consequence of this partnership was the misbelief of the PRC's leadership not only that China has a right to receive this all for nearly nothing – since it served the cause of international communism – but also, that it was so much easy to develop modern combat aircraft.

This – especially in the chaotic time of revolutional fever during the Great Leap Forward and the Cultural Revolution – lead to the ignorance, shown by political and military leaders of any facts: no-one was willing to realise the amount of time and resources required to establish an industry, to develop an aircraft. To accept that the phase of testing naturally lasts years of failed efforts and costs a tremendous amount of resources and resulted in the void of left after the Soviet advisers left after the split in 1962. In fact, the Chinese aviation industry was unable to independently develop, manufacture and produce aircraft for many years to come.

The ironic effect of this was that this phase became one of the most enigmatic periods, while the Chinese industry tried to deal with unrealistic expectations from PRC leaders. The resulting 'paper planes' like the Dong Feng series, the J-9, original J-10 to J-13 and several bomber projects were highly innovative in concept and appearance, but all unrealistic. Only in the late 1970s and 1980s – after Deng Xiaoping's reforms gained some success – the Chinese industry was able to recover and gain some improvements especially again via cooperation projects with the West. However, even if there were some promising proposals included in the Peace Pearl project, there were still no successful indigenous designs and right after military embargo was imposed in 1989, the future again looked bleak for Chinese military aviation and PLAAF.

New Russian assistance since the 1990s

Even if at first in the 1990s the then-Soviet and later Russian participation was quite limited, there were several attempts to get into business already before the final Su-27 contract. The main reason was that the so far most capable fighter was the J-8C/D, which still lacked any BVR capability after the Peace Pearl project was cancelled. Additionally, the next generation multirole fighter, the later J-10 project was in its infancy – and in fact just on the edge of being cancelled – due to ongoing technical issues and most of all the lack of an engine. Nevertheless, before Russia got its chance, there was still little hope in 1985-86 since the Sino-US-relationship was still fine. A first relaxation was, when in 1983, the Soviet Union re-approved the export of Mikoyan and Ilyushin aircraft to China, which eased maintenance issues and this was expanded by 1986 to a point, where even the sale of MiG-23MLD and MiG-29 was discussed. Slightly later, this offer was expanded to include not only the delivery, but also licence production of the MiG-29 and its RD-33s turbofan engine in China was on the table. In the end, this deal did not come to fruition, above all since the Peace Pearl project was still ongoing, but at least – and most likely by pure coincidence – this failed deal at least saved the fate of the J-10.

One reason for this were some dramatic changes in perception, future strategic planning and industrial goals: first of all in 1989, the abrupt cancellation of the Peace Pearl cooperation – now a severe blow to any future PLAAF modernisation plans – did allow Chinese aerospace technicians and the PLAAF to interact with Americans and gave a much deeper experience in which way the West interpreted modern air warfare and high-end aerospace development. The success of this Western way of aerial warfare perception was clearly demonstrated by the 1991 Gulf War to liberate Kuwait and this was in fact a most rude wake-up call to anyone in the PLAAF leadership, since it demonstrated, how far China and its armed forces were behind world-leading air powers. The PLAAF had to accept, that any plans for its own strategic goals – to defend mainland China from any aggressor or even the liberation of Taiwan, was simply an impossible dream. Consequently, any direct purchase of any new aircraft was beyond question; the main goal was to acquire and understand the latest technologies in order to become self-reliant. In addition, the MiG-29 was no longer an option, since it was too small, too weak against the Western high-end types, so that the only option the PLAAF would agree was the Su-27.

It seems as if this was at first refused by the Soviet Union – or at least seen with scepticism – however with declining domestic orders at Sukhoi as well as other companies within the Russian military industrial complex were in spiral wind-down to a total collapse in orders. As such, Sukhoi was most eager to receive export orders from China. In parallel the dissolution of the Soviet Union already full under way put the entire Sino-Russian cooperation in jeopardy, since there were certain groups within

the Russian government led by Boris Yeltsin, who were enjoying a honeymoon with the West. Several reformists like Pyotr Aven, Yegor Gaidar, Andrey Kozyrev and Alexander Shokhin were eagerly discussing to follow a Western model of economics and were reluctant to align again with China. There were even reports; Russia would offer Su-27s to Taiwan so that the PLAAF was in real danger of not receiving any 'Flanker'. As Feng noted, 'Here is where Chinese diplomats really went to work to try to get its relationship with Russia back on order' and 'given the history between the two countries, USSR's decision to allow the export of Su-27 to China (first non-CIS country to receive this type) is quite astonishing.' In the end, the collapsing Russian economy, resulting in runaway inflation and economic hardship, not receiving help from the West – at least not enough loans from the International Monetary Fund (IMF) and World Bank – as expected, resulted in the rise of more conservative members like Yevgeny Primakov, which pushed for more engagements with China. In the end, Sukhoi's political influence too helped a lot not only to enable a direct purchase of the Su-27, but also several succeeding contracts on licence manufacturing as well as a closer military cooperation between both countries in several other fields too.

It is probably ironic, that again a time of very close cooperation begun, where China was able to gain as much as possible, even if now the circumstances were very much different: in the very beginnings based on the political will to spread communism and now simply based for industrial survival. For China, this situation was therefore a 'once in a lifetime opportunity to purchase technology and recruit scientists/engineers from Russia/Ukraine', so that within the following years the Russians were offering several deals for licence production including the wide transfer of technology. But it was not only the direct selling of technology and know-how, but also Russia's permission to send Chinese aerospace engineers to Sukhoi, Mikoyan and other design and construction bureaus and the famous TsAGI.

Additionally, it opened the option for Russian companies to take over abandoned former Peace Pearl projects, like the assistance on the F-8IIM project – which evolved into the J-8H and F models – and China's participation in the co-development of Zhuk-8II radar with NIIR including to be involved in the development, testing and certification stage. Undeniably, the probably biggest beneficent was the J-10, which finally received an adequate engine. This engine is sure a special issue, since China did not receive transfer of technology and licence production of the Saturn AL-31 turbofan, however it was able to purchase special tailor-made variants for the J-10 – and probably also the J-20 – and received high level of technology transfer, documentation, tooling and machinery for maintenance and repairs of this engine, so that China was able to establish the worldwide largest AL-31F MRO facility outside Russia. Today allegedly, all maintenance and repairs on any AL-31F and AL-31FN turbofan can be done in China.

This understanding of the engine and its technology proceeded even that far that China was able to extend the life of an AL-31 from 900 to 1,500 hours and there are even reports, the current J-10C and J-20A models are using yet another up-rated, special version, which was co-developed and is even manufactured in China. Altogether, the refinement of the Super-7 turbofan into the current CAC/PAC JF-17 again related to its Russian RD-93 engine are other examples and similar as the Peace Pearl project opened the option to include other Western companies in this case China was able to

leverage Belarus and Ukraine defence companies to receive insight in radar, avionics, missile and powerplant technology. This is probably the biggest difference to the brief cooperation with the West, where China to much frustration learned that Western companies guarded their secrets much more closely, so that Chinese companies rarely get any true transfer of high-end technology from the West.

On the other side – and often enough complained in the media due to the break of intellectual properties – the Russians probably underestimated the Chinese capabilities – or even overrated their own skills – since many believed that Russia would be able to stay ahead of China in aerospace, that this time of recession would be only a brief one so that there was only little need to worry about such cooperation. Most likely, in this phase the Russian side saw solely the benefits of having a more balanced foreign policy and economic gain from deals with China.

Moreover, even more in contrast to the success of China's economic reforms and its resulting rising economic, political and military might, the Russian reforms nearly completely failed to fruition, so that in the last nearly 30 years since the collapse of the Soviet Union, the PLAAF and the Chinese aviation industry have both transformed dramatically, so that at least several Russian military companies survived due to Chinese orders and were allowed to survive. In summary, it is amazing – and probably only few people predicted this – how fast the Chinese industry was able to modernise itself, to absorb technology it has gained in this brief period between 1985 and the early 2000s from several sources and to create its own versions, so that China's military aviation industry would surely not be where it is today without the high level of technology transfer between China and Russia. Especially since Western countries were never willing to provide the same level of assistance a Russia did.

A modern air force is created

Before a true modern air force was transformed from the numerical superior but capability wise rather shacked remains of the Cultural Revolution, the PLAAF needed to face their final combat engagements. According to official PLAAF data, the last time a PLAAF aircraft shot down a manned aircraft was in April 1967, when a US Navy F-4 was downed near Guangxi province in southern China and about one month later, when a PLAAF AAA unit stationed inside China shot down an aircraft in May 1967; allegedly this was a US Navy A-4 again near Guangxi province. The overall last time action, during which a PLAAF SAM unit shot down an aircraft, was on 5 October 1987, when a Vietnamese MiG-21 crossed the border of Guangxi province.

Consequently, even today, one major concern often mention is that it has been a long time since the PLAAF has engaged any true aerial combat, and very few – in fact today none – of its senior leaders possessed combat experience. How far reaching this lack of combat experience and how dated the old strategy was, became clear in 1981, when the PLAAF begun to organise several large-scale exercises. Interestingly, even though the PLAAF participated in several smaller-scale exercises, there were only two large-scale ones mentioned: the initial one in November 1955 was an anti-landing exercise on the Liaoning Peninsula; the second major example was in September 1981 in Zhangjiakou within the Beijing MR. The aim of these manoeuvres was to test PLA

changes in the structure related to its readiness in a potential border conflict but also to demonstrate some show of force against the Soviet Union and altogether 12 air divisions and three independent regiments with 476 aircraft operating from ten airfields, one airborne division were in action. Overall, about 30,000 troops were involved. Typically for official reports, it is then listed, that 20,600 sorties were flown for an amount of 15,810 hours, it is further reported, that each pilot flew in average about 32 hours and 55 minutes – which is remarkable in comparison to a then average flight hour of 8 hours per month – how many engines were replaced (371, meaning in average 49.9 hours before a change was necessary), how many aircraft were repaired and so on. In retrospect, the PLAAF begun immediately after the exercise to evaluate the results and to draw conclusions concerning a revised strategy, doctrine and training but also in mind of its organisational structure.

One first reform therefore was initiated in the mid-1980s, which included several organisational changes in order to improve the PLAAF's operational capabilities. As noted, the PLAAF had reached its peak number of divisions already by the third quarter of 1970 but only for the time of renewal international opening under Deng Xiaoping a bit more of information on the PLA's reorganisation up to the late 1980s became available. For example, it only became known, that nearly all but five of the original air corps were either disbanded or downgraded to command posts. The reform was done in order to eliminate unnecessary administrative functions and to form the command posts as operational – and not administrative – organisations. In a similar step, from 1993 on all remaining command posts – with the exception of Lhasa – were further reorganised as bases. Quite noteworthy from a geographical point of view, the PLAAF finally had units permanently assigned throughout China.

Also, the reduced number of 11, was further reduced to only seven by 1985–88. In essence, of the former 11 military regions – Shenyang, Beijing, Jinan, Nanjing, Guangzhou (including Hainan Island), Kunming, Wuhan, Chengdu, Lanzhou, Xinjiang, and Fuzhou – only the Shenyang, Beijing, Jinan, Nanjing (which includes the former Fuzhou MR), Guangzhou, Chengdu (incorporating the former Kunming MR) and Lanzhou (incorporating the former Ürümqi MR) Military Regions remained. Interestingly, while in most cases (as mentioned) smaller former MRs were simply merged into other larger entities, the Guangzhou and Jinan Military Regions both appear to include parts of the former Wuhan MR.

Another major reform of the MRs was, that these territorial entities were no longer organised in a common way, but now according to their missions. Anyway, the general structure of each MRAF was subordinated down the chain by air divisions, SAM brigades or regiments and AAA regiments, which were complemented by radar, communications and support units and subunits. So in essence, long structured along PLA lines, the aviation branch was and still is organised into operational areas, also known as air force districts (AFDs). Since 1985, each of the AFDs has mirrored the so-called MRs of the PLA, which are generally based according to the political and administrative organisation of the various provinces of the PRC, and therefore vary in size depending on the geographic area and its strategic importance. Each of the seven AFDs exercises direct control over its respective military region air force (MRAF). The MRAFs of the PLAAF were under the dual control of the air force and the relevant military region of the PLA.

However quite important to note is that even if the order of units structured by the MR in several publications often follows not a strict order (sometimes by number of the division, sometimes in alphabetic order), the order of the MRs plays an important role in the PLA's organisational structure and their own publications. This official protocol order simply follows the dates they were established and as such even the army (PLA), the air force (PLAAF) and navy (PLN) are always listed in the same order (lu hai kong).[3] Again following this order the seven MRAFs are always listed in the general order of:[4]

MR PLAAF official protocol order	Military Region AF	MR PLA official protocol order
1. Shenyang	1. Shenyang MRAF	1. Shenyang
2. Beijing	2. Beijing MRAF	2. Beijing
3. Lanzhou	3. Lanzhou MRAF	3. Lanzhou
4. Nanjing	4. Nanjing MRAF	4. Jinan
5. Guangzhou	5. Guangzhou MRAF	5. Nanjing
6. Jinan	6. Jinan MRAF	6. Guangzhou
7. Chengdu	7. Chengdu MRAF	7. Chengdu

Overall another – some would deem it a quite dramatic – decision was to gradually reduce the number of divisions, which still remained on that high level of 50 divisions to only 29 divisions until the end of the 1980s. This measure was clearly a huge reduction in numbers. However, in mind of how many of them were only ill-equipped with hopelessly outdated types, often poorly maintained and no longer adequate for modern aerial combat, it was also a necessary decision, rather than a reduction in power. On the other hand, the units, which remained, received not only new types of aircraft in due years, but more importantly aircraft able to meet the refined mission requirements. This was especially important due to a change in operational doctrine toward the goal of performing simultaneously defensive and offensive operations. Another rarely noticed fact besides all these changes, which were most often seen purely related to operational or structural consolidations was, that due to China's dramatic economic and urban development, several bases were abandoned. This was either necessary to provide space for further urban development or in line with the operational need to modernise the base. So in essence, the necessary force reduction was coupled with a modernisation of the operating aircraft and their bases to better meet operational requirements and to cope with new strategic considerations[5].

A modern air force in transformation

Throughout the late 1970s and early 1980s, the PLAAF slowly began to implement readjustments with regard to leadership, training, combat readiness and other aspects of peacetime operations. However, no significant improvement had occurred before 1985, when Wang Hai was appointed C-in-C PLAAF. Wang Hai succeeded Zhang Tingfa as Commander of the PLAAF in 1985 and with this promotion, for the first time an aviator became C-in-C. Wang Hai is one of the famous heroes within the PLAAF. He entered

Command Posts
1. Changchun CP (Shenyang MRAF)
2. Dalian CP (Shenyang MRAF)
3. Shanghai CP (Nanjing MRAF)
4. Tangshan CP (Beijing MRAF)
5. Nanning CP (Guangzhou MRAF)
6. Fuzhou CP (Nanjing MRAF)
7. Wulumuqi CP (Lanzhou MRAF)
8. Datong CP (Beijing MRAF)
9. Xi'an CP (Lanzhou MRAF)
10. Kunming CP (Chengdu MRAF)
11. Lhasa CP (Chengdu MRAF)
12. Hetian CP (Lanzhou MRAF)
13. Zhangzhou CP (Nanjing MRAF)

▶ Map showing the organisational structure of the seven military regions, which existed from 1985 until 2016 when they began to be replaced by the current theater commands.
(Map by James Lawrence)

the PLAAF in June 1946 and started his career at the Mudanjiang Aviator School, the PLAAF's first aviator training school to graduate in May 1950 to become a fighter pilot. Between 1950 and 1953 during the Korean War, he was a fighter pilot assigned to the 3rd Fighter Division, where he gained ace status by downing or damaging nine US aircraft. The MiG-15 is still an exhibit in the Military Museum of the Chinese People's Revolution in Beijing. After the Korea War, he became commander of an air force division, later Commander of the Guangzhou Military Region Air Force and finally in 1985 Commander of the People's Liberation Army Air Force. Until his retirement in 1992, he profoundly set the foundations of the modern PLAAF.

Hai initially concentrated on improving the training and education of his personnel, and then – during the brief Sino-Western honeymoon – on acquiring new aircraft and equipment based on advanced Western technologies. Meanwhile, operational-level doctrine began shifting primarily from being able to provide an adequate air defence capability for major cities and industrial areas, towards the goal of being prepared for simultaneous offensive and defensive operations. This also affected flight training, which urgently needed adjustments. Therefore, the PLAAF issued between 1986 and 1988 to convert at least one air division within each MRAF to a specialised MR training base. These division-level transition training bases replaced de facto the former third training regiment within each or at least most air divisions and their aircraft and missions were transferred to these MR training bases. This disbandment resulted at first in yet another reduction of operational units – especially the number of regiments, because since then only a few air divisions retained three operational regiments – but most of all in order to streamline the training procedure and overall the level of flight-readiness within the MR. At these units, the new graduates from the PLAAF's flight colleges receive one year of intensive transition training before being assigned to an operational unit. While in parallel during the late 1980s until 1989, various levels of cooperation with the US and several Western countries in Europe and Israel were established, the PLAAF was able to boosting its capabilities through the introduction to service of correspondingly modified, locally manufactured aircraft types which incorporated certain Western subsystems. However, most of the related projects came to a sudden end in 1989, when such ties were cancelled due to the unrest in Beijing and the massacre of demonstrators at Tiananmen Square.

Around the same time, the Chinese began also to study the changing nature of modern air warfare in small wars. Ultimately, the US-led operations during the war with Iraq in 1991 shocked the PLA into the realisation that it had to become capable of engaging in high-tech warfare or otherwise face the certainty of falling ever further behind other modern militaries. The results of this shock had a galvanising effect on Chinese military leaders. As early as 1993, the leadership of the CCP and the PLA issued *The Military Strategic Guidelines for the New Period* – equivalent to a new national military strategy. The objective of this was rapid modernisation in order to enable the PLA to fight and win wars based on high-tech weapons, joint operational concepts and high-tempo operations. This also included the reorganisation all of its command posts as bases to meet reduction-in-force requirements and to streamline the operational control of aircraft in critical areas.

Training reform – a reform on its own

Besides a general reorganisation and revision – including the one for the training syllabuses, which however most importantly changed only in 2011 – aimed to dramatically improve the PLAAF's operational readiness, was the increase of realistic combat drills and expanding exercises. For some time one major drawback of the PLAAF's doctrine was its inability to accomplish large-scale exercises within a generally inappropriate and unrealistic operational training. The main reason for this was the lack of an integrated training between different branches like the PLAAF and Naval Aviation and the limited number of aircraft a command post could guide. This did not even change after the overwhelming display of power and its success in the 1991 Gulf War so that certain members within the PLA top brass still did not understand the value of modern aerial combat. This persisted even with the introduction of the Su-27SKs, which were most often operated the same way as J-7s and J-8s, namely, armed with rockets and dumb bombs to destroy ground targets and strictly flown by the manual. Gradually, this thinking of just serving support ground units changed to formulate the aim of becoming a force on its own which was capable of running large-scale offensive operation. This was coupled with the acceptance that the key to any future success lies not only in a dramatic increase of new equipment, but most of all in fundamental changes in training and combat tactics.

A first step in this direction was the establishment of the so-called Flight Test and Training Centre (FTTC) on 1 April 1987, when the former 11th Aviation School at Yanliang was re-formed into the FTTC/2nd Regiment and transferred to Cangzhou/Cangxian. This unit is now called Flight Test and Training Base (FTTB) with subordinated brigades.

A second important step was the foundation of a specialised test centre for weapons integration, testing and tactical training at Dingxin in June 1999 as a dedicated detachment assigned to the Chinese Flight Test Establishment (CFTE), which has its regular flight test centre in Xi'an-Yanliang. The FTTC – or now FTTB – therefore has three primary missions: first, to test new aircraft under development in close cooperation with the manufacture; second, to train the initial cadre of pilots for these new aircraft before the aircraft are deployed to an operational unit for the first time; and third, to devise new air combat tactics especially related to this new type or in general[7].

Therefore, immediately after its establishment at Cangzhou, the FTTC formed three regiments initially flying J-7s and later J-8Bs and Su-30MKKs, dedicated to tacti-

A major effort to improve the operational training of pilots was the establishment of the FTTC at Cangzhou and the formation of dedicated Blue Force regiments flying J-7E (left) and J-8B (right) fighters. These regiments briefly also wore the FTTC badge. (Both via Top81.cn)

cal training for most of the early 1990s – rather than exploring flying techniques or playing an aggressor force – due to its lack of experience in modern tactics. From 1988 onwards, the FTTC received Project Grindstone to simulate a Blue Force aggressor and for most of this period, the regiments were simulating Soviet forces, changing slowly to later simulate ROCAF/USAF. With the political changes, also a cooperation agreement with the Russian base at Lipetsk was signed in order to train the best pilots and controllers at Lipetsk's Red Flag Composite Training and Research Unit. Another base also complementing the FTTC is located at Jiugusheng and currently operates a J-10 regiment. Concerning the workshare and responsibility, theoretical tactics are usually developed by the PLAAF Command College in Beijing, which are then explored and refined in practice at Cangzhou. In parallel, the development of combat methods begins at an operational unit and ends with testing and approval at Dingxin. In both cases, once these tactical regulations and combat methods are developed and approved, the PLAAF writes the corresponding manuals which all pilots have to study at their operational unit. Commonly, such a process takes at least one year but may last for several years.

The second important base is Dingxin: this base and unit originally reaches back to 1958, when the PLAAF authorised construction of the so-called Northwest Comprehensive Missile Test Base (NCMTB) at Shuangchengzi, close to Dingxin. This base was a large centre built to test AAMs and SAMs in the Gobi Desert. Somewhere in the 1970s, those units relevant for aircraft and aerial weapons tests moved from Shuangchengzi to Dingxin[8]. In the years that followed, the now separated new range – especially for AAM and SAM testing – was updated with advanced tracking and control equipment and somewhere around the late 1980s to early 1990s; the base was upgraded to accommodate a tactical training centre associated with the FTTC at Cangzhou, which was established in 1987. This centre was to be large enough to house multiple units. Since its establishment in 1999, the Dingxin base has been expanded to almost double its original size and now allows training for an entire aviation corps. While being able to handle roughly up to 20 aircraft in its early days, the numbers of aircraft performing the annual exercises and the complexity of simulated war scenarios have increased from year to year. Today the latest Red Sword exercises involve up to more than one hundred aircraft of different types including fighters and striker and special mission types sometimes up to Theater Command level.

Consequently, at the Dingxin Test and Training Base the tactics and flight techniques developed at Cangzhou were explored and verified and one outcome of the early evaluations dramatically showed not only which part of the PLAAF's tactics and training manuals were outdated and needed to be changed, but also the disparity in the training levels and intensities of different forces around the country, clearly showing which units are better trained than others. This resulted in 2005 in the merger of the three former different test facilities into the current PLAAF test and training base. Currently, the base features China's first integrated EW training range in Dingxin which is equipped with a fibre-optic network and comprehensive computerised monitoring equipment including OE and telemetry) to provide real-time information for one of the PLA's digitised command and control centres. Additionally, this base became China's first base to enable realistic training under intensive EM environment, it has tactical air-to-air and air-to-ground ranges, surface-to-air missile (SAM) and anti-aircraft artillery (AAA) positions, radars, simulated enemy command posts (even including

a mock-up of a Taiwanese Air Force Base), ammunition and fuel depots. All this has enabled the CFTE and FTTC to run integrated exercises since 2005, the Red Sword and Blue Sword which are comparable to the USAF's Red Flag exercises.

While the Red Sword exercises focus on interdiction, CAS, SEAD and OCA (offensive counter air) operations, the Blue Sword exercises are mainly related to aerial combat. Both are aimed at preparing PLAAF pilots for the possibility of future high-technology combat against tactically and technically more advanced adversaries. In addition, in 2011 the PLAAF established the so-called Golden Helmet air-to-air competition – comparable perhaps to the former William Tell contest – with the aim of improving and assessing individual pilots' skills and capabilities especially by demanding less scripted free aerial combat manoeuvring. Winning pilots were rated as elite pilots and their units were allowed to proudly wear special markings on their aircraft similar to those taking part in the Russian Aviadarts 2014 competition for the first time. The pilots of the national aerobatics team Ba Yi and 25 additional 'outstanding aviators', were honoured for demonstrating 'unrestricted or free air combat' capabilities and publicity praised to boost their morale.

Another effort in this direction is the PLAAF's aim to actively learn from other air forces, especially in recent years again from those in the West, by increasing its training with other forces. This includes as a first, the joint Sino-Russian, on which also other former CIS states take part, exercises like Peace Mission (since 2005), and Aviadarts (since 2014), and continuing through several joint Sino-Pakistani exercises called Shaheen (eagle, since 2011) up to exercises with Thailand (since 2015) and Turkey (since 2010). According to several unconfirmed rumours, although the PLAAF performed 'pretty unspectacularly', it rates such exercises as a steady input to learn important lessons in the process; and another positive side-effect is to strengthen its military relationships with foreign states. The degree of realistic training in different scenarios has increased so that pilots are now practising flying under challenging environmental conditions, such as at night and in extreme weather conditions. They practice flying at low altitudes over difficult terrain including through valleys, around mountains and over water and also by holding sophisticated multi-branch and inter-service exercises under complex electromagnetic environments and formidable air defence scenarios to mimic actual battle conditions that a potential military adversary may present. Most significantly, the PLAAF is still seeking to cultivate a greater autonomy among its pilots and has begun to shift training away from an emphasis on ground control to a system which encourages independent decision-making. All this helped to significantly improve the PLAAF's combat readiness, which is demonstrated also by the flying time: 'During 1998, pilots achieved a record of per capita flying time, the highest since 1985, in spite of heavy summer flooding and a programme to restructure the air force. Pilots paid particular attention to improving basic flying techniques. The fact that 66 per cent of air units conducted highly successful long-distance mobile manoeuvres under harsh weather conditions indicated that China's Air Force has greatly enhanced its combat readiness' as Wu Guangyu, PLA Air Force Deputy Commander stated in January 1998.

In parallel to the institutional changes – the introduction of the FTTC at Cangzhou and Dingxin – also the organisational structure of the flight colleges was reformed. As a first step, the PLAAF reduced the original more than 15 flight schools to only seven flight colleges in the 1990s and in May 2004, the Air Force Aviation University (AFAU) was founded in Changchun to replace the 7th Flight College. This was once composed

of the Flight Basic Training Base – in fact the former 7th Flight College – and the Flight Training Base. In January 2009 then, an official *Outline of Military Training and Evaluation* (OMTE) manual was published, formulating – in fact demanding – fundamental reforms concerning all conditions, particularly under complex EW circumstances and in joint operations in high-technology environments. For this, the PLAAF uses the term 'under informatised conditions', which is a concept comparable to the US network-centric warfare.

Close to the current status, in 2011 the flight colleges were consolidated into three flying academies at Harbin, Shijiazhuang, and Xi'an, each of which includes two of the previous flight colleges and has several different types of trainer aircraft rather than a single type of basic and intermediate trainer. Finally, in April 2012, the former 13th Flight College in Bengbu, was transformed into a flight instructor training base for flight instructors in the three flight colleges and at operational units and was subordinated to the AFAU. The final step not only resulted in the three current flight colleges, but also it consolidated at least four of the seven military region training bases (MRTB). The remaining transition training bases were merged with the PLAAF's new air brigades and often reformed as formerly disbanded regiments.

2011–12 and 2016–17: the most profound reform since its foundation

In parallel to the reform of the training establishment and its procedures, also the general structure of the PLAAF was throughoutly modernised. This still ongoing process includes both hierarchical changes, a numerical force reduction via the introduction of more latest generation types but most of all an organisational reform that was accomplished in several phases: already in 1998, the PLAAF reorganised its headquarters to match the PLA's newly created General Armament Department. A unique side effect was, that in order to establish – or in fact to re-create – some sort of stronger identity or esprit de corps, all PLAAF members are allowed to wear dedicated air force uniforms rather than the former army uniforms when they fill positions in the four general departments. In order to streamline its command structure, in 2003 the PLAAF reduced its former long-time five-tiered vertical command structure – if including down to the lowest operational level even seven tiers (PLAAF HQ – MRAF HQ – command post – air division – air regiment – flight group – flight squadron) for its aviation troops – to four – or similar a six-tiered structure (PLAAF HQ – MRAF HQ – base – air brigade – flight group – flight squadron).

The first change was the abolishment of the air corps level for command headquarters, some of which were called bases. Instead, it created several corps deputy leader-grade and division leader-grade command posts (CPs) and consolidated the operational chain of command for aviation troops under the seven MRAF Headquarters. In the end and in line with the overall force reduction during 2003–04 of 200,000 personnel (85 per cent officers), all combat units assigned to each MRAF were set under the direct leadership of the MRAF Headquarters. The only exception from that structure are the 15th Airborne Corps and the 26th Specialised Air Division, which were directly subordinated to the PLAAF's Headquarters.

A further step to consolidate the operational chain of command was under the seven former MRAF headquarters, the remaining 13 command posts[9] – which acted on behalf of the MRAF headquarters to command the organisations in their AOR – within their military region. This downgrading all of the air corps-level organisations however, even if originally intended to simplify the command structure, actually complicated the situation at first, but in the end led to the latest reform.[10] This probably most profound reform was initiated in late 2011 and included a major unit-reorganisation. For many years – until 2012 – the best-known hierarchical units within the PLAAF tier have been the air divisions and their corresponding air regiments, which formed the most suitable starting point for an overall review. Additionally each CP controlled a number of subordinated ground-based assets (including SAM brigades and regiments, AAA regiments, radar, communications and other support units), as well as several of the most important combat formations of the PLAAF: the former air divisions (ADs) and air regiments (ARs), which were mostly disbanded and superseded by the concept of bases and air brigades (ABs). In a first step, since January 2012 four bases (as corps deputy leader-grade) were formed from existing CPs within only four of the seven MRAFs – Guangzhou, Lanzhou, Nanjing and Shenyang. These four – Dalian, Nanning, Shanghai and Urumqi – execute command and control of their subordinated air brigades but also SAM, AAA, and radar units in their area of responsibility (AOR) and they are also responsible to coordinate joint training with army and navy assets in their AOR. Quite noteworthy, this shift to an air brigade structure occurred parallel not only in operational units but also in the PLAAF's flight colleges, when the seven flight colleges were merged into three flight colleges at Harbin, Shijiazhuang and Xi'an plus one Flight Instructor Training Base subordinated to the Air Force Aviation University.

Even if it is not entirely clear why, this reform including the creation of brigades and bases and any further reforms were put on hold at the end of 2012 only to be re-instituted in early 2017. In the meantime – since early 2016 the former seven MRAF HQs were reorganised into five TCAF HQs. One possible explanation why there was a near five-year hiatus in creating new bases and air brigades – most likely to gain about six years of experience with the new structure and their operational benefits – the PLAAF restarted this rapidly progressing reform with a much wider-reaching re-organisation in April 2017. Since then for several months not a single week passed by in which not a new brigade was confirmed, aircraft were renumbered, reports about newly established bases appeared and older divisions were either restructured, relocated or disbanded. Meanwhile, their former regiments were either converted to brigades or disbanded – the latter above all in the case of those equipped with obsolescent aircraft. And in the end, even if not entirely clear, it seems as if in early 2018, only two CPs remain active – Hetian in the WTC and Changchun in the NTC – and it appears that no brigades are subordinate to them but solely to their bases.

In essence, it is necessary to differ between an air base and a base. An air base is simply an operations centre for units of an air force, on which a certain unit is based. However, a base is a leader-grade organisation. So even if at first sight it looks as if regiments were replaced by brigades usually just by reusing their original numbers and the divisions are replaced by bases, the difference is most of all related to its leader grade. Each base – one could probably better say a command base – is directly subordinate to the relevant Theater Command Air Force HQ, which is a Theater Command deputy leader grade organisation. As such, each of the bases has command over all PLAAF air

brigades (division deputy leader grade), SAMs, AAA, and radar units in their immediate AOR. Usually each of these bases also have associated, specific forward operating bases assigned and perhaps a base even commands the supporting infrastructure like airfield units, construction units and mobile units that can prepare unused airfields to turn them into operating airfields.

By now, there are usually two bases within each TC, which command the individual brigades in each of the five formal TCAFs: in protocol order these are the Eastern TC (ETC), which takes responsibility for the Taiwan Strait and East China Sea, the Southern TC (STC), which is focused on the South China Sea and the Western TC (WTC) as the largest TC, which is responsible for the Sino-Indian border and Central Asia especially cross-border terrorism. The fourth TC in order is the Northern TC (NTC), which handles challenges emanating from the Korean Peninsula and Japan and finally the Central TC (CTC) is responsible for the defence of the capital and will provide support to other TCs in case of urgency. Consequently, with this change to the revised structure of Theater Commands, the PLAAF is currently organised into five Air Force Districts (AFDs), which therefore operate five Theater Command Air Forces (TCAFs). The manner in which these are usually presented in official Chinese publications is known as the Official Protocol Order and this order plays an important role in Chinese military hierarchy and essentially dictates the way in which the entire PLAAF structure is usually presented. A recent change however is, that each TCAF no longer exercises control over its subordinated units via command posts (CPs).

Airborne Forces – a true spearhead

As one can see, the modernisation of the PLAAF was or is not a one-piece effort, but a broad and far reaching reform, that effected several aspects. At first sight only a minor one, but in the end to transform the PLA and the PLAAF into a true modern joint-capable force was the transformation of the 15th Air Corps into a rapid-reaction force (RRF). This important change in campaign strategy was initiated already in 1992, soon after the airborne corps returned to a divisional structure with an overall increase of 25 per cent in strength. This year is also important in another way, since the PLAAF received their first Russian Il-76 transports in 1992. In line with this, most notably the percentage of specialised paratroopers rose in order to transform the Airborne Corps into a combined arms force rather than a mobile infantry force. This is indeed a remarkable change, since over the 30 years since their genesis, the Chinese airborne forces developed relatively slowly due to the dogma that the army is the most important service.

However, since the late 1990s the emphasis changed dramatically due to two major events. The first was the fast deployment and most successful assault by the US airborne forces in 1991 Gulf War assisted and/or aided by heavy equipment and secondly, the dramatic earthquake in Sichuan province in 2008. Since then the PLA has constantly expanded its operational capabilities and combat readiness of its airborne forces particularly by intensive, realistic and often international exercises. Prime examples are the Peace Mission joint military exercises carried out since 2005 and the establishment of the new Zhurihe Training Base in northern China's Inner Mongolia Autonomous Region, which was completed in the summer of 2012. That year also saw

Key

● Theatre Command HQ

● Base

○ Former Command Post

Locations

1. Hetian
2. Urumqi (Wulumuqi)
3. Lhasa
4. Lanzhou
5. Chengdu
6. Kumming
7. Nanning
8. Guangzhou
9. Zhangzhou
10. Fuzhou
11. Wuhan
12. Xi'an
13. Nangjing
14. Shanghai
15. Jinan
16. Datong
17. Beijing
18. Dalian
19. Shenyang
20. Changchun

▶ This map shows the organisational structure of the current five theater commands, which replaced the former military regions in 2016. (Map by James Lawrence)

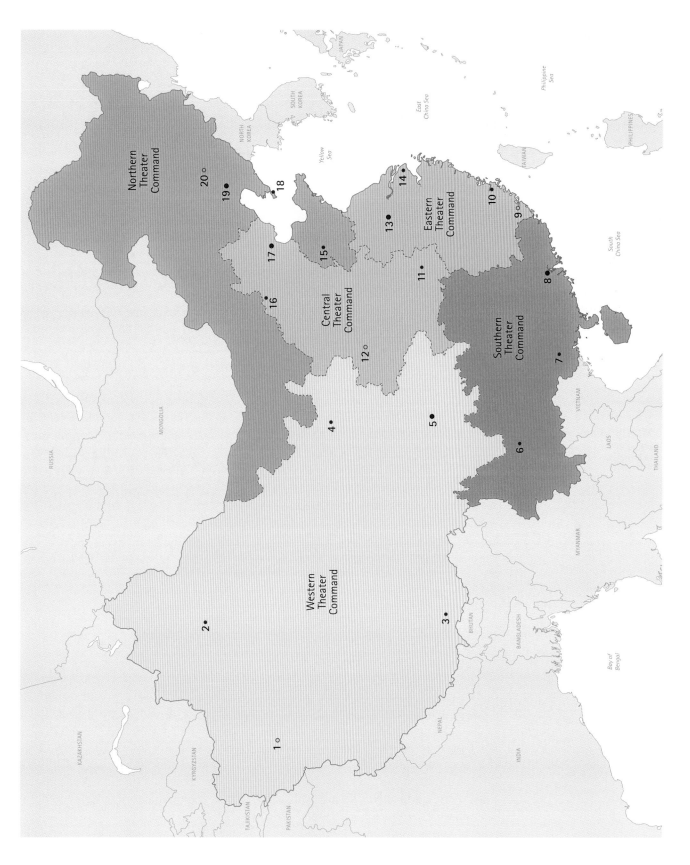

The current workhorse for transport duties is the Y-8C, which has played a major part in the transition of the airborne forces into a modern rapid-reaction force.
(Jiang Long via Chinamil.com)

the initiation of the current reforms to transform the airborne forces from a traditional light parachuting 'flying infantry' focused on rear-echelon combat to a combined air force corps featuring multiple services, full-time all-domain operation, and the capability of massive air-drops of heavy-duty equipment. Nevertheless, at first this change in doctrine excluded the aviation forces. True aviation rapid-reaction force units were allegedly under discussion since some time, however due to a lack in modern multirole aircraft types, the establishment of aviation RRF units did not occur until around the early 1990s. This once again was possible for the first time with the delivery of Russian Su-27s and later Su-30MKKs. A few units were also composed of J-7 and J-8s, which were later replaced by JH-7As, J-10A/Bs and J-11A/Bs until the end of the century. With the latest modernisation, the today's rapid-reaction aviation units are equipped with the latest J-10B/Cs, J-16s and surely soon the J-20.

Latest developments and future prospects

The periods describing the PLAAF's history often end with an epoch described as 'the future'. However, given the latest revolutions – which are no longer merely evolutional steps – it might be worth adding a sixth period. This began with the reforms initiated in 2012 and entered a second level in 2015 with the official unveiling of China's first white paper on military strategy on 26 May 2015 in Beijing. For the PLAAF, the current reforms mean that for the first time in its history, it will face the necessity of shifting its focus from primarily territorial air defence to the ability to conduct offensive and defensive operations as well, and which can meet the requirements of 'informationised' operations. This inevitably includes – and in public this is naturally what receives the most attention – the introduction of new hardware such as modern multi-role-capable

combat aircraft. Nevertheless, probably the most important reforms are largely unnoticed and these concern the PLAAF's tactics and training and its command structure.

Here the main focus lies currently in the proper use of these latest assets in order to better utilise their full potential and conduct different aerial combat missions which are no longer in a pre-exercised or directed manner through exercises with an increasing complexity of simulated war scenarios. In addition, the complexity of these latest exercises has been expanded in order to improve coordination between different units of the PLAAF but also in joint PLAAF/Naval Aviation exercises. One major component of this reform was therefore the transformation of the former seven military regions and their commands into the now established five Theater Commands in parallel with the introduction of the base/brigade concept, which replaces the former division/regiment structure.

By now – in mid-July 2019 – after a most spectacular year 2018, where after several months of continuous changes the speed of newly established brigades and their superordinated bases slowed so much down, that one might think, the mission is accomplished. Anyway, the reform is still ongoing and there are surely several issues not yet fully understood, but it seems as if at least the final structure has become visible. Consequently, the PLAAF not only expanded the base/brigade concept and adopted it for all Theater Commands but also that this re-organisation is much more profound than the 2012 reform. So far, the PLAAF entirely converted to this new organisation for the tactical combat units.

For the strategic assets – the bomber, transport and specialised EW and reconnaissance units – however it seems as if these divisions and regiments will survive and also the Naval Aviation has transformed its former naval air divisions in a similar way to naval air brigades. Besides the mentioned tactical operational combat brigades and the training brigades, the PLAAF created several more brigades: these are so-called transport and SAR brigade in each TC and one specifically assigned to the PLAAF's HQs, additionally several unmanned aerial vehicle (UAV) brigades were formed – and one can be sure that these units will even more grow in the near future. Also, the former FTTB and CFTE/TTC trails and evaluation regiments were converted to brigades and the PLAAF's airborne forces formed a dedicated transport aircraft aviation brigade. At the same time, it changed its entire force to a brigade structure similar to the reorganised group armies of the PLA Ground Forces and one can expect that the soon to be established marine corps aviation units will follow a similar structure. Nevertheless, there are still many uncertainties especially concerning which brigade is subordinated to what base even more since a few more brigades were confirmed since then, some of which were formerly thought to be disbanded. The biggest question however remains is this new structure working according to the original concept?

Also, what will come next? Which units will receive the latest equipment next and where will they based? Concerning this new equipment, the most modern types currently in production – and remarkably with barely any fact known concerning their current production numbers or schedules – are the J-10C, J-16 and J-20 for the fighters, the Y-20, the Y-9 and all its special mission types and the H-6K. However, will the PLAAF continue to use the concept of one brigade – one type or will it again try to create multi-role, multi-mission brigades as once planned? There are still reports that the PLAAF originally planned to establish multifunctional or multi-role brigades in which one brigade is equipped with each flight group equipped with a different type of air-

Following the two operational trials units at Cangzhou and Dingxin, the J-20 entered frontline service within the 9th Air Brigade in January 2019, facing Japan and Taiwan. (via @B747SPNKG)

craft, namely operational fighters and/or ground-attack or multirole and trainers. This was tested only by the 172nd Brigade, which operates a mix of Su-30MKK and JL-10 and the 176th Brigade, flying a squadron each with J-10C, J-16 and J-20A.

At least by now it appears as if this approach has been abandoned after the testing phase of 2012 to 2016 and gaining experiences in favour of the current structure. Reasons for this might be different and especially maintenance issue due to the higher complexity of operating small numbers of different types in one unit is the most often mentioned reason. A hint to this issue could be that on paper combat aircraft brigades might have three to five flight groups in theory, in reality all of the current operational brigades still have only the three flight groups inherited from the former regiments they upgraded from.

This in addition might be related to numbers since some types – like the JH-7A, J-10A and J-11A – are no longer in production or in case of the Su-30MKK only a limited number were imported, so that existing brigades cannot gain additional aircraft without disbanding at least one to spread its aircraft over the remaining brigades. However, maybe this concept might get a second chance and after installing similar changes to the logistics and maintenance systems, it could be resurrect someday. Another reason could also be that dispersing too few aircraft of the latest generation in too small numbers to too many different units caused logistic issues, which in the end might be solved after these types matured in service – and after eliminating various usual teething problems early in every career of an operational aircraft. How important the PLAAF rates logistics is clearly demonstrated by the formation of the PLA Strategic Support Force and the Joint Logistics Support Force. Both are seen as the most significant step toward enabling the PLA to act as a true joint military force on land, at sea, in the air, in the space and cyber domains.

And finally, in regard to new equipment the question remains, when will the next generation of aircraft currently under development be unveiled? This is most of all the rumoured new stealth bomber H-20, also – and less spectacular – new UAV and UCAV systems but even trainers, transports and liaison types. The other still open question remains on the issue of 'jointness', which includes joint training, joint logistics, and joint doctrinal development and its consequences. Besides the operational drivers, yet another issue is the desire to improve party supervision over an increasingly complex, corrupt and undisciplined rated system and finally improve the defence research and development system.

In summary the current PLAAF has already undergone – and is still undergoing – an impressive and wide-ranging process of modernisation not only during the last two decades but especially worthy to celebrate its 70th anniversary. The PLAAF proudly transformed itself into a far more capable force, able of at least limited joint operations with other Chinese military branches and services, something the PLA and PLAAF leadership not even dreamt for just a few decades before and especially remarkable from what it evolved after the Cultural Revolution. Therefore, the PLAAF's future appears bright and following this topic will remain similar interesting for the time that lays ahead as within the last decade. However, in mind of China's current political, economic and military power, there are also several endeavours ahead.

Largely unnoticed, a slightly upgraded JL-10A variant is also in service alongside the regular JL-10. The JL-10A features a small JL-10G fire-control radar as well as a new dorsal UHF/VHF antenna. It has been in service at the Shijiazhuang Flight Academy since late 2018. (via PDF)

Aircraft types

Xi'an H-6D (ASCC 'Badger')

Succeeding the earlier bomber models, the next dedicated variant to enter service was the first fully modernised version H-6D. This specialised AShM carrier for the PLAN Naval Aviation was under consideration since the late 1960s but development was much delayed. It was officially approved in October 1977 and aimed to feature the dedicated Type 245 target acquisition radar in order to guide the YJ-6 missile. The most obvious external change was therefore a much larger drum-like flat-bottomed radome and the missiles were carried on huge underwing pylons.

The first airframe was completed in 1980 but the prototype made its maiden flight only in August 1981. Flight testing continued until 1984 and it received certification in 1985, so that a first naval regiment was declared operational only in December.

Images of operational H-6Ds are rare and often of low quality. Today, all have been converted to H-6DU tankers and are assigned to Naval Aviation. (via Li Xueliang)

Xi'an HU-6/H-6U and HU-6D/H-6DU tankers

The most important specialised variant however is the tanker programme. This started in the mid to late 1980s during the brief Sino-Western honeymoon phase. Even if these efforts failed as a result of the arms embargo in 1989, it set the basement for the development of a H-6 tanker variants. The first is a dedicated PLAAF tanker revealed in the late 1990s called HU-6 or even HY-6 based on newly manufactured airframes featuring a solid nose and no chin radome.

The second type is designated HU-6D and all in use by the Naval Aviation are rebuilt H-6D naval bombers still featuring the standard glazed nose with the big chin radome. Altogether less than 20 examples of each version are believed to have been produced

The HU-6 – this example is from the 8th Bomber Division – was the first dedicated tanker in PLAAF service and the first H-6 to introduce a refined airliner-style cockpit section. (via Top81.cn)

and they were used to support the growing number of IFR-probe-equipped J-8Ds and J-8Fs as well as the J-10 fighters.

Later operational variants: H-6E/F, H-6H/M and H-6G (ASCC 'Badger')

The PLAAF in contrast did not receive the H-6D, but instead upgraded several H-6s during the 1980s with new onboard systems, to become known as the H-6E – often said to be nuclear capable – and the conventional H-6F, both having better navigation, more modern ECM and electronic support measures (ESM) equipment, an improved cockpit layout and more reliable engines. Both could be distinguished from non-modified H-6As by a new light-grey colour scheme, low-visibility markings and deleted forward cannons. Another more likely option might be that the H-6E entered service in the late 1980s with minor improvements and there was no real difference between nuclear and non-nuclear bombers, and that both were later updated during the 1990s again to receive the designation H-6F. Anyway, both still lacked a dedicated stand-off capability, which led the way to the next variants.

These later variants will only be mentioned, since a longer and more detailed description of them can be found in the books *Modern Chinese Warplanes* (2012 and 2018). The first of these three is the PLAAF H-6H, which was developed during the late 1990s as a dedicated missile launch platform to meet the requirement for long-range strike capability. Development began in January 1995, the first prototype was rolled out in April 1998 and the H-6H is reportedly equipped with a modified Type 245 radar, updated ECM equipment and the capability to launch KD-63 land attack cruise missiles. Its maiden flight took place in December 1998 and flight testing was completed in April 2000.

Yet a very similar model is the H-6M, which most likely evolved from upgraded H-6E/F bombers during the early 2000s featuring a much improved self-protection

The H-6H was for many years the standard long-range bomber within the PLAAF. Although still in use, it is slowly being replaced by the more modern H-6K and the latest H-6N. (via Top81.cn)

suite including RWR antennas, MAW sensors and chaff/flare dispensers. Overall, quite similar to the H-6H, even if it lacks certain systems, it differs since it was modified to launch the latest KD-20 ALCM. The H-6M became known in the West in about 2007 after it had entered service with one mixed PLAAF bomber regiment alongside the H-6H and until being replaced by the H-6K.

In addition, the next H-6D-based variant is the H-6G, which replaced the naval H-6D. It features four underwing pylons to carry YJ-83K ASMs or YJ-91 ARMs and often two large ECM/EW pods. The H-6G was introduced into PLA Naval Aviation service in 2005 and another updated subtype, able to use the YJ-12 AShMs is designated H-6L.

New generation H-6s: H-6K, H-6J and H-6N (ASCC 'Badger')

Again these members of a fully revised airframe are described in detail in *Modern Chinese Warplanes*, so they are only briefly mentioned for completeness: development of the H-6K was probably initiated due the lack of alternatives after the acquisition of an entirely new bomber was either postponed or completely abandoned during the 1990s. Thus, the PLAAF requested for a modern long-range strike platform and the result became the H-6K and its subtypes. The H-6K went unnoticed in the West for a long time until the first glimpse of the cruise missile carrier prototype was given in mid-December 2006 showing an H-6 with six ALCMs under its wings. After the basic H-6 airframe had been almost unchanged for decades, this version introduced a complete redesign with a new airliner-style non-glazed nose, a big radar and slightly larger air intakes. These were necessary because the H-6K is powered by two of the more economical Russian Aviadvigatel D-30KP-2 turbofan engines – or most likely currently the reverse-engineered WS-18 – as used by the Ilyushin Il-76MD and Y-20 transports. The H-6K made its maiden flight in January 2007, since then it is successively replacing all older models in PLAAF service. A naval variant entered service in late 2018 as the H-6J

An impressive line-up of nine H-6s assigned to the 36th Bomber Division. Interestingly, it shows a mix of earlier H-6As in white with the side gun visible, and the later H-6E or even H-6F in grey with the gun removed. (via CDF)

The H-6N is the latest member of the H-6 family and the first varaint to feature an in-flight refuelling probe. This variant was unveiled during the 70th Anniversary Parade on 1 October 2019.
(via Zhanghui)

armed with the YJ-12 and finally there is an IFR-probe-equipped version H-6N under test since 2015, which is said to act as a dedicated AShBM carrier.

Chengdu/Guizhou J-7III/J-7C and J-7IIIA/J-7D (ASCC 'Fishbed')

Following the success of the J-7B and the export F-7M, Chengdu was encouraged to start work on another improved, all-weather, day and night fighter similar to a MiG-21MF-equivalent at around 1977/78. The design became finally the J-7III or J-7C. The opportunity to improve the J-7 was provided by the access to several MiG-21MFs via Egypt and a first example arrived in China in February 1979. This effort to reverse engineer the MiG-21MF was undertaken jointly by the Chengdu Aircraft Design Company, the No. 611 Institute and the Guizhou Aircraft Company Base 011. The necessary drawings were finished until May 1980 and manufacture of the first of six prototypes began in October 1983, so that maiden flight was performed in April 1984. Compared to the basic J-7B, the J-7C was a much more sophisticated aircraft with about 80 per cent of its components re-designed and most of its equipment changed.

As a first it was fitted with a more capable JL-7 all-weather, day/night capable intercept radar, a HUD and a self-defence suite comprising countermeasure dispensers. Perhaps the most important change however, was the new and more powerful WP-13 engine. Despite the various improvements, the J-7C failed to meet PLAAF requirements and only a limited number were built in 1988, but not delivered to the PLAAF until December 1989.

As an attempt to save the programme, a project was started in 1988 for an updated version initially called J-7IIIA. It introduced the refined WP-13FI with increased reliability and upgraded avionics. It later became the J-7D and its most noticeable feature was a more prominent chaff/flare dispenser located on the sides of the dorsal fin.

The first J-7D prototype flew in August 1991 and limited series production began in November 1994. Again still hampered by several issues, only 32 were completed until 1999. In essence it was cancelled after that in favour of the more promising Shenyang J-8B/D and the later acquisition of the Russian Su-27.

The very first J-7III prototype wore several interesting colour schemes during its test phase, including this light blue one, which replaced the original colourful paint scheme.
(via Top81.cn)

Chengdu J-7E (ASCC 'Fishbed')

When it became clear that the once promising J-7C would be a failure, Chengdu returned to the drawing board and started again based on the trusted J-7B airframe. The main objective was to improve the aerodynamic performance as well as to add more fuel and the ability to use the latest AAMs like the PL-8 without dedicated modifications. Development of the resulting J-7E was started in 1987 and the biggest change was a new double-delta wing. This, and the use of a more powerful WP-13F, resulted not only in an overall new shape, but as desired in much improved manoeuvrability. In addition the J-7E was designed and manufactured using technology such as CAD/CAM which led to a much higher quality of manufacture in comparison to previous versions.

The J-7E is equipped with a Type 226 ranging radar, a modified cockpit with HOTAS and several more updated avionics. It flew for the first time in May 1990 and full rate

The J-7E – like this example from the 3rd Fighter Division – was for many years the standard fighter variant and the first to introduce the new wing. (via VF-154)

The J-7G is today the most capable PLAAF variant and introduced various updated avionics. Still, it lacks the capability to use BVR missiles. (via CDF)

A rare image of a JZ-8 assigned to the 4th Independent Reconnaisance Regiment in 'clean' configuration without its camera pod.
(via CDF)

production was reached in December 1993, so that until production ended in 2001, 263 J-7Es were delivered. Special subtypes were the J-7EH naval and J-7EB aerobatic version.

Final variants: J-7G and J-7L (ASCC 'Fishbed')

With the export success of the subsequent F-7MG and F-7PG, CAC was quick to introduce the latest changes into a final domestic version called the J-7G, even if there was indeed one last attempt to develop a radically altered version called J-7F, which was even tested in the J-7FS from 1998 but finally cancelled. The J-7G has further improved avionics giving it an all-weather air-to-air-combat capability and a one-piece windshield for a better pilot view. The heart of the upgrade was the new KLJ-6E Falcon pulse-Doppler optimised for the PL-5E and PL-8B AAMs. Assembly of a prototype began in March 2002 and it performed its maiden flight in June. Flight testing was concluded in June 2004 and allegedly 128 airframes were built until 2009.

The final J-7 to enter PLAAF service is a MLU variant of the remaining J-7E re-equipped with the J-7G's systems to be called J-7L.

Shenyang J-8I, J-8IE and JZ-8 (ASCC 'Finback')

The new J-8I or J-8A, featured several improvements like a revised canopy, a HTY-2 ejection seat and avionics like the Type 204 radar. It was also able to field up to four PL-2B or PL-5B AAMs and a new twin-barrel Type 23-III cannon. Design work on the J-8I was finished in February 1978 and the first prototype was completed in May 1980. After the loss of the first prototype, a second one had its maiden flight in April 1982 and flight testing was concluded in November 1985. However in the end, also the J-8I had not the desired improvement and production was therefore quite limited which ended in 1987. During the late 1980s and early 1990s, several J-8Is received some avionics derived for the J-7C/D and became the J-8IE, but already then, the much improved J-8II was already in development.

▶ For a brief period during the early 1990s, the PLAAF allowed a few units to wear unit badges, as evidenced by this J-8II from the 1st Fighter Division wearing the unit's Siberian tiger patch.
(via CDF)

Consequently, some were converted during the mid-1980s to the JZ-8 reconnaissance variant, which carried a large reconnaissance pod under its fuselage containing several cameras. The JZ-8 remained in service until the early 2000s, when the JZ-8F entered service.

Shenyang J-8II (ASCC 'Finback')

Since both the J-7C/D and the J-8I fell short of the PLAAF's needs, a new RfP was approved in September 1980. Concept studies began in April 1981 and the new J-8 variant was based on a proposed fighter bomber H-8 or JH-8. It used most of the fighter's rear fuselage and added a new front fuselage containing a radar two lateral MiG-23-style intakes plus a huge dorsal fin. Work on the resulting J-8II/J-8B began in 1982 and the prototypes were prepared in 1983, so that in June 1984 the first J-8II performed its maiden flight. Flight testing lasted through 1987 to 1988 but the PLAAF remained reluctant due to inferior performance and outdated avionics compared to other contemporary fighters and potential adversaries. An opportunity for a comprehensive modernisation with Western equipment came in the form of the Peace Pearl programme, during the late 1980s as in August 1987 Grumman was contracted to upgrade 50 J-8II with a decent avionics kit. Even two J-8IIs were shipped to the US in early 1989 and test flown by US pilots but due to the Tiananmen riots the whole programme was cancelled. In the end, even if the first J-8IIs were disappointing, between 1992 and 1995 a modest production run of estimated 54 aircraft were delivered.

A very interesting image of the 1st Fighter Division showing old J-8Is together with early J-8IIs and even (in the background) some J-8B Block 02s.
(via CDF)

Following the regular J-8II, the J-8B Block 02 and J-8D with refuelling probe are virtually identically. They can be recognised by the additional RWR on the tail and under the radome, as well as the different fin cap.
(via Top81.cn)

Nearly the full complement of J-8Fs assigned to the 1st Division's 3rd Regiment. This was the most capable interceptor variant in service, but its service career is slowly coming to an end. Today this unit operates the J-16.
(via Top81.cn)

Shenyang J-8B Block 02 and J-8D (ASCC 'Finback')

A slightly updated variant flew for the first time in November 1989 and went on to reach batch production as the J-8IIA, which became later J-8II Batch-02 or simply J-8B. The most significant improvement was a strengthened airframe and ability to carry larger payloads. In parallel SAC was developing a variant capable of aerial refuelling which was known as the J-8IIB or J-8D, which made its maiden flight in November 1990 and was delivered to the Naval Aviation.

Besides some additional minor updates, both the J-8B and J-8D had the Type 208B radar with a limited BVR capability, however it still lacked any beyond visible range AAM. Since the PL-11 entered service only much delayed after 2002. It seems likely that batch production of the J-8B/D started around 1995–96 until 2000–01 around 81 aircraft were built.

Shenyang J-8C, J-8H, J-8F and JZ-8F (ASCC 'Finback')

Following the cancelled Peace Pearl project, Russia and Israel stepped in during the early 1990s to complete an upgrade. The first attempt was the multi-role capable J-8III or J-8C, which was planned to fit a new pulse-Doppler radar. Some say the Elta EL/M 2034 was the basis for the Type 1471, which was compatible with the PL-11 radar-guided AAM, itself a copy of the Alenia Aspide. Otherwise, it was said to feature a digital FBW system originally tested in the J-8ACT, a removable IFR probe and an IRST system in front of the windshield, a modern glass cockpit included a HUD and two MFDs, and finally two WP-14 Kunlun turbojets. However, because of ongoing problems with the WP-14 all prototypes concluded testing with WP-13FIIs. A first example

flew in 1992 and altogether four J-8C prototypes were built, before it was cancelled during the late 1990 due to technical issues and most of all due to a shift in priorities by the PLAAF and the purchase of Russian Sukhoi Su-27SKs.

To save the J-8II project, there were several failed attempts, to develop a dedicated export variant F-8IIM fitted with the Phazotron Zhuk-8II radar and Russian AAMs. In the end, SAC was only left to put together the best and reliable elements of these failed attempts to further improved the PLAAF versions.

The first of these entered service as the J-8H is de facto a MLU based on the J-8B/D but refitted with the Type 1471 radar and PL-11 missile capability. It first flew in December 1998 and went into production in 2001. Only a small number of 24 new air-frames were built between 2001 and 2002 before production switched to the J-8F, but since then further airframes have been added through conversions from older models and these are operational as the J-8BH or J-8DH. Slightly later complementing the J-8H, development of the PLAAF's final variant began in 1997. The J-8F first flew in 2000 and in contrast to the J-8H, it featured the new Type 1492 pulse-Doppler radar, which is compatible with the advanced PL-12 AAM. It also has a modern glass cockpit with HUD, two MFDs and is powered by WP-13BII engines. Production of this version started in 2003 and about 56 aircraft were built until 2006 or 2008, before several more older ones were updated as J-8DF.

Besides these two fighter variants, there are two more specialised J-8s to mention; the first was a SEAD version called J-8G and eventually was only a research project having a first flight in June 2001. Armed with two YJ-91/Kh-31P ARMs, some sources say it entered service in 2005 or 2006 but this is unconfirmed. The final version is the tactical reconnaissance JZ-8F, which has a semi-recessed internal camera compart-ment right under the cockpit in place of the gun-pack. So far three different configured camera compartments with multiple windows of different sizes have been identified. It entered service in 2006 and was reportedly in limited production until 2011.

Chengdu J-10 and J-10A/AS Vigorous Dragon (ASCC 'Firebird')

The Chengdu J-10, China's first modern, single-engined fourth-generation multi-role fighter has been under development since the early 1980s. It was originally envisaged

A regular J-10A assigned to the 26th Brigade - the former 26th AR, 9th Fighter Division - during the Aviadarts 2018 exercise at Russia's Ryazan air base. (Yang Pan via chinamil.com)

that it would replace the obsolete J-7 fighter and Q-5 attack aircraft as the PLAAF's standard multi-role fighter but was delayed for several reasons, in particular by engine issues. Aerodynamically, as a tailless delta-canard design, it was based on the experience gained by CAC and No. 611 Institute on the J-9, which had been cancelled in 1980. In addition, there had been undeniable secret contacts between CAC and the Israeli IAI on the cancelled Lavi project most of all related to FBW development and FCS integration. Consequently, much has been written about the J-10's history, its long and protracted development based on several earlier concepts and its controversially discussed relationship to the IAI Lavi. Since some observers still assume the J-10 to be a phoenix-like resurrected Lavi, it is possible that this ancestry has led to the ASCC codename 'Firebird'. Regardless of all these discussions the J-10 became not only one of China's most modern multi-role fighter within the PLAAF, but also the most recent successful indigenous product of the Chinese aviation industries after many frustrating years of failed projects.

Development of the J-10 was conceived in 1984 and a design designated as the J-9VI or J-9B, with double-delta wing and canards, as well as a chin-mounted intake. The subsequent development proceeded very slowly, with most available funding invested in the J-8II and, during long development, the design went through at least one major redesign from the J-9B through an initial Lavi-like air-superiority fighter design to the J-10 we know today. Even if initiated in 1984, development in earnest begun only during the early 1990s. A full-size mock-up was completed in 1991 – still with the original WP-15 and later WS-10 engine – and the engine issue almost led to the cancellation of the entire project. This was only solved after once Moscow agreed to sell AL-31FN engines, which resulted in yet another re-design but it finally saved the project.

The first prototype made its first flight in March 1998. Flight testing was completed by the end of 2003 and the J-10 entered service in June 2004. Besides the J-10A, which features slightly improved avionics like the Type 1473G fire control radar and the naval J-10AH, there is also a tandem-seat trainer designated J-10AS, which features a prominent single canopy and a large dorsal spine to accommodate the electronics displaced by the rear cockpit. This type is also fully combat-capable and after its first flight in 2003 the trainer entered service in 2005–06.

Chengdu J-10B/C Vigorous Dragon (ASCC 'Firebird')

The next variant to follow the J-10A was the significantly improved J-10B, which was unveiled in December 2008, and in 2016 superseded by the J-10C. The most noticeable differences are a characteristic fixed diverterless supersonic inlet (DSI), a new indigenous IRST/LR dome in front of the canopy, a further-improved glass cockpit with a wide-angle holographic HUD and a new radome, which hoses an X-band PESA radar. This was later replaced in the J-10C by the definitive AESA radar. Overall the J-10B was built in one batch of about 56 aircraft and since 2015 from Batch 02 on aircraft have been called J-10C. Production is continuing.

Sukhoi Su-27 and Shenyang J-11/J-11A (ASCC 'Flanker')

For many years the PLAAF lacked a truly modern fourth-generation high-end fighter and, following the cancellation of the Peace Pearl treaty in mid-1989, the then Soviet Union was quick to step in and replace the West as China's number one arms resource. Following first negotiations in 1990 and after intensive evaluations, China decided to order 20 single-seat Su-27SKs and six Su-27UBK two-seat conversion trainers. The contract signed in 1991 was complemented by two additional orders in 1996 and 2000 for a total of 78 aircraft (36 SKs and 42 UBKs) delivered between in 1992 and 2000.

This agreement included also the licence-manufacturing of 200 additional Su-27SKs as the J-11 by SAC. Interestingly, this contract specifically excluded the AL-31F turbofan. After again several issues – the initial production block reportedly suffered severely on manufacturing quality – there was a steep learning curve, so that but by late 2002 the planned production rate had been achieved. After about 95 kits had been delivered from KnAAPO by 2004, a dispute between the Chinese manufacturer and the Russian designer occurred, since China demanded the J-11 with improved avionics and weapons systems. This issue was not entirely solved, and only a few more slightly improved J-11As were delivered. The J-11A, had its maiden flight in December 1999 and, including the updating of older aircraft up to the end of 2006, a total of 105 had been produced and modernised before production switched to the J-11B.

A unique formation and as such a useful comparison of Royal Thai Air Force JAS 39C Gripen and PLAAF J-10C fighters from the 131st Brigade during the Falcon Strike 2019 joint exercise.
(Xie Zhongwu and Zhou Yongheng via chinamil.com)

Chinese Air Power in the 20th Century

J-11As assigned to the 4th Brigade are recognisable by their prominent PRC flag under the cockpit.
(Tang Jun via chinamil.com)

Shenyang J-11B and J-11BS (ASCC 'Flanker')

The J-11B was a more ambitious programme, since it features a completely new set of indigenous avionics based around a Type 1493 radar compatible with Chinese weapons, and a modern glass cockpit, while the standard AL-31F engines were replaced by the Shenyang-Liming WS-10A Taihang. The first prototype powered by two WS-10s flew in 2004 but development was delayed by technical issues due particularly to engine reliability. Consequently, the first production batch once again had to use standard AL-31F engines, but since late 2009 these problems have been solved. Besides the J-11B, a naval variant J-11BH also exists and reportedly the final latest batches are equipped with FADEC and a further improved version of the WS-10A.

In parallel to the J-11B – and somewhat surprisingly since the licence agreement did not include the trainer – SAC managed to reverse engineer the Su-27UBK twin-seater,

A Batch 02 J-11B assigned to the 89th Brigade. This production block was the first to use the indigenous WS-10A Taihang.
(via Yang Pan via chinamil.com)

Besides the J-10C and J-20, the J-16 is currently the most capable frontline PLAAF fighter. This is a current Batch 05 production aircraft which differs from previous blocks by a new light grey radome.
(via SDF)

to produce the J-11BS. A prototype first flew in late 2007 and, after some delay, the type was certified in May 2010. Operationally, the J-11BS is not only assigned to J-11B units but has also replaced some of the older Su-27UBKs in J-11A units.

Shenyang J-16 and J-16D (ASCC 'Flanker')

Similar to the indigenous improved fighter version J-11B and the J-11BS twin-seater it had been speculated since 2010 that a dedicated multi-role strike 'Flanker' is under development. This version was unveiled in late July 2012 and appeared indeed to be based on the Su-30MKK since it featured most of those strike-specific changes like a retractable IFR probe and the reinforced twin-wheel nose gear to cope with the increased weight. As with all current Chinese 'Flankers' the J-16 is powered by two WS-10A turbofans and as for its avionics, it features an ASEA fire-control radar which is compatible with all Chinese-made precision guided weapons. A maiden flight was performed in October 2011 and by August 2015 that type had entered service.

Besides the regular striker, there is also a dedicated SEAD/EW version under development. The first J-16D made its maiden flight in December 2015 and it is expected to escort standard J-16s. By mid-2019 it was still in testing.

Chengdu J-20 Mighty Dragon (ASCC 'Firefang')

The CAC J-20 is not only the PLAAF's premier fighter but also the pride of China's aviation industries. Consequently, much has been written about it since its sudden appearance in late 2010. What at first was accepted with great scepticism resulted finally in a most successful project that lead to service entry in late 2016 as the world's third operational stealth fighter, after the F-22A Raptor and F-35 Lightning II The project leading to the J-20, as it was first disclosed in 1997 is officially named Project 718. It was then

The J-20 was officially unveiled to the public during the Zhuhai Airshow 2018 where it also demonstated its regular weapons configuration. As of today it is operational within two test and one frontline units. (Katsuhiko Tokunaga/D.A.C.T.)

known that both of China's major fighter aircraft manufacturers – the Shenyang Aircraft Industry Co. (SAC) and Chengdu Aircraft Industry Co. (CAC) – had been working in competition on advanced fighter designs for some time. Understandably, few facts became known and contradicting news items were often posted, but it seems as if the No. 601 Institute at Shenyang proposed a relatively conventional concept featuring a 'tri-plane' design with canard, widely canted tail fins and horizontal tails while the No. 611 Institute at Chengdu was researching a more radical tailless delta-canard design with two V-shaped tails and lateral DSI intakes. This was the chosen design and indeed a demonstrator flew successfully in January 2011. Following several slightly refined prototypes from late 2013 on, the first LRIP J-20As were handed over to the PLAAF in December 2016. By mid-2019, three units were operational.

As with all fifth generation fighters, the J-20 too carries its weapons in internal bays; there is one large central weapons bay for up to four PL-15 medium/long-range AAMs and two smaller lateral weapons bays behind the intakes accommodating one PL-10 short-range AAM each. Its avionics system is said to be built around a Type 1475 AESA-type radar. The biggest uncertainty remains its engine, since development of the final WS-15 lags behind the fighter's schedule; based on the most reliable reports, the demonstrators and prototypes are powered by AL-31FNs similar to those in the J-10B/C.

According to some reports, the J-20 might use a specially tailored version of the Salut AL-31 based on the AL-31FM2, but this is unconfirmed. The first definitive WS-15 powered J-20s are expected not before 2024–25 and currently CAC is testing a variant powered by an up-rated WS-10.

Xi'an JH-7 (ASCC 'Flounder')

The JH-7 is yet another prime example for the mixed fortune, the Chinese aviation industry had from the mid-1970s until today. However, this type was not only influenced by the usual technical issues and politics, but also by an internal rivalry between the PLAAF and the Naval Aviation. This type, which became in fact the only successful indigenous development during this time, was also born out of a requirement formulated after a military conflict, when, in January 1974, around the so-called Xisha Islands the PLAN and the South Vietnamese Navy were engaged. Despite being primarily a clash between naval forces, the conflict revealed some weaknesses, in particular regarding the lack of air support, so that in 1975 a RfP was issued for a new long range supersonic tactical bomber to replace both the H-5 and Q-5. What followed was a harsh rivalry between the PLAAF and the Naval Aviation, which both favoured different main performance requirements as well as airframe configurations. Following the official project start in June 1976, the design institutes at Nanchang and Shenyang responded quite quickly – Nanchang proposed the Q-6 development based on a heavily modified MiG-23 airframe, while Shenyang offered a ground attack version of its J-8 fighter – and Xi'an a bit later in 1977.

The design submitted by Xi'an was externally similar to the European SEPECAT Jaguar and it seems as if in the beginning, two alternative versions of the same airframe were studies with both with side-by-side and tandem-seating and alternative wing arrangements. In the end, besides all political and technical issues it was impossible to combine such vastly different designs into a common airframe, even more since the originally planned WS-6 turbofan finally failed. At around 1979–80 this approach

The JH-7A was the first dedicated all-weather precision strike aircraft in PLAAF service. Still in frontline use in several units, it is slowly being superseded by the more capable J-16.
(via CDF)

was dropped and decided to abandon the PLAAF H-7 variant and to concentrate on a simplified design re-designated JH-7. Between 1983–84 the design was finalised, and also it was decided to powered the JH-7 by the Rolls-Royce Spey 202 engines and later with a licenced version called WS-9, a decision which probably saved the project from being cancelled. By 1987, several prototypes were under construction and the first one made a successful maiden flight in December 1988. In the meantime, due to its protracted development and testing and the various technical issues, the PLAAF lost interest in the JH-7, and instead placed an order for Russian Sukhoi Su-27s and later Su-30MKKs. One of the main weaknesses was the JH-7's Type 232H Eagle Eye multi-function radar, which additionally delayed its service entry from 1992 to 1994 and also resulted in only a limited pre-production run of about 18 aircraft, which were all delivered to the navy. Only in 1998, additional Speys were purchased via Rolls-Royce and a licence-manufactured variant called WS-9 was initiated. Additionally, the original radar was replaced by a new JL-10A multi-mode radar, which resulted in an additional batch of 20 JH-7s were built between 2002 and 2004 as Batch 02. By now all Batch 01 aircraft have been upgraded accordingly.

Xi'an JH-7A and JH-7B (ASCC 'Flounder')

In the late 1990s, XAC developed a dramatically improved variant JH-7A, which also received renewed interest from the PLAAF. Reasons for this might be the high cost of the Russian 'Flankers' and so their limited numbers but also their incompatibility with Chinese-designed weapons and also related to the availability of the WS-9 turbofan since 2007. Several modifications were made to the airframe. The most prominent is a new one-piece windshield, additional pylons, a re-profiled wing without the wing fences and two large fins under the rear fuselage instead of the old central fin; besides that but even more important a completely new avionics system and cockpit was introduced. The first JH-7A made a successful maiden flight in July 2002 and flight testing was completed at around late 2003 or early 2004, so that the JH-7A entered PLAAF service in mid-2004. Altogether about 140 were delivered to the PLAAF and Naval Aviation.

By then, there have been several failed attempts to market a FCB-1 Flying Leopard export version and also Xi'an was working on a more improved version referred to as the JH-7B, which actually even flew but lost again against a 'Flanker' version; this time the J-16, so that the JH-7, which is also flying in the EW role since 2008 will at best receive a modest MLU package based on the JH-7B's advanced avionics until being retired.

The Q-5I and Q-5II were the first variants to replace the small bomb bay with a fuel tank and four pylons, clearly seen on this example assigned to the 5th Ground Attack Division. (via Top81.cn)

Nanchang Q-5I, Q-5IA, Q-5II or Q-5B and Q-5C (ASCC 'Fantan')

Next in line following the first Q-5s, the PLAAF requested an improved aircraft with more range. This version had its bomb bay replaced by a fuel tank and entered service as the Q-5I. Details are sketchy but flight trials began in August 1979 and the test programme lasted until October 1983. In service, this type steadily received minor upgrades like RWRs, an improved bombsight and the possibility of carrying a wider

The Q-5D is something of a rarity in PLAAF service, since it is the only type to wear a green colour scheme. This one was assigned to the 28th Ground Attack Division.
(via Top81.cn)

range stores and became the Q-5IA. It appears that certification was concluded in January 1985 and about 600 Q-5I and Q-5IA were built. After production of these had ceased, an improved version was manufactured in 1981 for export, which became the Q-5II or third Q-5B. Most likely new-built Q-5Bs featured additional systems like a laser-rangefinder and paved the way for the next version Q-5III or Q-5C. Development of this version, which was originally tailored to Pakistan as the A-5C, began in April 1981 and was most likely originally planned to be a PLAAF version using Western avionics. It again featured a revised airframe and the first one flew in September 1982, to be delivered between 1983 and 1984.

Nanchang Q-5K, Q-5M, Q-5D, Q-5L and Q-5J

The first truly westernised variants were then initiated at around the same time as two concurring variants: the first one was the Q-5K developed from 1987 on around several French systems like a Thomson-SCF TVM-630 laser rangefinder, a new HUD, INS and up-rated WP-6A engines. Prototype testing began in September 1991 within a regiment assigned to the 28th Ground Attack Division.

The alternative to the Sino-French Q-5K was the Italian Q-5M led by Aeritalia (now Alenia) which worked since August 1986 on this type. The core of the Italian avion-

The Q-5L was the final variant to enter service and eventually added a precision strike capability to the type. Seen here are two LS-500J LGBs and a rarely seen conformal fuel tank.
(via Top81.cn)

The Q-5J was developed in order to replace the JJ-6. Interestingly, most if not all were built from converted Q-5Ds after those were retired.
(via Top81.cn)

For some years, the Su-30MKK was the most potent strike asset in PLAAF service. However, the type is slowly getting old and is either on the verge of receiving a mid-life upgrade or being replaced by the J-16.
(Stanislav Bazhenov)

ics suite were several systems used by the AMX-like two digital central computers, a MIL-STD-1553B digital databus, a simple ELTA/FIAR Pointer-2500 ranging radar, an INS, RWRs and HUD. Otherwise the Q-5M had two additional hard points under the extreme wingtips. The first aircraft performed its first flight in August but tragically, it was lost in October the same year killing the test pilot. A second machine flew in March 1989 and altogether with a third both were tested until February 1991 for export customers. In the end, both programmes were reportedly successful but cancelled due to the Western embargo.

Consequently, in order to keep the Q-5 in service, another update programme was initiated in the late 1980s, which resulted in the Q-5D. This type picked up the experience acquired with the Q-5K and M programmes and replaced the Western avionics with an indigenous improved fire-control and navigation system including a new HUD and GPS/INS navigation. The Q-5D is noticeable via its unusual dark green colour scheme and a Doppler navigational radar in front of the nose landing gear. The first aircraft may have had its first flight during the 1990s, but all were replaced in the early 2000s by the Q-5L while others were converted to Q-5J trainers. Some also received a few Q-5L systems to become the Q-5N.

The bridge to the final Q-5L was formed by the Q-5E/F, which have been under development since the late 1990s in order to improve that type's precision strike capabilities. At first it was planned to develop them as the Q-5E 'killer' armed with two LS-500J LGBs and the Q-5F responsible for target illuminating acting as a 'hunter' carrying a target designator pod. In the end, both were merged into the single Q-5L, which was a major MLU of the Q-5B/C models carrying two LGBs and a targeting pod simultaneously.

The final and most unique variant was the twin-seat Q-5J, which most likely is a conversion of retired Q-5Ds. This type was needed after all obsolete JJ-6 trainers were retired as a cheap and rugged alternative to more specialised training aircraft. In addi-

The purchase of 24 Su-35s is still not fully understood and the reasons are likely manifold. They are currently operated by the 6th Brigade and routinely fly escort for the H-6K bombers along the SCS and ECS. (FanYishu via chinamil.com)

tion, the trainer was used as a FAC. The first flight took place in February 2005 and these aircraft are conversions or rebuilds of Q-5Ds. All Q-5s were retired by 2018.

KNAAPO/Sukhoi Su-30MKK/Su-30MK2 (ASCC 'Flanker')

One of the driving reasons behind the efforts to develop an indigenous 'Flanker' version was the missing multi-role performance. Additionally, the JH-7's development was troubled and the ordered Su-27 were only able to perform attack missions with 'dumb' munitions so that the PLAAF was looking for an alternative design suitable for precision strike. A solution was found in the multi-role Su-30MK and negotiations began in 1996. Following an initial order in late 1999 and even before this contract was completed, it was supplemented by a second one so that altogether 76 aircraft plus another 24 Su-30MK2 fighters for the Naval Aviation were purchased until 2003.

KnAAPO/Sukhoi Su-35 (ASCC 'Flanker')

Following the acquisition of the Su-27SK/UBK and Su-30MKK/MK2 and the many Chinese developments of them, the purchase of this latest Russian 'Flanker' variant seems surprising to many observers. Anyway, after long-lasting negotiations, a deal involving the delivery of 24 Su-35s was signed in November 2015. The first aircraft were delivered in December 2016 and by late 2018 all had been handed over.

Most mysterious in view of its own 'Flanker' developments including the J-11D and the J-20, it seems now as if this purchase was made for several reasons. First, it enables the PLAAF in exploring the TVC engines and their operational use, it also fulfils urgent operational needs particularly in the disputed South China Sea area and finally, it deepened the Sino-Russian political cooperation. Technically, the Chinese Su-35s are equipped in a similar way to their Russian counterparts and equipped with the Irbis-E PESA radar. In 2019 some news suggests that the PLAAF is considering a second batch.

1   https://www.cna.org/CNA_files/PDF/D0023640.A1.pdf

FINKELSTEIN, Dr. D., 'The Military Dimensions of U.S. – China. Security Cooperation: Retrospective and Future Prospects' (Washington DC: CNA China Studies, 2010) https://www.heritage.org/asia/report/arming-the-dragon-how-much-us-military-aid-china and LASATER, Dr. M. L, 'Arming the Dragon: How Much U.S. Military Aid to China?', (Washington DC: Heritage Foundation, 14 March 1986) http://thf_media.s3.amazonaws.com/1986/pdf/hl53.pdf and https://www.cfr.org/timeline/us-relations-china

2   http://countrystudies.us/china/128.htm and http://china-pla.blogspot.com/2011/08/chinarussia-military-cooperation.html

3   Note: the four general departments are always listed as GSD, GPD, GLD, and GAD, and the PLAAF's counterparts are always listed as the Headquarters Department, Political Department, Logistics Department, and Equipment-Technical Department.

See WANG HAI 'Wang Hai Shangjiang: wode zhandou shengya' [General Wang Hai: My Combat Career], Beijing; Zhongyang wenxian chubanshe [Central Literature Publishers], February 2000, p 300.

4   Note: one reason for a different order – especially in comparison to the PLA – is the fact that the MRs were established in a different order than the MRAFs. As such, the PLAAF uses the order listed above, while the PLA lists them as follows.

5   Note: see Kenneth Allen – The formation of these fifty divisions and five independent regiments is shown in Appendix G, note 921.

6   https://en.wikipedia.org/wiki/Wang_Hai#/media/File:MiG-15_-_079.jpg

By Tyg728 – Own work, CC BY-SA 4.0, https://commons.wikimedia.org/w/index.php?curid=62808297

7   Via Kenneth Allen: in February 1987, the PLAAF Flight Test and Training Center (kongjun feixing shiyan xunlian zhongxin) was established in Cangzhou/Cangxian), superseding the former 11th Aviation School. One reason was, that the PLAAF believed, that it was not receiving timely and accurate testing data from the aviation ministry during the ministry's development and testing of new aircraft at the CFTE at Xi'an-Yanliang. So that in consequence, the FTTC's main mission was to conduct independent testing.

8   In 1958, the CMC authorised construction of the Northwest Comprehensive Missile Test Base (NCMTB) at Shuangchengzi, to conduct testing of surface-to-surface, surface-to-air, and air-to-air missiles. NDSTC was the controlling authority but somewhere in the 1960, when construction was completed, the NCMTB apparently consisted of four basic entities: It consisted of the base with control organisations for SSMs, SAMs, and AAMs, and three separate test ranges. Between the mid-1960s and summer of 1970, a new launch site was constructed for the preliminary stage tests of long-range (medium and intermediate range) SSMs and launch tests for ICBMs. In July 1970, the AAM and the SAM test organisations (departments) were separated from the SSM organisational structure and placed separately under the PLAAF to form two independent SAM test bases, leaving the NCMTB as a specialised SSM facility only. Apparently, these two organisations moved from Shuangchengzi to nearby Dingxin airfield. In 1980, the Shuangchengzi facility changed its name to the Jiuquan Space Center and is one of the major launch sites for ballistic missiles and space launch vehicles, including military reconnaissance satellites.

See also http://china-pla.blogspot.com/2011/08/evolution-of-plaaf-doctrinetraining.html and http://www.china-defence.com/aviation/plaaf-ops/plaaf-ops_01.html

9   RUPPRECHT, A., *Modern Chinese Warplanes* (Houston: Harpia Publishing L.L.C., 2018) ISBN 978-09973092-6-3 , Chapter 6.

10   'People's Liberation Army Air Force 2010', [National Air and Space Intelligence Center (NASIC), 2010], Chapter 2, Organisational Structure.

See also ALLEN, K. W., 'Introduction to the PLA's Organisational Reforms: 2000-2012,' in POLLPETER, K. and ALLEN, K. W., (eds.), *The PLA as Organisation v2.0*, (Defence Group Inc., 2013).

And

ALLEN, K. W., 'PLA Air Force Organisational Reforms: 2000-2012', RAND, p 25. Kenneth Allen and Lyle J. Morris, PLA Naval Aviation Training and Operations: Missions, Organisational Structure, and Training (2013-15), (CASI, December 2017).

YAO WEI, editor, *China Air Force Encyclopedia* [中国空军百科全书], Vol. 2, (Beijing: Aviation Industry Press, November 2005).

ALLEN, K. W., 'Introduction to the PLA's Organisational Reforms: 2000-2012,' in POLLPETER, K. and ALLEN, K. W., (eds.), *The PLA as Organisation v2.0*, (Defence Group Inc., 2013). Accessed at www.china.com.cn/military/txt/2012-02/01/content_24523647.htm and http://club.mil.news.sohu. com/newclub/show.php?forumid=shilin &threadid=4114990 on 25 March 2012.

RUPPRECHT, A., *Dragon's Wings, Chinese Fighter and Bomber Aircraft Development* (Hersham: Ian Allan, 2013) ISBN 978-1-906537-36-4

APPENDIX I

Brief history of the final seven military region air forces[1]

1. Shenyang MRAF

The Shenyang MRAF traces its linage back to the Dongbei MRAF, which was founded in July 1950 using the Dongbei MR Aviation Division as the core. Its name was changed to the Dongbei MRAF in May 1954 and finally in April 1955 it was renamed again to the Shenyang MRAF. In May 1957 the Shenyang MR Air Defence Force was merged into the Shenyang MRAF.

Geographically the PLA Shenyang MRAF covered the northeastern provinces of Liaoning, Jilin and Heilongjiang provinces.

2. Beijing MRAF

The Beijing MR traces its lineage to the former North China Military Region established in May 1948 but the Beijing MRAF was established in October 1950 as the Huabei (North China) MRAF based on the Huabei MR Aviation Division as its core. In May 1954 it was renamed the Huabei Air Force Department and in May 1955 it received its current name the Beijing MRAF. Following the downgrading of the Inner Mongolia MR to a MD this was added to the Beijing MR. In line with the merger with the AD Forces in June 1957, the Beijing MRAF and Beijing MR ADF were combined into a single air defence system now covering also Beijing, Hebei, Neimenggu, Shanxi and Tianjin.

Geographically the PLA Beijing MR covered the Hebei and Shanxi provinces and the Inner Mongolia Autonomous Region (AR) as well as the capital Beijing and the important city of Tianjin.

3. Lanzhou MRAF

The Lanzhou MRAF was originally established in May 1952 as the Xibei (Northwest) MRAF with the 6th Army and the Xibei MR Aviation Division as its core. Shortly thereafter its headquarters moved to Xi'an and in May 1954 the name was changed to Xibei MRAF. One year later this was changed again – now covering Gansu, Ningxia, Qinghai, Shaanxi and Xinjiang – in May 1955 to the Lanzhou MRAF. Originally the Lanzhou MRAF also included Sichuan and Tibet, which were later transferred to the Chengdu MRAF CP in 1965 and 1969 respectively.

Geographically the PLA Lanzhou MR covered the the Ningxia Hui AR and Xinjiang Uyghur AR, as well as the Gansu, Qinghai and Shaanxi provinces.

4. Nanjing MRAF

Historically the Nanjing MRAF dates back to the Huadong MR Aviation Division and was founded in August 1950. Already in September the headquarters moved to Shanghai and merged with the Shanghai Air Defence Headquarters, where it was renamed to Huadong MRAF and simultaneously the Shanghai Air Defence Headquarters. In November 1954 it was renamed again to Huadong MR Air Force Department and finally in June 1955 to the Nanjing MRAF.

In September 1957, the Nanjing MR Air Defence Forces merged into the Nanjing MRAF. However, in July 1958 the Fuzhou MRAF was created at Jinjiangxian by using staff from the Nanjing MRAF 1st and 5th Air Corps as the core.

Finally in September 1985 the Fuzhou MRAF merged back into the Nanjing MRAF. Geographically the PLA Nanjing MR covered the six provinces of Anhui, Fujian, Jiangsu, Jiangxi and Zhejiang, as well as the city of Shanghai.

5. Guangzhou MRAF

The Guangzhou MRAF traces its linage back to the Zhongnan MRAF, which was established in Wuhan September 1950 with the Zhongnan MR Aviation Division as its core and was officially created as the Zhongnan MRAF in October 1950. In May 1954 it was renamed to the Zhongnan MR Air Force Department and during July 1955, this Air Force Department moved to Guangzhou, where it was renamed the Guangzhou MRAF. However, forces stationed in Henan and Hubei were transferred to the Wuhan MRAF. Again in May 1957 the Guangzhou MRAF and Guangzhou MR Air Defence Force were merged into a combined air defence system.

When the Wuhan MRAF was disbanded in September 1985, all PLAAF units in Hubei were transferred to the Guangzhou MRAF.

6. Jinan MRAF

The Jinan MRAF has its roots in the former 6th Air Corps and portions of the Beijing MRAF headquarters, when it was founded in September 1967 in Jinan, Shandong province. At the beginning the Jinan MRAF covered only the Shandong province but when the Wuhan MRAF was disbanded in 1985 all PLAAF units in Henan were added into its responsibility.

7. Chengdu MRAF

In contrast to the more or less established other six MRAFs, the last of the seven current military region air forces, the Chengdu MRAF, had a quite mixed history. It traces its origins back to the Xinan MR Headquarters Aviation Division, originally established in January 1950 in Chongqing. There the Xinan MRAF was established in September 1950 by using the resident aviation division as its core. Its main purpose was to control the aviation assets and to support ground forces entering Tibet. As such the Xinan MRAF was relocated to Chengdu in September 1950, where it was disbanded in June 1955 and its forces being transferred to the Lanzhou MRAF.

In August 1960, however, the Kunming MRAF CP was created as well as the Chengdu MRAF CP in October 1965. In April 1976 the Kunming MRAF CP became the 5th Air Corps and the Chengdu MRAF CP the 8th Air Corps. In November 1978 the 5th Air Corps was renamed the Kunming MRAF CP and similar the 8th Air Corps became the

Chengdu MRAF CP. In 1969 the Chengdu MRAF CP received responsible of the PLAAF forces based in Tibet from the Lanzhou MRAF. Finally, in September 1985 both MRAF CP's were merged and reorganised into the Chengdu MRAF.

Brief history of all disbanded MRAFs

Wuhan MRAF and Base (Wuhan CP)
The Wuhan MRAF was created in July 1955 by the merger of the Xinan MRAF and PLAAF's Guangzhou CP, covering Henan and Hubei. In September 1985 however the Wuhan MRAF was disbanded and replaced by the Wuhan CP. Its name was later changed to the Wuhan Base sometime after 1993 and all forces in Henan were transferred to the Jinan MRAF, and those in Hubei were subordinated to the Guangzhou MRAF. Following the 2003–04 restructuring the Wuhan Base soldiered on as the Wuhan CP.

Fuzhou MRAF (Fuzhou CP)
In preparation to the Taiwan Campaign in July 1958, the CMC decided to move aviation troops into Fujian for air defence duties of the southeast coast. As a consequence, the Fuzhou MRAF was created at Jinjiangxian by the end of July using staff officers from the Nanjing MRAF, the 1st and 5th Air Corps as the core. In June 1960 the headquarters was transferred to Fuzhou, but in September 1985 the Fuzhou MRAF was merged into the Nanjing MRAF.

Quite noteworthy, between 1958 and 1985 more than 130 aviation regiments have been deployed or stationed in the Fuzhou MRAF.

Table according to the mentioned primary source from Kenneth Allen

MRAFs		Air Corps (AC)		Command Posts (CP)		Air Divisions	
1955	Beijing	1951	1st AC	1955	Wuhan	1950	2nd – 9th Divisions (7)
1955	Nanjing	1951	2nd AC	1960	Fuzhou	1951	10th – 25th Divisions (16)
1955	Lanzhou	1951	3rd AC	1962	Lhasa, Hetian	1952	26th – 28th Divisions (3)
1955	Wuhan	1952	4th AC	1965	Chengdu	1954	29th Division (1)
1955	Shenyang	1952	5th AC	1976	Tangshan	1960	30th – 33rd Divisions (4)
1955	Guangzhou	1956	6th AC	1978	Kunming, Zhangzhou	1963	34th Division (1)
1958	Fuzhou	1962	7th AC	1979	Wulumuqi	1965	35th – 36th Divisions (2)
1965	Jinan	1962	8th AC	1985	Xi'an, Dalian	1966	37th Division (1)
				19??	Shanghai		
1985	Chengdu	1962	8th AC			1967	38th – 39th Divisions (2)
		1964	9th AC			1969	40th – 46th Divisions (7)
		1969	11th AC			1970	47th Division (1)
		1969	12th AC			1971	48th – 50th Divisions (3)
		1970	13th AC				

Air Corps, Command Posts and Bases

Following the MR within the PLA's grade structure, the corps were organisational headquarters between the MR and the individual divisions. Originally, they were established during the 1950s and 1960s in order to control the aviation and air defence units within a certain geographical area on behalf of the MRAF headquarters. Interestingly, the PLAAF seperates two types of organisations with the name corps which are the air corps and the airborne corps and adding even more confusion, there are several more corps-level adequate organisations without the specific term 'corps' in their name like the Air Force Command College and the Air Force Equipment Research Academy. Quite unusual for an uninformed reader, an air corps carried its pennant number between the two characters; as such the 1st Air Corps was called 'kong 1 jun'.

As already noted it is not an unusual habit within the PLAAF command structure that several of these organisations (MRAF, air corps, command posts and bases) have been downgraded, upgraded, disbanded or even re-established during reorganisational or consolidated efforts, sometimes even several times. In consequence, regarding their origin, command posts usually were either the former regional PLAAF headquarters before the number of PLA Army MRs had been reduced from 11 to seven military regions in 1985 or they were formed from previous air corps (jun/kongjun jun).

The tiers with the most changes are the air corps and command posts. Following a mixed history until 2002–03 only five ACs remained active and already by around 1993 the PLAAF began to rename six of the seven existing CPs into bases, which resulted in five corps-level-grade ACs, six corps-level-grade bases and three division-level-grade CP's, all of which were subordinate to their respective MRAF headquarters.

This mixed structure of ACs, CPs and bases standing side-by-side was then consolidated in line with the PLA's 2003–04 force reduction, when the PLAAF – with the exception of the 15th Airborne Corps, which is directly subordinated to the PLAAF HQ – disbanded all the air corps. During this process most, if not all, of the ACs and bases were downgraded to division-level grade and finally redesignated to common command posts. Their former responsibility for all aviation and air defence units was consolidated in each MRAF directly under the respective MRAF headquarters.

Brief history of all 13 air corps & four command posts[2]

1st Air Corps (Changchun CP)

The 1st Air Corps was most likely founded in November 1951 in Changchun, Jilin province. In order to prepare for the Taiwan campaign schedulded for the autumn of 1958, the PLAAF transferred during July 1958 the core staff of this AC to Jinjiang, Fujian province, where it was re-established in Changchun in October 1958. It was only ambolished in 2003–04 and later became the Changchun CP.

2nd Air Corps

The 2nd Air Corps was also established in November 1951 at Andong, Liaoning province, had only a brief career. It was later disbanded and not replaced by a CP.

3rd Air Corps (Dalian CP and Dalian Base)

The 3rd Air Corps was originally formed in November 1951 at Kaiyuan, Liaoning province and simply changed its designation to Dalian CP (*Dalian zhihuisuo/Dazhi*) at around 1985. Finally by 1993 it was renamed again to Dalian Base (*Dalian jidi/Daji*) only to be named again Dalian CP after 2003–04.

4th Air Corps (Shanghai CP and Shanghai Base)

The 4th Air Corps was established in August 1952 in Shanghai and was renamed to the Shanghai CP (*Shanghai zhihuisuo/Shangzhi*) also at around 1985. After that it was renamed again to Shanghai Base (*Shanghai jidi/Shangji*) by 1993 and finally received its current old former designation Shanghai CP since 2003–04.

5th Air Corps (Kunming MRAF CP and Kunming Base)

The 5th Air Corps has two roots: it was formed as the 5th Air Corps in August 1952 in Weifang, Shandong province. After a brief residence there it was relocated to Hangzhou in 1954 until April 1976 when it was disbanded. Besides that the Kunming MRAF CP (*Kunming junqu kongjun zhihuisuo/Kunzhi*) was founded on 1 August 1960 and when the 5th Air Corps command staff was moved to Kunming in April 1976 the Kunming MRAF CP was renamed the 5th Air Corps.

In November 1978 it was renamed again back to Kunming MRAF CP and several reports claim it was disbanded too. However it was renamed the Kunming Base (*Kunming jidi/Kunji*) sometime after 1993 and is now active again as the Kunming CP.

6th Air Corps (Jinan MRAF, Tangshan CP and Base, Tangshan CP)

The 6th Air Corps had quite a mixed history. It was founded in March 1956 at Yangcun, Hebei province but was already transferred in June 1956 to Weifang, Shandong province. In September 1967 it was relocated again, when it moved to Jinan, Shandong, where it formed the basis for the Jinan MRAF (*Jinan junqu kongjun/Jikong*).

One year later in December 1968 the 6th Air Corps was re-established in Tangshan, Hebei province, where it was active during the earthquake in 1976. Slightly later it was renamed to Tangshan CP (*Tangshan zhihuisuo/Tangzhi*), which was again changed to Tangshan Base (*Tangshan jidi/Tangji*) by around 1993 only to receive again the name Tangshan CP after 2003–04.

7th Air Corps (Shantou CP and Nanning CP)

In contrast to the other air corps, the 7th AC was established in Chenghai, Guangdong province in November 1959 as the Shantou CP (*Shantou zhihuisuo/Shanzhi*). From there it was relocated in 1960 to Xingning, Guangdong province and quite confusing after 1960, another Shantou CP was apparently established.

In June 1962 this newly established CP became the 7th Air Corps, which was slightly later transferred to Xingning. In August 1964 it had to move yet again to Nanning, Guangxi Autonomous Region, where it still exists today but once again renamed to Nanning CP after 2003–04.

8th Air Corps (Fuzhou MRAF, Fuzhou CP, Jinjiang CP, Chengdu MRAF CP)

One of the most changing histories of all CPs has the 8th AC. It was originally founded in September 1955 in Fuzhou, Fujian province as the PLA ADF's 1st Corps (*fang-kongjun diyi jun*). Following the ADF Corps' merger with the PLAAF in 1957 it was replaced in July 1958 by the Fuzhou MRAF (*Fuzhou junqu kongjun/Fukong*), which was formed at Jinjiang, Fujian province from a core of the 1st Air Corps in order to command PLAAF units in Fujian and Jiangxi in preparation for the campaign to liberate Taiwan.

Even more confusing, in February 1960 the PLAAF created the Fuzhou CP (*Fuzhou zhihuisuo/Fuzhi*) and already by June 1960 the MRAF and CP staffs changed locations. In line with this exchange the Fuzhou CP was renamed to Jinjiang CP (*Jinjiang zhihuisuo/Jinzhi*) only to be renamed again in June 1962 to the 8th Air Corps. After quite a stable time it was again transferred in April 1976 to Zhangzhou, Fujian province, where it was disbanded but immediately reconstituted in Chengdu to replaced the Chengdu MRAF CP.

In November 1978, the 8th Air Corps was replaced by the Chengdu MRAF CP but by around 1978 the 8th Air Corps had moved from Chengdu back to Fuzhou again. After the Fuzhou MRAF Headquarters was disbanded in August 1985 it became one of the primary PLAAF command authority and still exists today; once again as the Fuzhou CP.

9th Air Corps (Xinjiang/Wulumuqi CP)

The 9th Air Corps was created in Wulumuqi, Xinjiang Autonomous Region in November 1964. During November 1978 it was renamed the Xinjiang MRAF CP (*Xinjiang junqu kongjun zhihuisuo/Xinzhi*) only to be renamed again on 16 April 1979 to Wulumuqi MRAF CP (*Wulumuqi junqu kongjun zhihuisuo/Wuzhi*). The 9th AC itself was then noted again in Xinjiang (probably Wulumuqi) as early as 1993.

The most likely explanation is a re-establishment by around 1985 to replace the Wulumuqi CP after the consolidation process when the PLA reduced its 11 MRs to seven by the merger of the Xinjiang MR into the Lanzhou MR.

10th Air Corps (Datong CP)

One of the most longstanding units, the 10th Air Corps was established in January 1969 at Datong, Shanxi province and still exists today as the renamed Datong CP.

11th Air Corps (Xi'an CP and Base)

The 11th Air Corps was created in June 1969 in Hetian, Xinjiang Autonomous Region, where it replaced the Lanzhou MRAF Headquarters at Xi'an, Shaanxi province in November 1969, when the Lanzhou MRAF (*Lanzhou junqu kongjun/Lankong*) headquarters moved from Xi'an to Lanzhou, Gansu province.

By August 1985 it was renamed the Xi'an CP (*Xian zhihuisuo/Xizhi*) and this name was changed again to Xi'an Base (*Xian jidi/Xiji*) sometime after 1993. Currently it is still active again under its old name Xi'an CP.

12th Air Corps (Shantou and Xingning CP)

The 12th Air Corps was originally established in November 1959 as the Shantou CP (*Shantou zhihuisuo/Shanzhi*) in Chenghai, Guangdong province. From there it was transferred in 1960 to Xingning, Guangdong, but by around 1960 another Shantou CP had been established. In June 1962 it became the 7th Air Corps and in June 1969 the Xingning CP was renamed to 12th Air Corps. In April 1976 it was disbanded.

13th Air Corps

Similar to the 2nd, 5th and 12th Air Corps, the 13th Air Corps was disbanded in March 1976 after only a brief career – it had been founded in August 1970 in Shijiazhuang, Hebei province.

Lhasa CP and Base (Lhasa CP)

The Lhasa CP (*Lhasa zhihuisuo/Lazhi*) was established in November 1962. It was subordinated to the Chengdu MRAF in January 1969 and in August 1985 downgraded to a general office (*bangongshi*).

After an upgrade in 1987 to a command post, it remaint the PLAAF's smallest CP. It seems as if the Lhasa CP never was restructured as a base (*jidi*) during the 1993 command structure changes.

Hetian CP

Not much is known about this CP, but the Hetian CP (*Hetian zhihuisuo/Hezhi*) was established in July 1962 in Xinjiang. It was later downgraded to a maintenance field station (*changzhan*) in April 1967, but is now active again as the Hetian CP.

Zhangzhou CP

In October 1978, the Fuzhou MRAF re-established the Zhangzhou Command Post (*Zhangzhou zhihuisuo/Zhangzhi*) in Fujian province. This command post was probably originally established in 1958, but was later disbanded.

Wuhan MRAF and Base (Wuhan CP)

Not listed in the regular air corps or command post list, the Wuhan CP traces its lineage back to the Wuhan MRAF, which was created in July 1955. When the Wuhan MRAF was disbanded in September 1985 it was replaced by the Wuhan CP and its name changed to Wuhan Base sometime after 1993. Following the 2003–04 restructuring it is now once again the Wuhan CP.

---

1   See ALLEN, K. W., *PLA Air Force Organisation*, Chapter 9, Appendix G: Origins of PLAAF MRAFs, Air Corps, Command Posts, pp 441–443.

2   See ALLEN, K. W., *PLA Air Force Organisation*, Chapter 9, Appendix G: Origins of PLAAF MRAFs, Air Corps, Command Posts, pp 443–449.

Air Corps/ Command Post	Date of Establishment	Location	Re-established or Renamed	Status prior to Force Reduction (1993–2002)	2012 status/ designation
1st	1951 November	Changchun, Jilin		Active in Changchun	Changchun CP (Shenyang MRAF)
2nd	1951 November	Andong, Liaoning		Disbanded?	
3rd	1951 November	Dalian, Liaoning	Dalian CP (1985)	Dalian Base	Dalian CP (Shenyang MRAF)
4th	1952 August	Shanghai	Shanghai CP (1985)	Shanghai Base	Shanghai CP (Nanjing MRAF)
5th	1952 August	Weifang, Shandong	Kunming MRAF CP (1978)	Disbanded (1978)	
6th	1956 March	Yangcun, Hebei	1976 Tanshan, Tangshan CP (?)	Tangshan Base	Tangshan CP (Beijing MRAF)
7th	1962 June	Shantou, Guangdong	Shantou CP	Active in Nanning	Nanning CP (Guangzhou MRAF)
8th	1962 June	Jinjiang, Fujian	Fuzhou MRAF (1958) Fuzhou CP (1961) Chengdu MRAF CP (1978)	Active in Fuzhou	Fuzhou CP (Nanjing MRAF)
9th	1964 November	Wulumuqi, Xinjiang	Xinjiang MRAF CP (1979)	Active in Wulumuqi	Wulumuqi CP (Lanzhou MRAF)
10th	1969 June	Datong, Shanxi		Active in Datong	Datong CP (Beijing MRAF)
11th	1969 June	Hetian, Xinjiang	Xi'an CP (1985)	Xi'an Base	Xi'an CP (Lanzhou MRAF)
12th	(1959 November) 1969 June	Xingning, Guandong	Shantou CP (1962) Xingning CP (1969)	Disbanded (1976)	
13th	1970 August	Hebei		Disbanded (1976)	
Kunming MRAF Command Post	1960 August	Kunming	5th Air Corps (1976) Kunming MRAF CP (1978)	Kunming Base (1976)	Kunming CP (Chengdu MRAF)
Lhasa CP	1962 November	Lhasa, Tibet			Lhasa CP (Chengdu MRAF)
Hetian CP	1962 July	Xinjiang, Tibet		Downgraded (1967)	Hetian CP (Lanzhou MRAF)
Zhangzhou CP	(Probably 1958) 1978 October	Zhangzhou, Fujian			Zhangzhou CP (Nanjing MRAF)

APPENDIX II

Brief history of all 50 PLAAF air divisions

1st Fighter Division

This division is considered the 'elite' within the PLAAF and traces its lineage back to the earliest days of the air force. It was formed on 19 June 1950 as the 4th Mixed Brigade of the PLAAF in Nanjing, created from the 90th Division of the 30th Army. What later became the 1st Division was originally established as the 10th Regiment within the 4th Mixed Brigade in Xuzhou, with jurisdiction over the 28th, 29th and 30th Brigades and one squadron. On 25 July 1950, it was transferred to Shanghai Longhua air base, and later to Shanghai Dastadium air base and Hongqiao air base.

It originally consisted of three more regiments: the 11th AR was established in Nanjing on 23 June 1950 (with jurisdiction of the 31st, 32rd and 33rd Brigades and an additional squadron) but was transferred to Shanghai Jiangwan air base on 29 July 1950. The 12th AR was established the same day (with jurisdiction of the 34th and 35th Brigades and one squadron, adding the 36th Brigade on 6 October 1950). This regiment was the PLAAF's first bomber unit.

Finally, the 13th AR was established in Xuzhou on 1 August 1950 (with jurisdiction of the 37th, 38th and 39th Brigades) as the PLAAF's first ground attack unit. These regiments experienced a fairly turbulent history, since they were reassigned to become the 'cores' of the subsequent divisions, were later re-formed, and were often reassigned more than once.

On 19 June 1950 the 4th Mixed Brigade was reorganised as the 4th Pursuit or Fighter Brigade in Liaoyang. Following the outbreak of the Korean War, several more changes were introduced, including the change from three regiments per brigade to only two regiments – the 2nd AR was added in addition to the original 10th AR – while the 7th Regiment of the 3rd Brigade was also assigned to the 4th Brigade albeit with its number changed to the 12th Regiment. The original 11th, 12th and 13th ARs were used to form other units. In the end, the 10th and 12th ARs were to remain under this brigade and on 31 October 1950 the 4th Air Brigade was officially renamed as the 4th Division. During that time, both ARs were the PLAAF's first combat regiments equipped with jet fighters, namely MiG-15s (plus a few Yak-12s), which were reassigned from Soviet stocks.

In this form, the 4th Division entered the Korean War in December 1950, where it showed extraordinary courage during two years and eight months of duty. Altogether

A line-up of J-7Es from the 1st Division's 2nd AR taken before 2005, when the unit was briefly allowed to wear a unit badge. (via CDF)

A J-10A assigned to the 2nd AR in 'clean' configuration. This unit is now – as the 2nd Brigade – flying the latest J-10C.
(Longshi via Top81.cn)

A superb image showing a J-11B in standard air-to-air configuration with two PL-8B short-range AAMs and two PL-12 medium-range AAMs. This is an aircraft from Batch 01.
(Wan Quan via Top81.cn)

it served four tours of duty, flew over 4,000 combat sorties and was engaged in more than 900 air combats (downing a total of 64 enemy aircraft).

Following the war, on 30 March 1956, this unit was ordered to deploy to Anshan, in Liaoning province, where it was finally reorganised as the 1st Division, consisting of three regiments.

During the 1950s and 1960s the 1st AD achieved some remarkable firsts: in 1958, the 1st and 3rd ARs were dispatched in emergency to Fujian Liancheng, to participate in the fight to recapture the coastal area in Fujian and eastern Guangdong. It was the first unit to down a BQM-147G UAV over the Suixi area, Guangdong province, and on 28 January and 18 April 1965, respectively, two more US reconnaissance UAVs were shot down over the Guangxi Ningming and Yunnan Mengzi regions. Also, in 1959, the 1st Fighter Division was one of the first units to re-equip with the J-6 fighter, and ever since has often been the first to introduce the latest and most modern fighters to service. This included the introduction of the J-11B – albeit from Block 01, still with AL-31F engines – which replaced the Su-27SK in 2008, within the 1st AR. Similarly, the 2nd AR replaced its J-7Es with J-10As in 2007 and in 2003 the 3rd AR gained J-8Fs to replace its older J-8Bs.

Today, the 1st, 2nd and 3rd ARs are no longer regiments; in mid-2017 all three were transformed into brigades. In late 2017 the 3rd Brigade was merged with the former 62nd AR and moved from Anshan to Qiqihar where it is currently receiving J-16s.

2nd Fighter Division

The 2nd Division, similar to the 1st Division, was formed in Shanghai on 25 November 1950 from the basis of the 90th Division of the 70th Army, 208th Division. It soon became the 2nd Brigade and then the 2nd Division, with the 4th and 6th Regiments subordinated, of which the 4th AR was established from the original 4th Mixed Brigade's 11th AR equipped with La-11 fighters. This unit was initially responsible for air defence of Shanghai, but also took part in the Korean War. It entered combat on 4 November 1951. It gained several achievements during the Korea War and through later campaigns. On 30 November 1951, while escorting Tu-2 bombers from the 8th Bomber Division, it shot down a USAF F-86. Another aerial victory followed on 15 April 1957, when MiG-17s from the 6th AR downed a ROCAF RF-84 reconnaissance fighter and a US Navy P4M-1Q reconnaissance aircraft was shot down over Zhoushan, Zhejiang province. In total, the 2nd Division achieved 17 kills.

A Su-27UBK together with a J-11A assigned to the 6th AR during the first joint Sino-Thai Falcon Strike exercise at Korat Royal Thai Air Force Base in November 2015. (via CDF)

In September 1968 the 2nd Fighter Division was relocated from Shanghai to its present location in Guangdong province, and in the mid-1990s became only the second PLAAF unit to convert to Russian-made Su-27 fighters.

Since then it has had an eventful history, comparable to the 1st Division. The 4th, 5th and 6th ARs are no longer regiments since the reforms of mid-2017 transformed them into brigades. Of these, the 4th Brigade – which was originally the 9th Division/27th AR – flew J-8DHs and J-8DFs before becoming assuming its current identity. In turn, it replaced its J-8D fighters with J-11As from the 6th Brigade. Meanwhile, the former 5th AR operated the J-10A/AS from 2006 but replaced this type with J-10Bs in November 2015. The former 6th AR operated J-11As for many years before the first Su-35s were delivered in December 2016, together with a few Su-30MKKs to serve as trainers for the newly established 6th Brigade.

Shortly before being converted into a brigade, the 4th AR introduced a falcon or eagle tail art.
(via www.81.cn)

3rd Fighter Division

A typical flight line of four J-11As and one Su-27UBK during an exercise, allegedly in Tibet. This unit now flies the Su-35 as the 6th Brigade. (via CDF)

Together with the 1st and the 2nd Fighter Divisions, the 3rd Division is one of the oldest and most decorated units of the PLAAF. The 3rd Fighter Division was originally established with Soviet assistance as the 3rd Pursuit Brigade (itself created from the former 209th Independent Infantry Division PLA) in Shenyang on 5 October 1950, with the 7th, 8th and 9th ARs as subordinated regiments. Following the PLAAF's decision

Crews hurry to their Su-30MKKs assigned to the 9th AR during an exercise. This scene is now consigned to history, since this unit – as the 9th Brigade – became the first in the PLAAF to operate the J-20.
(via FYJS Forum)

to reduce all divisions to a two-regiment system, the 7th AR was transferred to the 4th Division and the original 8th AR became the new 7th AR.

On 7 November 1950, the 3rd Brigade was officially converted to become the 3rd Division. At that time, it was equipped with MiG-15 fighters (plus a few Yak-12s).

The unit was involved in the Korean War from 19 October 1951 and distinguished itself in the course of close to 3,500 combat sorties and 255 aerial combats, claiming 87 enemy aircraft shot down in the process. In fact, it ranks first in the PLAAF order of downed aircraft. After the Korea War the 3rd Division initiated a complex training programme under all-weather conditions from August 1953 and thereafter became the PLAAF's first unit able to operate under 'all-weather, day and night' conditions. During the 1950s, the 3rd Fighter Division took part in clashes with Nationalist forces along the eastern Zhejiang province and helped seize control of the coastal area around Fujian and eastern Guangdong. Here, on 10 November 1956, a MiG-17 shot down a ROCAF C-46 transport over the Xiaoshan area. During the 1960s the division was redeployed to the south and southeast coasts of China, where it saw engagements with USAF fighters and UAVs over Hainan Island.

The 3rd Division was often first recipient of the most modern types: it was the first PLAAF unit to be equipped with J-7 fighters, and in the 1990s it was the first to receive the Su-27SK and later the Su-30MKK. Today its regiments are no longer active since all three were transformed into brigades in June 2017.

The former 7th AR flew J-7Bs until 2011, replacing them with the J-7E/L, but in 2017 this unit gained J-16s, while the J-7Ls were passed on to the 21st Brigade. The 8th Brigade replaced its J-7Bs with the J-10A/AS in early 2006, and these are still operational. Finally, the 9th Brigade replaced its original Su-27SK/UBKs dating from the 1990s with Su-30s around 2001 and is now the first PLAAF frontline brigade to operate the J-20A.

4th Fighter Division/Transport Division

This division is quite unusual, since the current 4th Transport Division has almost nothing in common with the original 4th Division. The decision to establish the division was made on 27 October 1950, when the 10th Regiment of the original 4th Mixed Brigade in Shanghai moved to northeast Liaoyang and founded the new 4th Fighter Brigade. Following another decision on 2 November to establish a second sub-unit, the 7th Regiment and the 7th Supply Brigade of the 3rd Brigade were ordered to be transferred to the 4th Brigade; consequently, this brigade was renamed the 4th Division with the 10th and 12th Regiments subordinated. Subsequently, the division received equipment from the 28th Division of the Soviet Air Force at Liaoyang air base; a total of 60 MiG-15 fighters and two Yak-12s as well as all necessary ground equipment were transferred.

However, on 30 March 1956, the PLAAF decided to realign the numerical system and consequently this first 4th Division became the new 1st Division. The second 4th Division was then reconstituted on 16 April 1956, again with jurisdiction over the 10th Regiment, which was formed from the 15th Division's 44th Regiment and the 12th Regiment, which was established from the 21st Division's 62nd Regiment. The two regiments were equipped with J-5 (or perhaps more likely MiG-17) and MiG-15bis fighters. At first based at Liaoyang, Shenyang province, the division was also successively stationed in Shenyang Yuhong Tun, Dongta and Liaoning Pulandian air bases. In August 1968, the 10th Regiment stationed at Kaiyuan was deployed to Shenyang Yuhongtun, and in May 1969 the 11th Brigade was transferred from Chengshahe air base to Dalian Zhoushuizi air base, while the 10th Brigade was transferred from Pulandian.

Equally confusing, the translation varies between the designation of regiments and/or brigades. As with several other units, this division saw extensive operational service and served tours of duty during the Korean War. Additionally, on 6 December 1973, the 12th Regiment transferred to Liancheng for combat duty and returned on 5 January

An interesting image showing several very early J-7Is without and some later J-7Is with the the tail-mounted brake chute. Both are from the 3rd Division's 9th AR.
(via CDF)

Today the 4th Transport Division operates both the latest Y-9 and Y-20A, but the Y-8C is still the workhorse within the 11th AR.
(Feng Jian)

The 4th Transport Division was the first PLAAF unit to operate the latest Y-9 (top), which is operated by the 10th AR, and the Y-20A (left), assigned to the 12th AR.
(Both Feng Jian)

1975. Similar, the 10th Regiment went to Yunnan Mengzi in February 1985 and returned in September 1985.

The next change occurred in 1989, when the 12th Regiment became a dedicated night-fighter group. It was originally equipped with J-6As but later received the J-7D. Another operational deployment followed in February 1992, when the 11th Regiment (it is unknown when this third regiment was added) deployed to Lushan. This mission ended in late November. Another change occurred in 2002, when the division was rated as a military training unit. Since its establishment, the division has mostly been stationed in the Liaodong peninsula, where it is responsible for air defence missions in the Bohai Bay area along the Beijing-Tianjin front.

Even though the first 4th Division was well known, this second 4th Division has remained largely unknown. Consequently, in line with another round of reorganisations in 2003, the division's 10th and 12th Regiments were retained but transferred to the 30th Division within the same military region. As such, the second 4th Division was de facto disbanded.

Thanks to good luck and in order to carry forward the traditions of the 4th Division, the PLAAF reconstituted the third 4th Division in July 2005. This time, however,

it was no longer a fighter unit, but a transport division at Qionglai subordinated to the Chengdu MRAF. During 2009-12 the base at Qionglai was refurbished and expanded. In mid-2012 the 10th AR received ithe first Y-9 transports and in mid-2016 the 12th AR became the first regiment to introduce the Y-20A.

5th Ground Attack Division

The 5th Division's origins lie within the 206th Division of the former 69th Army. It was established at Kaiyuan, in Liaoning province in December 1950 and was initially equipped with Il-10s left behind after the withdrawal of the Soviet forces. From the beginning it had two regiments subordinated, the 13th and 15th Regiments, and later the 14th Regiment was added.

The 13th and 15th Regiments completed several tours of duty during the Korean War and on 21 August 1958 both were ordered to prepare an emergency transfer to take part in the bomber attack on Kinmen Island. In addition to Il-10 ground-attack aircraft, the unit received the MiG-15bis before transitioning later to the indigenous Q-5.

In November 1967 the 5th Division was ordered to take part in the PLAAF's test mission to research the use of tactical nuclear weapons and it was decided to use a modified Q-5. The resulting Q-5A was ready by 1970 and in October 1970 six modified Q-5As were transferred to Dingxin on standby. However, due to several problems with the bomb, the unit was again withdrawn in early 1971. After solving these issues, the unit was reassigned again on 8 September 1971, and on 30 October a Q-5A from the 14th Regiment took off with a live bomb loaded. Unfortunately, technical problems prevented release of the bomb (after three failed attempts). In the end, the test was successfully repeated on 7 January 1972 at Lop Nor.

Very little is known about its subsequent history except that at some point this division had three regiments equipped with several Q-5 variants. The 13th and 14th regiments were disbanded in June 2017, while the 15th AR – which had replaced its Q-5s with JH-7As in 2007 - was transformed into the 15th Brigade at around the same time.

A very rare image depicting not only the full complement of 28 early Q-5s assigned to the 13th AR, but also the two-tone brown-tan camouflage and white serial numbers.
(via Top81.cn)

Another rare image of a Q-5D from the 15th AR in its typical green camouflage. Unusual, however, is the red serial number, which was later applied in white only.
(via CDF)

These two Q-5 variants were the last to be flown before the 13th AR was disbanded in June 2017. At top is a Q-5J and below a Q-5L with the rarely seen K/PZS-01H laser designator pod. (Both via CDF)

6th Fighter Division

The 6th Division was established at Anshan in Liaoning in November 1950, based on the 170th Division of the original Independent Infantry. It had jurisdiction over the 16th and 18th Regiments with its main task to provide air defence over key industrial cities in northeastern China. Reportedly, the unit was equipped with MiG-9s and MiG-15s.

In December 1951 the 6th Division deployed to take part in the Korean War and the division's first kill was logged on 22 February 1952 when the 18th Regiment shot down a B-26 bomber. The unit completed several tours of duty during the Korean War and was credited with downing 26 enemy aircraft plus five damaged, ranking overall fifth in the PLAAF's combat record.

In April 1966 the 6th Division was transferred to the Lanzhou MRAF in order to strengthen the air defence forces in the northwest region. By mid-April it had arrived at Linyi air base, where it became the first fighter unit within the Lanzhou MR. On 17 June 1967, the 16th Brigade was involved in China's first hydrogen bomb test and provided seven J-6s for sampling particles in the cloud after the explosion. After Korea, the next operational deployment was in June 1971, when the 18th Regiment dispatched 19 J-6

A line-up of J-7Bs from the 16th AR in the typical scheme worn from the 1970s to the 1990s: plain white colours overall and red serial numbers. (via CDF)

fighters to Liancheng air base facing Fujian. Overall, a total of 668 sorties were flown including 167 aerial combats before the unit returned to Zhongchuan air base in Gansu in December.

Another first came in mid-December 1971 with the first assignment of J-6s to Lhasa Gongga air base in Tibet, becoming the first fighter unit to begin training on the Tibetan Plateau. During the 1980s, the 6th Division successively organised several regular detachments of the 18th Regiment to Tibet.

Much less is known about its recent history, and only two of its regiments survive after being transformed into brigades in July 2017. The 16th Brigade is the successor to the original 16th AR, which was disbanded in 2003 and eventually transformed into a military region training base (MRTB) flying J-7Bs. Sometime later the former 47th Division, 140th AR, took over the regimental number: this was the final unit to operate the original J-8IE and in line with this transfer the unit had re-equipped with J-11As by 2002.

The 16th AR became the 16th Brigade around July 2017 and, unusually, the unit's aircraft wear a prominent unit marking in the form of a yellow lion's head. The 18th Brigade is the second surviving regiment, formerly assigned to the 6th Fighter Division, but very little is known about its subsequent history. It flew J-6s for most of the 1960s and 1970s, receiving J-7s in the 1980s. The unit merged with the deactivated 47th Attack Division in 2003-04 and regained a third regiment by incorporating the former Lanzhou MRTB. In 2017 the 18th AR was transformed into the 18th Brigade – still flying J-7Hs. Its aircraft wear a prominent red and yellow hawk's head as the unit marking.

Images of Su-27s and, later, J-11s assigned to the 6th Division are extremely seldom. This is the only known example showing a J-11BS assigned to the 16th AR. (via CMA)

7th Fighter Division

The 7th Division was established on 8 December 1950 at Dongfeng in Jilin province and was based on the 168th Infantry Division's 512th and 503th Regiments. It had two subordinated regiments, the 18th and 19th Regiments. However, on 23 January 1951 the 18th Regiment was renamed as the 21st Regiment. On 10 December 1951 the division moved to Beijing Nanyuan, with other elements being based at Yangcun air base,

Similar to the 6th Division's 16th AR, the 7th Division's 21st AR also flew J-7Bs. The only difference was their serial numbers.
(Weimeng via Top81.cn)

where they received the pilots and 67 MiG-9 fighters from the 17th Division. In this form, the 7th Division was mainly used as a supplementary training division and it was not until August 1953 that it assumed the task of providing air defence for the capital and northern China, as well as continuing training pilots for the combat regiments. On 15 December 1953 elements from both the 19th and 21st Regiments were brought together establish the 20th Regiment, also equipped with MiG-9s. Between October 1954 and January 1955, the 19th and 21st Regiments completed training to convert to the MiG-15bis, followed by the 20th Regiment from March to April 1956. Interestingly, besides serving as a fighter unit and still being responsible for training, the 7th Division was tasked in 1956 with establishment of the air force's 81st 'Ba Yi' aerial demonstration team for aerial escort of Chinese and foreign political leaders and aerial demonstration tasks.

On 28 November 1959, the 7th Division was ordered to transfer from Luqiao air base to Jinjiang and on 23 January 1960 the 19th Regiment was relocated to Hui'an air base to take part in combat missions. It returned home to Yangcun in July.

Another change was introduced in January 1960, when an independent night-fighter brigade was formed. Two years later, on 29 January 1962, in accordance with Premier Zhou Enlai's instructions, the 19th Regiment was formally formed as the PLAAF's Escort and Air Show Brigade, which became the predecessor of the PLAAF's 'Ba Yi'. This unit was at first equipped with JJ-5 trainers and was officially still listed as the 19th Regiment's 4th Brigade (?) stationed at Yangcun. In July 1968, this unit was assigned to the 38th Division and in August 1964 both the 19th and 20th Regiments were reorganised into the 19th, 20th, 21st Brigades plus the dedicated 1st Flight Performance Brigade.

During one of the numerous clashes between the PRC and ROC forces on the southeastern coast on 26 August 1965, the 20th Brigade provided air cover during 124 sorties and ensured that the navy was able to sink two enemy ships. Another first was the re-equipment of the 19th Brigade in April 1967 with four J-7 prototypes; later, this unit became the first to receive J-7 fighters. On 10 August 1969 a new 20th Brigade was formed at Zhangjiakou based on elements of the 21st Brigade and the original 20th Brigade, which was transferred to the 41st Division.

These very early J-7Is were also assigned to the 21st AR.
(via CDF)

The 7th Division's 19th AR briefly flew Su-27SKs, J-11As and Su-27UBKs before it converted to the latest J-11B/BS in 2016. (via CDF)

In line with the 1970 reform, the three brigades were renamed the 19th, 20th and 21st Regiments. Between October 1970 and June 1978 this division took part in six missions to counter enemy air balloons and shot down 56 examples. Consequently, in early 1976 the 19th Regiment formed a dedicated anti-balloon team. Yet another operational mission was in February 1979, when the 19th Regiment and its J-7s were transferred from Zhangjiakou to Tianyang, to take part in the conflict against Vietnam. A total of 714 sorties were flown between 17 February and 31 May. Another deployment was then ordered between May 1982 and July 1983, detachments of the 19th Regiment with J-7s being transferred from Zhangjiakou to Mengzi. A first round of force reductions was initiated in October 1985, when the independent brigade was disbanded, but at the same time the 20th Regiment began training on the latest J-7B variant. Between April and August 1989, the 19th Regiment was again ordered to go to Lhasa Gongga air base in Tibet. The next round of reductions occurred in November 1992, when the 21st Regiment (the JJ-5 training group) was withdrawn only to be re-established shortly afterwards, when the 38th Division was abolished and its 113th Regiments became the new 21st Regiment.

Little is known about its subsequent history except that today the 7th Division is no longer extant, since it was disbanded in July 2017 and the regiments became brigades. As such the 19th AR flew J-7s before it gained J-11Bs in 2016 before becoming the 19th Brigade. The still unconfirmed 20th AR was most likely a regiment of the Beijing MRTB prior to October 1988, when the 17th Division was reorganised and that training regiment was subordinated in 2012 as the 20th AR, still operating J-7Bs. However, since 2017 its status is unconfirmed and it is likely to have been disbanded. Finally, the 21st AR – which was transformed into the 21st Brigade in 2017 – replaced its old J-7Bs with J-7Ls at around the same time, the new jets being reassigned from the disbanded 7th and 42nd ARs.

The new, only partly glazed airliner-style nose section gives the HU-6 a sleeker and more modern appearance than the regular bomber variants. (zhang81zhang via Top81.cn)

8th Bomber Division

This bomber division was formed on 27 November 1950 at Siping, Jilin province, on the basis of the 168th Division, from the former Northeast Military Region. As such it belonged to the Northeast MRAF. At the beginning, the division consisted of a high-altitude transport brigade and some other troops, which together formed the 22nd Regiment, reportedly under the jurisdiction of the original 504th Army Infantry Regiment. Meanwhile, the original 510th Army Infantry Regiment formed the 24th Regiment. Each regiment had three flight groups (or brigades?). The flight cadres were essentially drawn from the original 12th Regiment of the very first 4th Mixed Brigade.

Early in this period, the 8th Division was equipped with 70 aircraft: 64 Tu-2 bombers, four Tu-2U trainers and two liaison/communication aircraft. On 13 October 1951 it was transferred to Shenyang Yuhong to participate in the Korean War. During the conflict, the division was praised for its morale and combat effectiveness and it was involved in several bombing raids. On 30 October 1950 a Tu-2 from the 24th Regiment was able to down an F-86. However, in this same raid, a total of four Tu-2 bombers and three escorting La-11 fighters were lost. In July 1952 six Tu-2 bombers, together with several La-9s from the 9th Division, were merged into a mixed regiment and based at Guanghan air base in Sichuan, to assist ground forces of the Southwest MR. After Korea, the next operational deployment was in August 1958, when the 22nd and 24th Regiments were transferred from Wuhu, Anhui province and Nanjing, Jiangsu province to Jiangxi Yushu (Changshu) air base. From here they participated in the struggle to seize air superiority along the coast of Fujian and eastern Guangdong and assisted in the blockade of the enemy-occupied Kinmen/Quemoy Islands. Immediately after the Taiwan crisis, the 22nd Regiment with its Il-28 bombers, and several Tu-2s from the 23rd Division, were relocated to Wugong in Shaanxi in April 1959 to strengthen

This H-6H wore an unusual serial number with an '8' as its second digit. The reson for this is not known, but this aircraft was on display at the Zhuhai Airshow in 2010.
(via CDF)

Today the 8th Bomber Division operates two regiments flying the latest H-6K. This aircraft is assigned to the 22nd AR and carries an unusual missile training store.
(via PDF)

the Western Front. From there they took part in several counter-insurgency missions against rebels and were also detached to Qinghai Golmud.

Much less is known about its more recent history. It was based at both Datong and Wenshui prior to 1999, but after 1 October 1999 it was merged with the 48th Bomber Division from the Guangzhou MRAF and has been based at Leiyang since 2003. The status of this important division was long unclear, though it was understood to have been reduced to two regiments, when the original 23rd AR was disbanded in August 1985. In July 1999 it gained a third regiment once again, when the former 48th Division's 143rd AR – since 1992 an independent regiment – was reassigned to the 8th Bomber Division and finally renumbered to become the 23rd AR in 2002.

When the 8th Division gained its first H-6 is unclear; it is also unknown when these first H-6As were replaced by H-6Es and then by H-6H models. In mid-2012 the 24th AR started receiving the first operational H-6Ks and in 2015 the 22nd AR followed suit, replacing the H-6H. Since then this division has operated three regiments, two flying the latest H-6Ks and the 23rd operating all HU-6 tankers from the former 48th Division.

9th Fighter Division

When the 9th Air Division was first formed at Jilin in December 1950, it was mainly responsible for air defence duty around key industrial cities in the northeast. It was initially equipped with La-9 fighters and consisted of the 25th and 27th Regiments as subordinated units. However, it was transferred to Naval Aviation on 25 September 1955 and was re-formed on 7 December as the 6th Naval Aviation Division.

The second 9th Division was re-established on March 1956 in Guangzhou, in order to strengthen air defence capabilities in the southern sector, especially in Guangdong. This division achieved its first kill on 5 January 1958, when a MiG-15bis assigned to the 27th Regiment damaged a ROCAF F-84 over Pingtan Island, Fujian province; the Taiwanese fighter later crashed. In August the same year, the 27th Regiment was ordered to make an emergency transfer to Zhangzhou, Fujian province, to take part in the campaign to establish air superiority over Fujian and the eastern coastal areas of Guangdong. In this campaign, another kill was credited on 7 August, when a J-5 damaged an F-86 over the Jinjiang area.

In another aerial combat over Zhangzhou on 25 August 1958 two ROCAF aircraft were downed, but due one J-5 was mistakenly shot by 'friendly fire', killing the pilot. Since then, there have been several more air defence operations in the southwest and south-central regions and the 9th Division has been frequently involved. One such inci-

A line-up of J-6s and even a J-5 (far right) from the 25th AR, with serial numbers clearly visible. Interestingly, it shows both early J-6s in the foreground and radar-equipped J-6As.
(via CDF)

Two J-8Ds from the 27th AR with their removable refuelling probes. The green radome was characteristic for the J-8D and J-8B Block 02. (via CDF)

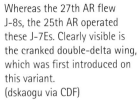

Whereas the 27th AR flew J-8s, the 25th AR operated these J-7Es. Clearly visible is the cranked double-delta wing, which was first introduced on this variant. (dskaogu via CDF)

dent, on 24 December 1965, involved a J-6 that downed a US BQM-147 UAV above the Mengzi area in Yunnan. Another incident occurred on 5 October the same year, when four J-6s from the 25th Regiment shot down a US reconnaissance aircraft over the Guangxi, Pingxiang and Longzhou area in Guangxi. On 5 March 1966 another UAV was shot down over the Nanning area of Guangxi. These events combined with the division's overall performance resulted in a very good reputation within the PLAAF.

Very little is known about the more recent activities of this unit. Until 2012 it was a standard division operating three regiments equipped with J-7Bs, and later J-7Ds, plus J-7Es and J-8Ds. The 27th AR was transferred to the 2nd Division as the new 4th AR, the 25th AR disbanded and the remaining 26th AR became the 26th Brigade in 2017. It is noteworthy that the 26th AR was formerly the 35th Division, 103rd AR, which was disbanded in December 2009 before the unit received J-10A and J-10AS fighters.

A fine image of a regular H-6A from the 28th AR. Today this unit flies the H-6K, including one example with the same serial number.
(via Top81.cn)

10th Bomber Division

The 10th Division was formed on 17 January 1951. It originally consisted of the former 66th Infantry Division's 196th Regiment, the 12th Regiment from the original 4th Mixed Brigade, and the 12th Supply Brigade at Nanjing, in Jiangsu province. It was initially equipped with Tu-2 bombers and commanded by a former Nationalist B-24 pilot. The 30th Regiment received its pilots on 5 February and flight training begun on 12 February. Consequently – since its origins can be traced back to the very first PLAAF bomber unit – the 10th Bomber Division is one of the oldest units of its kind within the PLAAF. Due to its excellent flight safety record for the tenth consecutive year, this division received the honorary title of 'Flying Safety Red Flag Division' in April 1964. This is the most prestigious honorary title awarded by the highest commanding department of the PLA in peacetime.

Soon after its foundation this division began to be regularly called into action for special missions including bombing ice floes on the frozen Yellow River. This has been undertaken since March 1951 and is still a routine duty of the division. The unit was also involved in several nuclear tests and experimental exercises.

In early April 1951, a combined large-scale exercise of fighters and bomber trained together for the first time. This involved La-11s from the 2nd Division's 4th Regiment from Shanghai Jiangwan and Tu-2s from the 28th Regiment from Nanjing. Besides that, the 10th Division participated in the Korean War, while it was active in the provinces of Hebei and Shenyang during the 1950s. Soon after its foundation, the division was relocated to Liaoyang in northeastern China. Its first combat mission was allegedly in the night of 29 November 1951, when Tu-2 bombers from the 28th Regiment took off from Liaoyang air base and bombed three US warships. Lacking any night bombing experience, the pilots were unable find the target and all bombs missed; this was the first time the PLAAF carried out a night bombing mission. After the war, in January 1955, the unit received equipment from the Soviet Air Force in the Luda area. Reportedly, the 3rd Brigade of the 28th Regiment received its first Il-28 bombers to form a dedicated reconnaissance brigade. In November 1955 the 30th Regiment participated in an anti-landing exercise on the Liaodong Peninsula. Around one year later in September 1956, the 10th Air Division was transferred from Qijiahar Sanjiazi air base in Heilongjiang province to Tangshan in Hebei province, and was placed under the command of the Beijing MRAF. New equipment was introduced in August 1957, when the first Il-28

A rare image of an HD-5
electronic warfare aircraft
assigned to the 10th Bomber
Division. This particular aircraft
is today on display at the China
Aviation Museum, the former
Datangshan Museum.
(via FYJS Forum)

electronic reconnaissance aircraft were imported from the Soviet Union; they began
to undertake electronic reconnaissance missions in spring 1958. New capabilities were
added in November 1959, when a modified Il-28 electronic reconnaissance aircraft was
refitted with two jammers, making it the PLAAF's first electronic jamming aircraft.

In the 1970s, the 10th Division was involved in several nuclear tests, including on
25 April 1968, when H-5 bombers were transferred to No. 20 Base (Lop Nor). However,
the first true drop of a nuclear device occurred only on 27 June 1973. Another successful test followed on 17 June 1974, again from an H-5. Consequently, in November
1976, the division was declared a strategic force and is believed to be the PLAAF's first-
line nuclear strike division that plays an important part in China's nuclear deterrence.
In November 1980 the indigenous HD-5 electronic warfare variant of the H-5 became
operational within the 10th Division.

Once again, more recent history is much less documented. The unit must have
gained indigenous H-6 bombers sometime during the 1970s and 1980s to equip two of
the three regiments, while the third regiment was used to establish the 48th Division
and later re-formed as an independent electronic warfare regiment, before being re-
equipped with a mix of specialised Y-8 variants and reassigned to the division in 2003.

An H-6K operated by the 28th
AR. Following the 8th Bomber
Division's 24th AR, this was the
second regiment to re-equip
with this variant.
(Yang Pan via chinamil.com)

In 2012 the 30th Air Regiment was disbanded, its base at Nanjing/Dajiaochang was closed and the Y-8s were transferred to re-establish the 20th Division. In parallel, the 28th AR gained the first H-6K and transferred its older H-6Hs to the replace H-6As within the 29th AR in 2013. By 2017 the 30th AR had been re-established, gaining H-6Ms from the 36th Division's 108th AR; currently this division operates all air force H-6 variants.

The 30th AR was re-established in 2017 and is today the sole regiment operating the H-6M, an interim variant capable of using the KD-20 cruise missile and fielded before the H-6K became operational.
(via CMA)

11th Ground Attack Division

In January 1951, the 11th Division was established in Xuzhou, Jiangsu province, consisting of the original 86th Infantry Division's 256th and 258th Regiments. Ever since, this has been a ground-attack division and initially had three subordinated regiments: the 31st, 32nd and 33rd Regiments. However, its affiliation has been changed several times, and it has belonged to the East China MRAF, the Nanjing MRAF and – after 1999 – to the Shenyang MRAF.

In July 1951 the newly formed 11th Division was ordered to prepare for the Korean War and on 13 October the same year it arrived at Dongfeng air base in Jilin province. However, it returned to Xuzhou in December. Then, between November 1954 and August 1958, the 11th Division saw involvement in battles with Nationalists along the eastern coast of China, where its Il-10s participated in the liberation of coastal islands in eastern Zhejiang.

A total of 78 sorties were flown, especially against facilities on Dachen and Yijiangshan Islands. Allegedly, its main task during the first strike wave was suppressing enemy artillery positions in order to provide security for the subsequent 20th Division and their Tu-2 bombers. Other important missions until the end of the campaign were attacks against command posts, long-range artillery positions and against radar positions on Dachen Island.

The next operational deployment began on 25 August 1964, when the 33rd Regiment entered Fuzhou air base and reportedly claimed a – still-valid – record for ultra-low-altitude bombing (130ft/40m). A minor change occurred in June 1970, when the 31st, 32nd and 33rd Brigades (it is not clear when these became brigades) were again changed to the 31st, 32nd and 33rd Regiments and Siping air base was formally established.

Even though the 11th Ground Attack Division operated Q-5 variants for a long period, images of the Q-5D are quite seldom. These are from the 31st AR.
(Both Top81.cn)

On 8 October 1984 the 32nd Regiment relocated to Lushan in Yunnan and in April 1985 it returned home. However, the following October the 32nd Regiment was disbanded, and merged with the 33rd Regiment.

The next round of reorganisations and downsizing occurred on 30 September 1992, when the 11th and the 22nd Divisions were merged into the new 11th Division and the 22nd Division was disbanded together with the disbandment of the 33rd Regiment. The two former 22nd Division regiments, the 64th and 65th, were then renamed as the new 32nd and 33rd Regiments respectively and assigned to the 11th Division.

Since then not much is known: the Q-5Ds were replaced by JH-7As in 2009, prior to the merger in 2012. Today, the only confirmed active unit is the 31st Brigade, whereas operations for the 32nd AR most likely ended in 2017. The former 33rd AR was transformed in 2012 to become the 90th Brigade, but there are still reports of a new 33rd Brigade operating J-7s since 2018.

Successor to the Q-5D within the 31st AR was the JH-7A, introduced from 2009. This regiment is the only one to have survived the merger with the 22nd Division. Today it is the 31st Brigade.
(via CDF)

12th Fighter Division

The 12th Division's predecessor was the 66th Division of the 22nd Army of the former Third Field Army. On 23 December 1950, on orders from the Central Military Commission (CMC), it was reorganised into the 12th Division in Xiaoshan County, Zhejiang province. At first, the 34th and 36th Regiments, plus two supply brigades, were subordinated. As of late January 1951 the 12th Division was stationed in Shanghai, with the 36th Regiment based at Hongqiao, both responsible for the protection of Shanghai. At around the same time, the division received its personnel and on 13 February 1951, formation was completed. Its first fighters were accepted on 1 April 1951, when it received equipment from division of the Soviet Air Force in Shanghai, which transferred 62 MiG-9s, five Yak-17s, two Yak-11s and two Yak-12s. Thereafter, on 17 September 1951, it became responsible for air defence in Shanghai, but on 24 December that year the division was ordered to prepare for the Korean War. On 20 March 1952 the division arrived at Dagushan air base and joined the ranks of the Chinese People's Volunteer Air Force.

Actual combat began on 10 June 1952, when the 12th Division entered the fight, and a first aerial battle for the division took place on the 11th, when the 34th Regiment scrambled eight aircraft in the south of the Zhangzhou area and encountered several USAF F-86s. Altogether, three Sabres were shot down. Several more encounters took place between June 1952 and March 1953 and altogether 3,075 sorties were logged. The division was involved in 84 aerial combats and shot down or damaged 67 enemy aircraft, putting it in overall third place in the PLAAF combat record. In late March 1953 the 12th Division was transferred from Dagushan to Liaoyang air base in order to defend the second line and train new pilots. Therefore, the 34th Regiment continued to serve as a combat unit, while the 36th Regiment was reassigned to the training role.

Unfortunately, little is known about its more recent history: it is not known if the division also participated in fighting against the Nationalists in the late 1950s.

The 36th Regiment was later re-equipped with J-6As and even J-6IIIs from the mid-1960s, and received J-7Is, and later J-7Bs, from the mid-1980s. Since then its history

Images of older types showing their full serial numbers are rare. This image of J-6As is especially so, since the nearest aircraft displays the old pre-2005 serial number system.
(via Top81.cn)

The 12th Division's 35th AR was one of the last units to operate the original J-8II and is now most likely disbanded. This interesting image showing one J-8IIs with an engine flame-out was taken in 2007. (via Top81.cn)

This J-10AS is flown by the 12th Division's 34th AR, a unit that is today the 34th Brigade. (via Top81.cn)

is somewhat confusing but the division was reported to comprise regiments based at Jinan, Gaomi and Wendeng. Around the same time, a 35th Regiment was also formed, and this flew the oldest surviving J-8IIs from 2003. Its current status is unclear and it is most likely disbanded. The 36th AR was based at Jinan until 2010, when that air base was abandoned due to urban developments and relocated to a new air base at Qihe.

In 2012 the 36th gained new J-10As and changed its number plate to the 34th AR. At the same time the old 34th AR became the new 36th and renumbered its J-7Gs accordingly when both units became brigades in 2017. Since 2012-13 it has operated the J-7G, replacing J-7Bs. Interestingly, the former 'old' 34th AR stems from the previous Jinan MRTB, which was formed in 1988 from the original 31st Division, 91st AR. Later, the Jinan MRTB was merged with the Nanjing MRTB – which was, in fact, the former 32nd Division, 94th AR prior to 1988 – as the 34th AR.

13th Transport Division

The 13th Transport Division traces its heritage back to the PLA's Southwest Military Region Airlift Group, established in April 1950 at Xinjin Xi'an in Sichuan province. It was originally equipped with C-46s and C-47s left behind by the Nationalists. On 24 November 1950, immediately after it had received its first Il-12 transports from the Soviet Union, the group was expanded and re-designated as the High-Altitude Airlift Regiment, with three brigades under its jurisdiction. It was equipped with 36 Il-12s and nine C-46s. Approval to be transformed into a division was granted by the Central Military Commission (CMC) on 17 March 1951 and, by using personnel transferred from the 2nd Flying School at Changchun, this regiment was finally expanded to become the 13th Transport Division on 24 April 1951. At the time, the division was mainly responsible for airdrop missions to supply the 18th Army of the PLA.

The division was officially established in Sichuan Xinjin, Sichuan province. During that time it had jurisdiction over the 37th Regiment, which was a dedicated high-altitude transport group, and the 39th Regiment, acting as a 2nd Flying School high-altitude transport training brigade with a total of 48 aircraft (36 Il-12s, 11 C-46s and one C-47). Throughout the 1950s its units were intensively involved in operations against the insurgencies in Tibet and western China.

During the early 1960s and through the 1970s, the unit was in action on the Sino-Indian border, in the Paracel Islands/Xisha Island conflict with Vietnam and on the Sino-Vietnamese border. In 1962 the 13th Division was assigned to the 15th Airborne Corps. In 1964 one of its Il-12s was used to collect atmospheric samples following China's first nuclear bomb test. In 1966 the 13th Transport Division was partially re-equipped with Soviet-made An-12 transports, and two years later was reassigned from the 15th Airborne Corps to the Wuhan MRAF, to which it remained subordinated until 1985. Besides operational missions, this division proved valuable in different emer-

When the Il-76MD entered service with the 13th Transport Division during the early 1990s it wore this quasi-civil colour scheme. Today, nearly all have been repainted in a tactical light grey and this division's 38th and 39th ARs are the only two units flying the Il-76. (via Top81.cn)

The 13th Transport Division's third regiment is the 37th AR, which still operates Y-8Cs, which are often used by the airborne forces.
(Hunterchen via Top81.cn)

gency situations, including flood and earthquake relief and transporting heavy equipment to fight forest fires. It was also involved in several scientific test flights and supported civil aviation transport.

Currently, the division still has three subordinated regiments. The 37th AR still operates Y-8C transports regularly assigned to the airborne troops. The 38th AR flew the An-26 and Y-7 for many years, replaced in 2013 by Il-76MD/TDs and three Il-78 tankers. The final regiment, the 39th AR, was for a long time the only PLAAF operator of the Il-76MD transport.

14th Fighter Division

The decision to form the 14th Division was issued by the Central Military Commission (CMC) on 18 August 1950 and it was officially established on 14 February 1951 at Beijing Nanyuan air base on the basis of the 95th Infantry Division from the East China MR. The newly established division was placed under the command of the North China MR and had two subordinated regiments: the original 95th Division's 284th Regiment was reorganised into the 40th Regiment, while the original 285th Regiment became the 42nd Regiment. The newly formed division received its equipment on 7 April 1951 from a Soviet Air Force division. Then based in Nanyuan it was responsible for air defence of the capital and comprised 58 MiG-9s and two Yak-17s. Between November 1951 and August 1953, the 14th Division participated in the Korean War and was credited with 12 enemy aircraft downed. Although in retrospect the division's Korean War record seems average, it played a crucial and celebrated role in the air battles on the Fujian front line.

The most important raid occurred on 10 October 1958, when the ROCAF launched an air offensive, dispatching 44 waves comprising 182 sorties to provoke the mainland. During one aerial battle, a flight of six F-86s rushed into Fuqing and Longtian in Fujian

The J-7L is the final PLAAF version of the venerable 'Fishbed' family, here operated by the 42nd AR. Its current status is unclear.
(VF-154 via Top81.cn)

and a flight of eight MiG-17s from the 42nd Regiment scrambled to intercept them. During the aerial combat that followed, one pilot shot down two enemy aircraft but his own aircraft was seriously damaged and he was killed in the subsequent crash. Altogether, the 14th Division shot down three enemy aircraft during this air battle.

Much less is known about its more recent history. On 17 September 1968 the division was transferred to Xiangtang, Jiangxi province, and placed under the Fuzhou MRAF until this MR was disbanded in August 1985. After operating J-5s and J-6s during the 1950s and 1960s, the unit was re-equipped with J-7s in the 1980s and somewhere in between it gained the 41st Regiment as its third subordinated regiment. Currently the status of these three former regiments is only confirmed for the 40th and 41st, which became brigades in June 2017.

During the first round of reorganisations in 2012, the original 41st AR was transferred to become the 86th Brigade in 2012. However, it was soon replaced by the former 86th AR, 29th Division, which was renumbered as the 41st Air Regiment in due course before moving to Wuyishan. Subsequently, both the 40th AR and 41st AR were re-equipped with J-11As and Su-27UBKs; by around June 2017 both had been turned into brigades. Since December 2017 the 40th Brigade has been equipped with J-16s, with its J-11s going to the 55th Brigade in the CTC. The status of the 42nd AR is still unclear.

A J-11A from the 40th AR in 'clean' configuration with only the typical Sorbtsiya ECM pods on the wingtips. This unit is now the 40th Brigade and has flown the J-16 since late 2017.
(via FYJS Forum)

15th Ground Attack Division

The predecessor of the 15th Division was the 71st Division of the 24th Army within the 3rd Field Army, which was reorganised in October 1950 into a PLAAF unit within the Minhang District, Shanghai. Two months later, in December 1950, the 71st Division was temporarily assigned under the PLAAF's headquarters of the Central South MR, where from early May onwards it was stationed at Jilin Gongzhuling air base and officially reorganised as the 15th Division on 31 May. The 1st and 2nd Regiments under the original jurisdiction were re-formed into the 43rd and 45th Regiments, respectively, and in September the division received a total of 84 aircraft from the Soviet Air Force. Around a year after its foundation, in October 1951 the 15th Division was ordered to participate in the Korean War. Beginning on 19 February 1952, it took part in operational missions. During the months from mid-April it was involved in numerous aerial combats which included the downing of several enemy aircraft. In early September, it was transferred to Dongfeng air base and, by mid-September, the original MiG-15s were replaced by 52 MiG-15bis fighters, while the MiG-15s went to the 6th Division. Following completion of the conversion, the 15th Division was ordered to enter the war for the second time, in November 1952. The division was involved in a total of 76 aerial battles, flying 2,927 sorties and shooting down 51 enemy aircraft as well as damaging 16 more; with this, the division achieved fourth place in the PLAAF ranking.

Very little is known of its history following the end of the Korean assignment, except that it received Q-5s from the former 50th Attack Division during the 2003–04 reorganisations, when it became a ground attack division. Somewhere in between the 44th Regiment was added. As of around 2012 it was the only PLAAF division known to operate from bases within another MR, since one of its regiments was based at Suizhoung, in Liaoning province (Shenyang MR). Today, only two of its former regiments survive as reorganised brigades: the 43rd Brigade remained after the 15th Division was divided in 2017 and the 44th was transferred to the Northern Theater Command (NTC). The 43rd AR was one of the last units to operate the J-7C/D, which it did until February 2012, when it received J-10As.

In 2017 the 43rd AR was transformed into the 43rd Brigade. The 44th Brigade was transferred to the NTC, while the other two remained within the Central Theater Command. It was originally assigned to the 7th Division as the 20th AR flying J-7Bs, but

Another rare image showing three of the few J-7Ds in operational service wearing the old pre-2005 serial numbers. (via FYJS Forum)

Although rated as a ground-attack division, the 15th Division usually operated fighter types like the J-10A (left) within the 43rd AR and the J-7G (right) within the 44th AR.
(Left: via Top81.cn,
Right: via CDF)

gained J-7Gs in 2010 from the 'Ba Yi' demonstration team, and in 2012 it was merged into the 15th Division as the new 44th Regiment. In 2017 the 44th Regiment became the 44th Brigade. The status of the 45th AR is currently unconfirmed and it is most likely disbanded. Established once in August 1985 as the 50th Division's 149th AR, this was subordinated to the 8th Bomber Division in May 1986, still as the 149th AR. In April 2005 the 149th AR was resubordinated to the 15th Ground Attack Division as the new 45th AR and by 2017 the final remaining Q-5s had been withdrawn from use.

16th Fighter Division/Specialised Division

Dating back to 28 February 1951, the 16th Division was formally established at Liuting air base in Shandong province, based on the 58th and 60th Regiments of the 7th Army Division. It then had two regiments under its jurisdiction, the 46th and the 48th Regiments. Its initial equipment of 44 MiG-15s and nine Yak-17s was transferred on 15 May from a Soviet Air Force division based in Qingdao. Around two years after, on 25 January 1953, the division were relocated to Liaodong Dagushan air base to participate in the Korean War and, on 26 March 1953, the 48th Regiment downed its first US aircraft.

Another rare image of several early J-6s without the brake chute installed and with the original pre-2005 serial numbers.
(via hangkongnet.com)

Like all transport, bomber and specialised divisions, the 16th Division is still active, today flying JZ-8F reconnaissance aircraft within the 46th AR. (Longshi via Top81.cn)

Until the end of its deployment, the division clocked up 693 sorties and shot down and damaged one enemy aircraft each.

After the war, in May 1954, the 47th Regiment was added as the division's third regiment. It was formed in Sanyuanpu, Jilin province and in November 1954, the 16th Division received new MiG-15bis fighters, again from a Soviet division in Langtou and Dadonggou. On 10 May 1955, eight 46th Regiment MiG-15bis were involved in an intense combat against 12 F-86s and during the battle one fighter from each side was downed. On 27 April 1956 the 48th Regiment of the 16th Division participated in a joint military intercept exercise between the Shenyang MRAF and the Soviet Air Force in the Far East Military Region. From mid-August 1958 onwards, the 16th Division was stationed at Longtian air base and was one of the first units to enter the fray in that crisis, to seize control of airspace above the far eastern provinces and islands. Several battles were fought, again downing some enemy aircraft. In total, the 163th Division shot down six enemy aircraft and damaged four, as well as downing three reconnaissance balloons. Then, on 4 April 1959, the 16th Division returned home from Liancheng to Shenyang Yu Hongtun. Slightly earlier, in March 1959, a dedicated night-fighter brigade was established at Pulandian.

In February 1960 the 47th Regiment was transferred to the 32nd Division and renamed as the 96th Regiment. In June 1961 the night- fighter brigade was re-formed into a divisional independent brigade. Furher changes occurred through the mid-1960s: in August 1964, the 46th and 48th Regiments were changed into the 46th and 48th Brigades; at around the same time, the 47th Brigade was re-established and the independent brigade became an independent regiment (possibly the 4th Independent Regiment). Overall, the 16th Division had an eventful history and several relocations were implemented: in November 1966, the division was again on alert for combat duty and the 47th Brigades remained at Shenyang Yu Hongtun to defend Shenyang. Meanwhile, the other brigades were stationed at Yunnan Mengzi and Wujiaba, where they replaced the 21st Division. As of early September 1968 the 16th Division was stationed at Shenyang Yu Hongtun and Liuhe.

In May 1970 – starting with the 1970s reforms – the three brigades became the 46th, 47th and 48th Regiments. On 20 December 1982, the 48th Regiment relocated to Liancheng and in June 1983 returned to Sanyuanpu. In contrast the 46th Regiment went to Yunnan Mengzi in July 1984 only to go from Jilin Liuhe air base to Tianyang and finally returned to Jilin Sanyuanpu in September. The first round of reforms, that

Left: Besides the regular operational types, the 16th Division always operated a dedicated flight for transport and liaison duties equipped with Y-5C transports.
(via CDF)
Right: The main operational type within the 47th AR today is the rarely seen Y-8CB (Y-8GX-1) ELINT platform, which still wears a quasi-civil livery, in contrast to most other special mission types.
(via CYJB Forum)

lead to its current status were initiated in August 1988, when the 16th Division was re-formed into the Shenyang Military Region Training Base, with the three regiments being re-formed as the 1st, 2nd and 3rd Training Regiments.

Again, there is a lack of information for more than 20 years, before in mid-2012 reports indicated that the former 4th Independent Regiment had been re-formed as the 46th AR and assigned to the re-established specialised division. At around the same time the old JZ-6s were retired and that unit gained JZ-8Fs. The 47th AR gained special missions Y-8s of different variants as well as a transport flight. Very little is known about the history of the former original 4th Independent Regiment, but it can probably be traced back to the former 4th Independent Bomber Regiment established in December 1952. It was later divided into a separate photo-reconnaissance unit, while the EW unit was equipped with a miscellany of Y-7 and Y-8 variants. Also it seems as if the 1st AR of the Beijing MR Training Base was merged with the Shenyang HQ transport Regiment to form the new 48th AR at Shenyang-Dongta, however this is unconfirmed.

17th Fighter Division

According to official reports, the 17th Division was established in Tangshan, Hebei province, on 8 April 1951 and was based on certain units of the North China MR: the 29th Army's 86th Division, 257th Regiment and the 32nd Army's 95th Division, 283th Regiment. It had command over the 49th and 51st Regiments and, as an immediate measure, received its equipment directly from a Soviet Air Force division based in Tangshan. This comprised 60 MiG-9s, five Yak-17s and a pair of Yak-11s. On 1 July 1951 it received 58 MiG-15s and at that time was mainly responsible for air defence of the capital as well as cities in the Tang and Tianjin regions. It was established under the North China MRAF.

On 25 March 1952 the 17th Division was transferred to Dadonggou to participate in the Korean War. Soon after, the first aerial combat took place and the 17th Division scored its first kill by downing a US Navy F4U. Several more aerial victories followed and in the end 23 enemy aircraft were shot down and three more damaged. On its side, the division lost 11 fighters and had two more damaged. It ranks sixth overall in the PLAAF combat record. Between May and October 1953, the 17th Division received 56 MiG-15bis fighters.

Images showing fighters from the 17th Division are not available, but this J-7B and JJ-7 are from the Beijing MRAF Training Base, which was formed from the 17th Division. (Both via CDF)

After the war, on 8 December 1953, the 51st Regiment and 26 MiG-15bis were transferred to the PLA Navy, and finally, on 20 May 1954, the entire 17th Division followed suite. In early June all its aircraft (55 MiG-15bis and three trainers) arrived in several batches in Ningbo, Zhejiang province, at Shandong Jiaoxian air base, where the division was re-formed as the 4th Naval Air Division of the PLA Naval Aviation. In this form, the original 17th Division's 49th Regiment became today's well-known 'Sea and Air Eagle Regiment' (10th Regiment, flying Su-30MK2s). Around two years later, in March 1956, the Central Military Commission (CMC) approved the reconstruction of the 17th Division, which was finally re-established on 6 April 1956 at Shahe air base in Beijing. Its regiments were the 49th Regiment, which was the reassigned 7th Division's 21st Regiment and the 51st Regiment, established from the 14th Division's 41st Regiment; both were equipped with MiG-17 fighters.

Then placed under the command of the Beijing MRAF, the reconstituted 17th Division successfully completed several operational missions, engaged seven times in combat, and took part in complex exercises; special operations included particle sampling after nuclear tests. A total of 29 reconnaissance balloons were shot down and the division excelled in training. In September 1956 it received the first batch of indigenous J-5 fighters. Between 1960 and 1961 its regiments were temporarily based at forward locations, including the 51st Regiment at Jiaxing air base in Zhejiang province in April 1960, while the 49th Regiment was transferred from Baitayu air base to Zhangzhou in April 1961. Both returned home to Tangshan in December.

In September 1963 the 51st was ordered to transfer to Wujiaba in Yunnan to perform the combat missions during the crisis with Vietnam. In the same month, a not entirely understood reorganisation took place, when the original 49th and 51st Regiments were split into three brigades, of which the 51st Brigade was responsible for training. In 1967, the 50th Brigade received its first J-6 trainers at Tangshan, and on 3 June 1970 the three brigades and the independent squadron were re-formed into the 49th, 50th and 51st ARs as well as an independent squadron.

On 15 February 1987 the 50th AR was transferred to Shaoshan air base in Yunnan for air defence duties but a year later, in June 1988, the PLAAF General Staff decided to convert the 17th Division into the Beijing MRAF Training Base. This took place on 26 October and the three regiments became the 1st, 2nd and 3rd Training Regiments.

In October 1992 the training mission of the three regiments was revoked, and in November the same year, the base repair shop and the Y-5 squadron were decommissioned. In April 1995 the base's command post was relocated to Tangshan, and on 30 May it was officially placed at second-class combat readiness.

18th Fighter Division

The 18th Division was established on 5 May 1951, as the first unit within the Central South MRAF at Guangzhou Baiyun air base. It was based on the original 4th Division of the army and had jurisdiction over the 52nd and 54th Regiments. On 23 June 1951 the division received its equipment from a Soviet Air Force division in Guangzhou. In July, flight training began with these MiG-15s in order to assume responsibility for air defence operations in Guangzhou. The 18th Division participated in the Korean War. Between May and December 1952 it was involved in seven aerial battles and claimed a total of six enemy fighters downed, and three damaged, with the loss of one of its own pilots. In early December 1952 the division was withdrawn to the second line in order to undertake air defense missions in the rear sector. On 26 February 1953 the 52nd Regiment was ordered to transfer from Dongfeng to Baiyun air base to take over the 19th Division's air defence mission.

In the mid-1960s, the 18th Division – and particularly the 54th Regiment – was redeployed to southeast China to protect PRC airspace against incursions by US combat aircraft and reconnaissance UAVs. Its pilots were credited with shooting down three US aircraft during the Vietnam War. The 54th Regiment transferred to Shanghai Hongqiao to strengthen Shanghai's air defences. In January 1954 the 53rd Regiment was formed, and in November 1954 the 52nd and 53rd Regiments were transferred to Anshan. By that time, at least the 54th Regiment had gained MiG-17s, since on 31 January 1956 a ROCAF RF-86 was forced down during a reconnaissance mission over Huiyang, Guangdong; the Sabre land at Kai Tak Airport in Hong Kong. Several more aerial battles were fought during subsequent operations against the Nationalists while these were still regularly operating over the mainland. More kills were claimed between October 1956 and September 1958, before in October 1958 the 18th Division ended operations and returned to Guangzhou Shadi air base. Aerial clashes continued through the 1960s; for example, a ROCAF B-17G electronic reconnaissance aircraft was downed in the night of 29 May 1959 by 'MiG-17s' from the 52nd Regiment. Reports mention that this engagement was the first time radar-equipped PLAAF interceptors had been used. The aircraft must have been MiG-17PFs, which is surprising since plans for licence manufacture were only obtained in 1961, and the resulting J-5A appeared in 1964.

In August 1964 the three regiments within the division were renamed the 52nd, 53rd and 54th Brigades. The 54th Brigade was receiving J-6 fighters as of early 1965, and soon after was ordered to form two detachments to perform combat missions in eastern Guangdong and Guangxi. During March and April several interceptions were made, including the downing of a ROCAF RF-101 reconnaissance fighter on 18 March. During April, several US UAVs were downed over the Chongzuo area in Guangxi. Including kills from Korea and during the Taiwan Crisis, a total of 27 enemy aircraft were claimed shot down or damaged and nine reconnaissance balloons were downed. This tour of duty ended in June 1967 – other reports say August – and the brigades returned from Nanning to Changsha. During the Vietnam War a total of 293 combat sorties were flown and two US Navy A-6As were downed in three aerial battles. After the war, the 53rd Brigade was reorganised in August 1969 as the 125th Brigade of the 42nd Division, located at Guilin, and subsequently the 53rd Brigade was re-established. In June 1970, all three brigades were renamed as the 52nd, 53rd, and 54th Regiments.

One of the few images showing old J-5 fighters with the original four-digit serial system and which includes mention of the unit in the accompanying caption. However, it is unconfirmed if they are indeed from the 18th Division. (via CDF)

Not much is known about more recent history but, on 7 October 1986, the General Staff issued a notice stating that the 18th Division was now declared a strategic reserve, and in early November 1992 the 53th Regiment was disbanded. However, during the 1980s the remaining regiments flew J-6s, J-6IIIs and subsequently J-7s until 2003, when the 52nd was disbanded and the 54th Regiment converted to Su-30MKKs. Interestingly, when the 54th AR received Su-30MKKs in 2003 it was long thought to be the 53rd AR, due to its serial numbers.

In 2012 the division once again gained the 53rd Regiment from the former military region training base (MRTB), also equipped with J-7Bs. Finally, in March 2017, the 54th Regiment traded base and aircraft with the 'true' 53rd AR, before both were converted to brigades in June 2017. Today, the 54th appears to be the sole surviving former regiment from the 18th Division. Even though some reports still mention a 53rd Brigade – allegedly transferred to the Northern Theater Command – both the 52nd and 53rd are thought to be disbanded. The Su-30MKK unit is unique in several ways since some of its aircraft wear – or at least temporarily wore – a green-tan/brown-tan camouflage scheme for disimilar air combat training and the unit's aircraft carry a prominent eagle patch below the cockpit.

Another rare image showing early J-6s and a J-6III with serial numbers visible. (via CDF)

19th Fighter Division

In accordance with an order from the Central Military Commission (CMC), a large contingent of troops from the Central and Southern MRs was selected at Wangjiadun air base in Wuhan, Hubei province, to establish the 19th Division. This was executed on 1 October 1951 with jurisdiction over the 55th and 57th Regiments and two supply brigades. The division received its pilots and MiG-9 fighters on 25 December 1951 and began flight training under the leadership of a Soviet Air Force division. In February 1952 it officially took over responsibility for air defence operations in Wuhan under the command of the Central and Southern MRAF. Interestingly, since its training was unfinished, the division was ordered not to take part in the Korean War. However, it was involved in several other campaigns including clashes in Fujian and eastern Guangdong, claiming several kills. For example, on 16 February 1960, for the first time in PLAAF history a ROCAF F-86F was downed by a J-5. In June 1960 a detachment of the 19th Division was stationed in Zhangzhou as part of preparations for the campaign

The 18th Division is the only PLAAF unit to operate a few of its frontline fighters in special camouflage, as demonstrated by these two Su-30MKKs (left) alongside several others in the standard colour scheme. (Both via Top81.cn)

against Taiwan. Besides these operational deployments in which the 19th Division was credited with 26 downed reconnaissance balloons, it was also responsible for 'chase duties' during China's first and second atomic bomb tests in 1964 and 1965.

During the mid- to late 1970s, there were several fairly confusing movements and structural changes: in mid-January 1967, the 55th Regiment was moved to Liencheng, and by late November 1969 the 55th Brigade was transferred from the 19th Division to form a new unit and a new 55th Regiment was soon re-formed. In late July 1970 the division was moved from Zhengzhou to Liancheng and Zhangzhou, with the 56th Regiment stationed at Zhangzhou air base and the 57th Regiment remaining at Liancheng. The 56th, however, was again moved in February 1977, from Zhengzhou to Fuzhou and, on 7 October 1977, the 56th Regiment was re-established.

During November 1980 the PLAAF organised a first mobile exercise of aviation units to Xinjiang, and the 19th Division's command led the 56th Regiment as well as an independent brigade together with 38 fighters – aided by eight transport aircraft – from Zhengzhou in Henan province to Malan air base in Xinjiang. The exercise was completed on 2 December and the unit departed from Malan back to Zhengzhou. In September 1985 the independent brigade was disbanded and the division transferred to the command of the Jinan Military Region.

Several more noteworthy events occurred during the 1980s. In April 1988, the 56th Regiment arrived for the first time with J-7 fighters at Lhasa Gonggar air base, before the PLAAF established an aviation training base there on 11 June 1988. For this purpose, the 57th Regiment became the Jinan MRTB. On 19 June 1990, the 55th Regiment was transferred from Lushan air base (the air force aircraft storage centre) to Zhengzhou. In another first, in August 2005, the 19th Division participated in the Sino-Russian Peace Mission 2005 joint military exercise, and on 12 July 2011 the Chairman of the US Joint Chiefs of Staff, Admiral Michael Glenn Mullen, visited the 55th Regiment, equipped with Su-27SK/UBK fighters.

In 2012, the decision to convert one regiment into the Jinan MRTB was reversed and one of those training regiments – allegedly one that was formerly from the 31st Division – was added again as the new 57th Regiment. However, its current status is unconfirmed, and it has likely been disbanded. The 55th Regiment gained Su-27SKs from the 9th Regiment in around 2001 before replacing these with J-11Bs sometime before mid-2017 – at which point it was transformed into the 55th Brigade. Finally, the 56th began to replace its J-7Bs with J-10Bs sometime in late 2015 before it too was transformed into the 56th Brigade in 2017.

Images of 19th Division aircraft are seldom published and most often depict 'Flankers' of different variants, such as these examples assigned to the 55th AR. The image on the right reportedly shows the arrival of the first J-11B while on the left is one of the original Su-27UBKs.
(Both via CDF)

20th Bomber Division/Specialised Division

The 20th Division – together with the 58th and 60th Regiments as its two subordinated units – was established at Bengbu within Anhui province on 15 September 1951. It was founded as a bomber division based on the former East China MR Teaching Corps and a guards battalion. Equipment was received by the newly established division in January 1952 in the form of 46 Tu-2 bombers, six Tu-2U trainers and a single Yak-12. Flight training began on 4 February 1952 but on 8 February 1953, the 58th Regiment's 1st and 2nd Brigades as well as the 60th Regiment's 1st Brigade were merged and re-formed into a combat readiness training group that moved to the Nanjing University base. Additionally, on 16 May 1953 it was decided the 60th Regiment would be transferred to Kaifeng air base in Henan for training, where it arrived in late August. In July 1953 the 58th Regiment and the 28th Regiment of the 10th Division were merged, and the former 28th Regiment was renamed as the new 58th Regiment. Its first operational mission was during the First Taiwan Strait Crisis on 10 January 1955, when 28 Tu-2 bombers were put into action against a naval target, sinking the tank landing ship *Zhongquan* and damaging the escort destroyer *Taihe*. More bombing missions followed within this campaign and the Tu-2s were successful against enemy fortifications, artillery positions and command facilities on Yijiangshan Island. On 27 March 1956 the 20th Division was transferred from Nanjing to Qiqihar in Heilongjiang province and between April and June the division began training for the more modern Il-28, which replaced the Tu-2 from August. From early August 1958 the 58th Regiment was stationed at Gongzhuling and the 60th Regiment was based at Zhengjiatun Datushan.

The division gained its third regiment on 3 October 1964, when the 59th Regiment was formed and on 5 October all three regiments were renamed as the 58th, 59th and 60th Brigades. This system was revised again on 1 May 1970, when they again became regiments. Several more changes were introduced in the following years: in February 1971 it was decided to transfer the 59th Regiment to the 48th Division on 1 March, and a new 59th was re-formed on 19 July 1971, from elements of the two remaining regiments.

One special operation was ordered in April 1985, when due to the thawing of the Heilongjiang River, an ice dam was formed and the water level rose to a dangerous level. The 20th Division was called upon to dispatch three H-5 aircraft and successfully bombed the ice dam. Soon after, on 25 September 1985, the 59th Regiment was deactivated and a process of force reduction began.

As well as from the 16th Specialised Division, the 20th Specialised Division also operates a few Y-8CB (Y-8GX-1) aircraft; this example serves with the 58th AR. (via CJDBY.net)

Among the special-mission types in service with the 59th AR is the Y-8G (Y-8GX-3) ECM variant. In recent years these have been updated and can be recognised by new, dark grey ECM antenna fairings. (via CDF)

By December 1990 the division had jurisdiction over the 58th and 60th Regiments based at Gongzhuling and Shuangliao, but only two years later, on 30 September 1992, the 20th Division was disbanded. Surprisingly – and most likely to continue the tradition of this unit – in late 2012 or early 2013 a new 20th Division was formed; this time as a specialised division, which can trace it lineage back to the 30th Regiment of the original 10th Division. This regiment was first used to establish the 48th Division and later re-formed as an independent electronic warfare regiment, before being re-equipped with a mix of specialised Y-8 variants and reassigned to the 10th Bomber Division in 2003.

In 2012 the 30th AR moved from Dajiaochang to Guiyang/Leizhuang and became the re-established 20th Division, operating from 2013 as a specialised or special mission division. At around the same time the new 60th AR was formed as a dedicated reconnaissance regiment.

21st Fighter Division

This division was formed on 1 November 1951, at Shanghai Dachang air base, on the basis of deployed troops from Sanyo and the East China MR. It included the 61st and 63rd Regiments under its jurisdiction and was transferred from Shanghai to Jilin City, Jilin province, in August 1954. Initially it was equipped with materiel from the Soviet Air Force division based at Libao (?) air base in the Dalian/Luda area in January 1955. Confusingly, other reports mention that it was established at Mudanjiang-Hajlang, in the far north. Therefore, this division, since established in the 'Northland', is sometimes regarded a direct successor of the old aviation school that reflected the spirit of the Northeast Tigers.

On 29 March 1960 the 63rd Regiment was transferred to Fujian Liancheng air base for operational service. During the years that followed, the division had mixed fortunes. On 12 May 1966 a fighter from the 63rd Brigade shot down a USAF RB-66 over Maguan, Yunnan province. However, during that battle one of its own fighters was shot down by a USAF F-4C. During the 1970s to 1980s several more changes occurred: on 6 September 1975 the 63rd Regiment was transferred from Mudanjiang Hailang to Zhangzhou air base; on 18 January 1985 the 61st Regiment was relocated to Tianyang, Guangxi; and on 21 February 1987 the 62nd Regiment returned home to Jiaohe air base in Jilin. Another notable event was the defection of a J-6 assigned to the 62nd Regiment to the Soviet Union on 25 August 1990. However, only a few days later both the fighter and its pilot were returned. On 18 October that year the 63rd Regiment returned to Mudanjiang air base. There followed a series of reorganisations resulting in several changes since the early 1990s. In 1998 the former 39th Division was merged with the 21st Fighter Division but only in 2003 was the reassigned 117th AR renamed as the 62nd AR. Later – some sources say on 30 September 1992 – the 62nd Regiment was disbanded – at that time it was flying a mix of refurbished J-8DHs, new J-8Hs and J-8Fs – but at the same time the 61st Regiment was transferred to the 30th Division. Others sources say the 62nd Regiment was merged with the 3rd Brigade; the status of the 63rd Brigade is unconfirmed, but it is likely disbanded.

An impressive image showing two J-8Hs from the 63rd AR behind a JJ-7A. The latter is the standard trainer in J-8 units since no dedicated twin-seater exists for this type. (via Top81.cn)

A J-10B from the 61st AR, dating from the brief period the unit also flew this type with full 21st Division serial numbers, before being converted to the 61st Brigade. Here, however, the serial numbers have been removed to conceal the unit's identity.
(via CDF)

Today only the former 61st Regiment soldiers on. Since 2014 it has operated J-10Bs, which replaced J-7Es; in 2017 it became the 61st Brigade.

22nd Ground Attack Division

The 22nd Division was established on 20 September 1951 in Hengyang, Hunan province with the 4th, 5th and 6th Regiments assigned. The 5th Regiment was transferred in October to the 9th Division and on 1 November this division received its number as 22th Division with the three regiments being renumbered to the 64th and 66th Regiments both equipped with the Il-10. On 17 November both moved to Xuzhou and the division was under the command of the East China MRAF. On 31 March 1953, it was transferred to Gaomi in Shandong province and on 1 April 1955, it was placed under the command of the North China MRAF.

The next reassignment occurred on 19 November 1961, when the 22nd Division was reassigned to the Beijing MRAF, where the 64th and 66th Regiments were joined by the 1st Brigade at Jiaxing. Finally, on 19 October 1964, they were reorganised into the 64th, 65th and 66th Brigades. Yet again a reassignment occurred on 1 October 1967, when that division was transferred under the Jinan MRAF and briefly moved in June 1969 to a base close to Jixian, before the brigades returned home and became the 64th, 65th and 66th ARs on 22 March 1970.

In early 1976, the 65th AR was transferred to the 45th Division and on 25 May a new 65th AR was formed from elements of the 64th and 66th ARs. The downsizing begun 1985, when on 16 September the 66th AR disbanded and the 65th AR transformed into a training regiment. Also on 15 October 1985 it was placed under the command of Dalian CP under Shenyang MRAF and in October 1992, the 22nd Division was finally withdrawn.

Quite an interesting side note: there is still a 66th Brigade active even today, which is probably one of the most secretive units. Even its serial number – which usually fits nicely – is a non-standard number that would fit to a 177th Brigade. Barely anything is known on its history other that it is a quite new unit formed in 2014 and it is the PLAAF's new dedicated OPFOR unit replacing the former small OPFOR unit, which was more the size of a dadui with a true brigade-level unit. This unit operates J-10C and J-11B/BS.

One of the few known images showing an aircraft assigned to the 22nd Ground Attack Division; unusually, it shows a J-7B fighter.
(via Top81.cn)

23rd Bomber Division

This bomber division was originally named on 4 January 1952 even if a predecessor unit was established already in October 1951 in the Hubei, Jiangxi and the Hunan Military Region, when troops were deployed to Nanchang, Jiangxi province. Later, these units moved to Hengyang, Hunan province, with three subordinated regiments, namely the 67th, 68th and 69th AR all equipped with Tu-2 bomber. Following its official establishment as the 23rd Bomber Division in September 1953 it was based first at Changsha Datopu air base and from October 1954 on at Zhengzhou in Henan province.

In July 1959, the division was transferred to Shenheji (?), which became in April 1960 the PLAAF Lixindian Station. In May 1969, the 23rd and the 25th Divisions were deployed operationally, and the 23rd Division was transferred to Shaanxi Linyi. From there this division was the first PLAAF bomber division to deploy in September 1974 its H-5 to Shigatse for special training, this was the first time a bomber unit deployed to Tibet. Anyway, 11 years later, on 27 August 1985, the 23rd Division was disbanded.

24th Fighter Division and Ba Yi Aerial Demonstration Team

On 28 September 1951, the 7th Army of the Central South MR and some elements drawn from the Henan and Guangxi MRs formed the so-called Zhengzhou Air Force Division and the 1st, 2nd, and 3rd Regiments. This unit was renamed the 24th Division on 4 January 1952 with jurisdiction over 70th, 71st and 72nd Regiments. On 17 November 1952, it was transferred to the Nantang Xiangtang air base and in February 1953, it received its first MiG-15 fighters. Altogether 64 aircraft, including 60 MiG-15, 2 MiG-15U and 2 Yak-17 trainer were delivered by March and flight training began on 22 April. The following years saw some organisational changes, when in March 1955, the Central South MRAF was transferred to the East China MRAF and in August 1958, it was again re-formed as the Fuzhou MRAF.

In parallel, the division's first operational deployment was its participation in the battle to liberate the Yijiangshan Island, where the division shot down three enemy planes as well as two balloons in the 1960s and another interception occurred on 19

A rare image of an updated J-8IE assigned to the 70th AR. This was the final PLAAF unit to operate the original early 'Finback' version. (via Top81.cn)

June 1963, when the 20th Division's Independent Night Fighter Brigade shot down a P2V electronic reconnaissance plane. Besides the operational duties, the division was responsible to organise the flood relief work in Fengcheng, Jiangxi province in June 1962. Not much more is known for the following years besides, that in 1965, the division converted to J-6 fighters and reportedly in parallel the 70th Regiment may still have operated J-5 fighters. On 13 January 1967 another kill was claimed, when a fighter from the 70th Regiment from Zhangzhou shot down a F-104. Other structural changes were initiated in the late 1970s, when in September 1968, the division was transferred under the command of the Beijing MRAF and during December participated in the nuclear test. Slightly later in January 1970, it relocated to Zunhua air base and was responsible for the security of the capital before in 1985, it gained its first J-8 fighters. Another non-military operation was the participation in 1976 during the earthquake relief work in Tangshan and Fengnan.

Between 1984 and 1986, the 24th Division again was successful as a fighter unit, when seven balloons were shot down. At that time in January 1986, the 71st Regiment was already transferred from Pingquan to Fuzhou air base and returned home in late November and during the 1990s all of its regiments were equipped with indigenous J-8 interceptors.

Another interesting change was the reassignment of the famous BaYi (August 1st) Aerial Demonstration team to the 24th Division on 30 September 1992. This team originally belonged to the 38th Division and in memory of the founding day of the PLAAF on 1 August 1927 it is named 'Ba Yi'. Itself founded in 1962 it was originally equipped with JJ-5 jet trainers, which were replaced later with J-7EB and in April 2005 with J-7GB. Since 2009 that team operates the dedicated J-10AY and J-10SY variant.

The famous 'Ba Yi' aerial demonstration team is a relatively recent addition to the 24th Division, being assigned in 1992. It has operated J-10AY and J-10SY aircraft since May 2009.
(Katsuhiko Tokunaga/D.A.C.T.)

Otherwise, the history of this division is less well documented: on 27 November 1993, the 72nd Regiment was transferred from Zunhua to Yangcun and equipment-wise, there have been some interesting changes, so that only two former regiments – besides the Ba Yi – remain active until today.

The 70th Regiment replaced its legacy J-8IE with J-7G in 2011 and in 2017 was renamed as the 70th Brigade. In early 2018 the J-7s were replaced by J-10A coming from the 72nd Brigade, which converted to the latest J-10C. Concerning the missing 71st AR, there was once a regiment assigned to the Beijing MRTB before it was subordinated to the 33rd Division and renamed into 99th AR. However there are still reports concerning a J-7B regiment, which is sometimes called the 71st AR or even a brigade, although this is not confirmed. The 72nd, similar to the 70th replaced its J-8IE – and at least one image is known, showing J-8B fighters – in 2009 with J-10A, which again were replaced in early 2018 with new J-10C and similar to its sister brigade, the 72nd became a brigade in early 2017.

25th Fighter Division

The 25th Division was established on 10 May 1952, at Xi'an (Huyi District) in Shaanxi province, based on the 16th Division of the 6th Army with two subordinated brigades, namely the 73rd and the 74th. At first the unit was equipped with Tu-2 and Tu-2U bomber and personnel came at first from the 8th, 10th and 27th Divisions. Already on 6 October 1952, the division departured Xi'an to Zhengzhou but in January 1954 transferred to Linyi air base.

The 26th Division was the final operator of the original JZ-6 reconnaissance version before this type was replaced by the JZ-8F (JC-8F) in 2006. (via Top81.cn)

Operationally, the most important event occurred on 19 November 1960, when two modified Tu-2 from the 74th Regiment from Zhengzhou intercepted a ROCAF P2V reconnaissance aircraft but unfortunately lost one bomber.

Following a period of combat readiness training, the 25th Division returned home to Linyi on in late August 1962. In 1970, the 25th Division began to convert to the domestic H-5, but the division disbanded on 27 August 1985.

26th Fighter Division/Specialised Division

According to a Central Military Commission (CMC) decision from 12 December 1952, based on certain cadres of the Central South MR and the 23rd Division's 67th Regiment as well as the 24th Division's 71st Regiment the 26th Division was established in 22 December in Liuzhou, Guangxi province. Under its jurisdiction were the 76th Regiment – formerly the 67th Regiment – and the 78th Regiment – formerly the 71st Regiment. At the beginning of 1953, the division began to receive Soviet Air Force equipment, including 39 La-9 and 20 La-11 fighters. Soon thereafter combat flight training began in early April 1953. A first relocation occurred in mid-April 1956, when the division was transferred to Guangdong Suixi under command of the Guangzhou MRAF. Its first combat deployment was between late March and mid-October 1957, when eight La-11 and one La-11UTI was dispatched to cooperate with the army to quell the rebellion in parts of southern Gansu and southern Qinghai. Its first true combat missions however were undertaken from 22 July 1960 on, when the division's 76th Regiment and the Independent Night Fighter Brigade were transferred from Suixi to Kunming Wujiaba and placed under the command of the Kunming CP, officially assuming the task of air defence combat duty on the southwest border.

On 24 September 1961, it was transferred back to Guangdong Suixi but its assignment was changed to the Guangzhou MRAF. About four years later in August 1964, the two regiments became to the 76th and 78th Brigades and also the 77th Brigade was formed, which only one year later in August 1965 however was transferred to the newly established 35th Division as the new 105th Brigade and subsequently, a new 77th Brigade was reorganised. Re-equipped with J-5, it was redeployed to Yunan province in April 1966, to boost PRC air defences during the Vietnam War, where the 78th Brigade arrived on 3 April at Ningming.

Altogether a total of 393 sorties were flown, it participated in eight aerial battles its pilots were credited with two confirmed kills against US aircraft including one A-3B and one F-4B and damaging one more type. The brigade returned home on 2 March 1968 only to be replaced by the 76th Brigade, which deployed to Ningming in late February 1968. On 5 September 1968, the division was transferred to the Nanjing MRAF and later the same month both the 2nd and the 26th Divisions were transferred from Ningming and Suixi in Guangdong to Shanghai Jiangwan and Hongqiao air bases. The 76th Brigade and an independent regiment (?) were based at Hongqiao, while the 77th and 78th Brigades were stationed at Jiangwan.

The only known image of an H-5 assigned to the 25th Bomber Division. (via CDF)

The next organisation change occurred in June 1988, when the PLAAF decided to set up a dedicated training base and the the 32nd Division's 94th and 95th Regiments as well as the 26th Division's 77th Regiment – most likely changes from brigades in 1970 – were re-formed. In return, the 32nd Division's 96th Regiment was assigned to the 26th Division.

In late July 1991, the next operational deployment was ordered, when on 27 July the 76th Regiment sent a detachment of 10 J-6 fighters to Zhangzhou; they returned home on 29 December. About one year later in October 1992, 11 J-6 from the 78th Regiment formed a similar detachment at Zhangzhou, and their deployment ended on 29 March 1993.

The changes, that led to the current status were initiated in the early 2000s, when in 2003, the 78th Regiment was transferred to the 29th Division and reorganised as the 87th Regiment. Subsequently, the division was reorganised from a fighter to a special aviation or special mission division comprising of three dedicated regiments each assigned to a specific role such as AEW&C, search and rescue as well as transport, and reconnaissance.

By 2017 the division was reorganised again with now only two regiments left, when the 77th Regiment dedicated to search and rescue duties was turned into a dedicated Theater Command subordinated transportation and search and rescue brigade.

27th Fighter Division

On 29 December 1952, the 27th Division was established in Tongxian County, Beijing, based on the 8th Division of the army and the 79th and 81st as subordinated regiments. At first this fighter division was equipped with 55 MiG-15 aircraft, was established by the North China Military Region Air Force. Flight training began on 5 April 1953. The division has successively been based in Qingdao, Dalian Chengsha River, Zhoushuizi, Suixi in Guangdong, Mengzi in Yunnan, and Hubei Shanpo air base and has participated in the counter-attacks against Vietnam. During these missions, the 27th Division carried out air defence operations, destroyed 15 surveillance balloons and it was involved in sampling particles after nuclear tests.

This mysterious image shows a lineup of J-8B Batch 02 aircraft with serial numbers from the 76th AR. However, the type is not known to be flown by this unit. (via CDF)

Today the 76th AR operates a mix of AEW types comprising the KJ-500, KJ-2000 and this KJ-200. In recent years, this unit apparently underwent some internal changes since all types have been renumbered. (via Top81.cn)

Already in March 1955, the 27th Division was moved from Shandong Liuting to the Jinzhou air base in Liaoning, where it received equipment from a Soviet Air Force Division based in Jinxian County within the Shenyang MRAF. Later on, it moved to Dalian Zhoushuizi and Shenyang Yu Hongtun and Anshan.

On 9 April 1956, a MiG-15bis from the 79th AR chased and damaged a US RB-50 reconnaissance aircraft over Bohai Bay. On 18 March 1959, the 79th AR returned from Liancheng to Dalian Zhoushuizi. Strangely, in August 1964, the 79th and 81st ARs were renamed the 79th and 81st Brigades and the 80th Brigade was established at the Chengshahe air base in Liaoning province.

On 26 August 1968, the 27th Division was transferred under command of the Kunming MRAF and its two brigades were relocated from the Zhoushuizi and Pulandian air bases to Mengzi. The division was now conducting complex meteorological training at Jiangxi Yushu air base. The third brigade and an independent squadron were stationed at Wujiaba. Somewhere in 1970, the three brigades were re-formed as the 79th, 80th and 81st Regiments. Another reorganisation occurred in December, when the 27th Division moved to Zhongxiang in Hubei and was placed under the Wuhan MRAF, before the 27th Division's Night Fighter Brigade again moved to Mengzi in Yunnan in December 1978. In August 1985, the 27th Division was transferred to the Guangzhou MRAF. In early 1986, the Guangzhou MRAF identified the 27th Division as a pilot unit for the training system reform which aimed for a centralised training within the individual MRs. This system was officially executed and on 11 June 1988, the 27th Division was reorganised into the Guangzhou Military Region Training Base (MRTB), with the three regiments becoming the 1st, 2nd and 3rd Training Regiments respectively.

In February 1990, the Guangzhou MRTB was placed under the command of the Wuhan CP and on 30 September 1992, the 3rd Regiment was disbanded. The start of the downgrading begun in July 1998, when the Guangzhou MRTB was downgraded to regiment level, albeit still using the original name, but basically the strength of the original training regiment and the training base department was withdrawn, and moved to Laohekou, Hubei and in November 2003, the training base was redesignated (and merged) with the 18th Division.

28th Ground Attack Division

This division was founded on 18 December 1952 in Gucheng, Hebei province on the basis of the 143rd Infantry Division, the 4th Regiment of the Southwest MR's Infantry Base and the 533rd Infantry Regiment. Its two initial regiments, the 82nd and the 84th were equipped with 40 Il-10 and assigned to the North China MR. Already in January 1953, the division was transferred to Tangshan, Hebei province to succeed the 17th Division. On 10 March 1953, it began with flight training only to be relocated once again on 27 December 1954 to Siping in Jilin province. About one year later in November 1955, the 82nd Regiment took part in an anti-landing campaign exercise in the Liaodong Peninsula and in November 1959, the 84th Regiment participated in a large tactical exercise in conjunction with the 46th PLA Army near the Yinma River in Jilin City. Several more dedicated exercises followed through the 1960s and 1970s before in August 1964, the 82nd and 84th Regiments were renamed the 82nd and 84th Brigades. At around the same time personnel and equipment was drawn from these two brigades to form the 83rd Brigade. Another base change occurred in July 1969, when the 28th and the 11th Division – all from the Zhengjiatun air base at Siping were transferred to the Jiaxing air base in the Zhejiang province and placed under command of the Southern MRAF.

At the end of 1972, the 82nd and 83rd regiments were deployed to Hangzhou Luqiao air base, and the division's independent brigade (?) remained at Jiaxing air base. In 1976, the 84th Regiment was transferred to the 50th Division and renamed the 148th Regiment. Soon thereafter a new 84th Regiment was formed. In 1979 the 83rd took part in the operations against Vietnam and deployed with 36 Q-5 to Yunnan.

For the following years again much lesser is known. In 1987, the Central Military Commission (CMC) officially approved that the 28th Division should open to the outside world, and so far they have hosted more than 200 military delegations from more than 100 countries. In that role, this division has become some sort of foreign relationship partner for many years and is often regarded as the 'proudest' PLAAF attack unit.

Otherwise a new era began in 2004, when the 83rd Regiment exchanged its Q-5Bs for JH-7As, while the 84th Air Regiment exchanged its Q-5Ds for JH-7As in late 2011. The 82nd Regiment has not received JH-7As, but has partially been re-equipped with LGB-capable Q-5Ls, while the remaining JJ-6 conversion trainers were replaced by Q-5Js in 2010. In line with the latest round of reorganisations, some more changes followed: quite surprisingly this most capable Q-5 variant was retired first and the 82nd Regiment disbanded in March/April 2017. In parallel the 83th AR became a brigade in

Another rare image showing several J-6 and JJ-6 jets from the 27th Division
(via Top81.cn)

The 28th Division is probably the best-known PLAAF ground-attack unit and flew Q-5 variants through most of its history. Here are two of this family flown by the 82nd AR, comprising an immaculate Q-5D (left) and a much earlier image showing a Q-5I and a JJ-6 trainer (right). It finally flew the Q-5L before being disbanded in 2017.
(Both Top81.cn)

Successor to the Q-5 in both the 83rd and 84th ARs was the JH-7A, which is still in use today, albeit in the re-formed 83rd and 84th Brigades. (via Top81.cn)

June 2017 and the current status of the 84th AR was long unconfirmed before being confirmed only in 2018 as the 84th Brigade however still using their old serial numbers.

29th Fighter Division

Established on 17 December 1953 in Jiaxing, Zhejiang province, the 29th Division was formed from a regiment of the 71st Army Division and certain units from the East China MRAF. Originally it the 85th and 87th Regiments, both equipped with La-11 as subordinated regiments. Already in August 1954, the division was ordered to carry out combat missions to support the army in liberating Yijiangshan Island, and according to a decree from 10 March 1955, it was transferred under the command of the North China MRAF. This was executed on 1 April 1955 and the division was stationed at Luting air base in Shandong province. Only four years later in early August 1959 it was moved again to Xuzhou in Jiangsu province. On 22 July 1954, the 85th Regiment was deployed to Haikou air base to carry out an escort mission for Soviet tankers from Hainan Island to Huangpu Port. This was the first time a unit was stationed at Hainan Island. During that mission however the division was involved in a tragic event, when a Cathay Pacific Airways C-54 airliner was shot down off the coast of Hainan Island, where the plane was en route from Bangkok to Hong Kong, killing 10 of 19 passengers and crew on board. In return on 26 July 1954, during the search operation for survivors, two La-11s were shot down by a pair of A-1s from the aircraft carriers USS *Philippine Sea* and USS *Hornet* in the same area.

The regiment returned home to Xuzhou only in May 1967. In mid-November 1968, the 29th and the 12th Divisions were redeployed again; the 12th Division from Luzhou,

Luqiao air base to Xuzhou, Baitayu air base, and the 29th Division was transferred to the former 12th Division's base.

In September 1977 the 86th Regiment was transferred from Jiaxing to Liancheng. Another deployment occurred in May 1992, when the 86th Regiment moved with its J-6 fighters from stationed Jiaxing to Zhouzhou and it returned in October. A few weeks later on 9 November 1992, the 87th Regiment – a JJ-5 training unit (?) – was disbanded.

What followed is largely unknown: most of its history it was equipped with J-6s facing Taiwan, the 85th Regiment must have flown J-7B until 2003, when they were replaced with Su-30MKK and the 86th Regiment gained J-7E in April 2012. At around the same time or slightly earlier under the 2011–12 reform, both the 85th and 86th Regiments were one of the first brigades established in 2011 and originally assigned to the Shanghai Base in 2012. The 86th Brigade was formed at Jiujiang/Lushan from the former 14th AD/41st AR and moved to Rugao in early 2013. And the 85th Brigade quite surprisingly in line with the second round of changes, had its assignment changed to the newly established Fuzhou Base in 2017.

30th Fighter Division

The 30th Division was established on 4 May 1960, based on the original 1st Division's 2nd AR and the 6th Division's 17th AR. It was formed at Donggou/Dabao air base (?) in Liaoning. With the 88th and 90th ARs it had two subordinated regiments equipped with MiG-15bis fighters. These two regiments were renamed as the 88th and 90th Brigades in August 1964 and a 89th Brigade was formed. In the following years, several changes were made: in July 1965, it moved from Dabao in Fengcheng County to Qianyang in Donggou County and in August 1967, it was moved back to Dabao. Also in 1967 an Independent Night Flight Squadron was formed.

According to the 1970s reform, in May 1970 the three brigades became the 88th, 89th and 90th ARs. Another change occurred in September 1985, when the air base from Dabao air base to Longtou air base and the 90th AR was disbanded, only to be re-established slightly later by transferring the 119th AR of the 40th Division to the 30th Division. Also, on 12 May 1990, the 88th AR was transferred from Fengcheng, to Dandong.

In 1998 the 30th Division was re-formed with the retirement of the 89th AR while in return the 61st AR was reassigned from the 21st Division. Five years later, in 2003, the air force again streamlined with the reassignment of the 61st AR to the 21st Division and the withdrawal of the 90th AR. In return, the 10th and 12th ARs from the 4th Division – then still a fighter division - when this was reorganised as a transport

A J-11A from the 86th AR, when this unit was still a regiment. Today, as the 86th Brigade, it operates J-7Es after its 'Flankers' were reassigned to other units.
(via Top81.cn)

division and were transferred to the 30th Division and renamed the 89th and 90th ARs respectively.

Equipment wise, the 30th Division flew J-6s for many years until being reequipped with aircraft taken over from other units, foremost the former 4th Fighter Division. In 2003 the 88th AR started replacing J-8IE with J-7E, and briefly also J-7C/D were noted that regiment gained from the former 43rd AR before they were retired in 2015-16. The 89th AR moved in 2009 from Dalian-Zhoushuizi to Pulandian and in 2010 its J-7E were replaced by J-11 with the J-7Es being transferred to the 88th AR.

Today the 30th Division is no longer extant, when in April 2012 all regiments were converted to brigades. The 90th was in fact the former 22nd Division's 66th AR, which was merged with the 11th Division in September 1992, creating the new 33rd AR; in 2012 it was reassigned to Dalian Base as the new 90th Brigade, which reportedly received new J-7Ls in 2017–18.

31st Fighter Division

On 29 March 1960 the decision to found the 31st Division within the Nanjing MR was made. This was implemented on 10 July, when the 31st Division was officially established in Yancheng, Jiangsu province. Its subordinated regiments were the 91st Regiment, the renamed 5th Brigade of the 2nd Division with 24 J-5 fighters and the 93rd Regiment, established by the 12th Division's 35th Regiment operational with 27 MiG-15bis and 5 MiG-15UTI. On 8 September 1963, the 31st Division together with both regiments were relocated to Fuzhou, where they were on combat duty to return home on 19 April 1964. On 17 August 1964, the 91st Regiment was allocated to Shuofang, to replace the 15th Division with the defence of Shanghai. Only slightly later, the division gained its third regiment, when on 1 December 1964, a flight squadron each was dispatched from the 1st and 3rd Divisions as well as some personnel drawn from the 91st and 93rd Regiments to establish the 92th Regiment at Yancheng. On the same day, all three regiments were re-formed into the 91st, 92nd and 93rd Brigades. However already on 8 January 1966, the 93rd Brigade was replaced by the 4th Independent Regiment only to be re-established on 1 July 1966 together with another independent squadron, which was formed in March 1967. Between August 1967 and June 1968, all three brigades of the 32nd Division were on combat duty also from Xintai, Jiangsu Ruyi (?) and Gaomi assigned to Jinan MRAF.

Two images from the era in which both the 88th (left) and 89th (right) ARs were regiments both flying J-7Es. The 88th still flies that type as the 88th Brigade, while the 89th Brigade gained J-11Bs in 2010.
(Left: via Top81.cn,
Right: Weimeng via Top81.cn)

With the reform in early 1970, all three brigades became regiments, so that the former brigade and the division's independent squadron became in turn the 91st, 92rd and 93rd ARs as well as a divisional detachment (sometimes still called independent brigade). The 92nd was responsible for training. Between August 1967 and August 1968 additional transfers followed to Rugao, Xintai and Gaomi.

Quite unique, in October 1975, a fifth subunit was formed, which was disbanded only in October 1999. In August 1976 the Independent Brigade operated J-5A fighters and the 91st AR flew J-6 fighters, several balloons were shot down and altogether until July 1984, the division shot down 18 balloons.

The time between September 1984 and March 1985 again saw several operational deployments and the division was regarded one of the best troops in the southern region. Similar to other units, the downsizing began in 1985, when in October the 93rd AR together with the division's independent brigade were disbanded. Anyway, due to the unrest in Tibet, in 1987 the division sent a small deployment and in 1988, the 92nd AR was re-installed from a training as a combat regiment.

But even further in 2003, the 91st AR was disbanded, the 92nd AR integrated into the 12th Division as the new 34th AR and as such, the 31st Division was dismantled.

One of the very few images showing an operational J-5A flown by the 31st Air Division. (via Top81.cn)

32nd Fighter Division

On 21 April 1960 on the basis of the Beijing MRAF Cadre Training Brigade, the 3rd Division's 8th Regiment and the 16th Division 47th Regiment a new division was formed in Jinghai County, Hebei province. This 32nd Division had two subordinated regiments, namely the 94th Regiment – from the re-formed 8th Regiment – and the 96th Regiment as the renamed 47th Regiment; both equipped with MiG-15bis. On 8 December 1961, the 32nd Division was transferred to Beijing Shahe air base. What followed is an unusual confusing time in which several quite surprisingly changes were made: already on 9 June 1962, the 94th Regiment was withdrawn, and its aircraft and pilots reassigned to other units in that area. However on 12 July 1962, the 1st Independent Regiment was transferred to the 32nd Division and on 13 September 1963, the division moved to Shandong Gaomi air base. Another change was in September 1967, when it was placed under the Jinan MRAF and on 12 May 1965, the 96th Regiment was divided into new 94th and 95th Brigades and nearly two years later on 21 March 1967 the 96th Brigade was re-established at Gaomi and during the second half of 1967, an independent night- fighter regiment was formed. On 23 November 1969 yet another brigade was withdrawn, when the 96th Brigade was transferred to the 47th Division and renamed the 140th Brigade only to be re-formed by the end of the month in Yancheng. At around the same time, some operational deployments were ordered and so one brigade and the independent regiment were moved to Jiangsu Yancheng, another brigade moved to Jiangsu Rugao and a larger detachment was stationed in Zhangzhou, Fujian. Later it was placed under the command of the Nanjing MRAF.

The next round of changes occurred in May 1970, when the three brigades became the 94th, 95th and 96th Regiments. This status lasted for about eight years, until in October 1978, the division was deployed from Jiangsu Yancheng and Rugao to Xuzhou and Baitayu. Otherwise almost nothing is known about the original 32nd Division, which was equipped with J-5s and probably J-6s until its disestablishment in 1988.

Another rare image of a J-7IIH armed with PL-8 AAMs at Nanning Guangxi, most likely taken before that regiment became a training unit. (via CDF)

This flight of J-11Bs from the 95th AR illustrates the re-established 32nd Fighter Division after 2012; this unit is still active today as the 95th Brigade.
(via Top81.cn)

On 16 December 1988, the 32nd Division was converted into the Nanjing Military Region Training Base with the 94th and 95th Regiments as well as the 77th Regiment of the 32nd Division were transformed into the 1st, 2nd and 3rd Training Regiments. The 96th Regiment in return was assigned to the 26th Division.

Only two years later on 5 January 1990, the same regiment was transferred back to the Training Base and renamed the 3rd Training Regiment. In that form, it soldiered on until 2012, when the 32nd Division was re-established in early 2012 with the 94th Regiment equipped with J-7Bs and the 95th Regiment flying J-11Bs, which were received from the 19th Division's 57th Regiment. The 96th Regiment is unconfirmed since then but in 2017 the 32nd Division and both the 94th and 95th Regiments were disbanded and as it seems only the 95th Regiment survived as the re-formed 95th Brigade. This was transferred to the Shanghai Base where it replaced the already established 85th Brigade, which was moved to the newly established Fuzhou Base.

33rd Fighter Division

The 33rd Division was founded on 12 April 1960 in Shanpo, Hubei province with jurisdiction over the 97th and the 99th Regiments both equipped with MiG-15bis. About already two years later on 4 July 1962, the 99th Regiment was disbanded and both its aircraft and pilots were reassigned to augment other units in the area. In return, the 2nd Independent Regiment was transferred to the 33rd Division on 15 July 1962 and on 24 March 1967 the 97th – now renamed as a brigade – ended its first round of operational deployment from Liancheng and returned home. During the second half of 1967, an independent night-fighter brigade (?) was formed and also a 98th Brigade is mentioned thereafter. In the following years several more deployments and base changes occurred, so on 20 August 1969, when the whole division was moved from Wuhan in Hubei to Sichuan; the 97th and 99th Brigade and the Independent Regiment to Dazu and the 98th Brigade to Chongqing/Baishiyi.

On 31 January 1979, the 98th Brigade and the Independent Night Fighter Brigade were deployed to Kunming and the 97th Regiment stationed in Luliang to participate in the counterattack against Vietnam. This period is quite confusing since often both terms regiment and brigade are used in reports.

In late May 1981 for the first time J-6 fighters were successfully deployed from the eastern frontline to Tibet and altogether 3 batches of 12 aircraft equipped with special high capacity fuel tanks were based at Lhasa Gongga. A similar deployment was repeated in mid-May 1987, when the 97th Regiment sent its J-7 fighters to Tibet to carry out an air defence missions; that was the first time, J-7s were deployed to the Tibetan plateau. During the following years, the 33rd Division specialised in this operational area and with the main goal to explore methods of warfare in mountainous environment and at high altitudes. By around 1990 the regular home of the 98th Regiment must be Chongqing, which even in September 1994 was still flying the J-6.

A process of downsizing was initiated in 1998, when the 99th Regiment was disbanded whereas the in the early 2000s, the remaining regiment began to upgrade their aircraft. Otherwise very little is known about its more recent history.

The former 97th Regiment gained J-7E from the 111th Regiment in mid-2011 replacing its J-7Bs and in 2017 it became the 97th Brigade. The 98th Regiment was long operating J-11A and both units wore a prominent winged 33 and eagle's head as its unit markings. In July 2017 it turned into the 98th Brigade and in early 2018 the 98th Brigade became the first PLAAF unit to operate J-16 with low visibility markings. The 99th Regiment was briefly re-formed in April 2012 at Liancheng, when the former 2nd Training Regiment of the Beijing MRTB became the new 99th AR assigned to the 33rd Division. The Beijing MRTB itself was established in October 1988 from the disbanded 17th Division. In line with this change it was reported to have moved from Xishan-Beixiang to Zunyi-Xinzhou, although most sources mention Chongqing/Baishiyi as its base. Today the unit is either disbanded or – as some reports suggest – has replaced its J-7Bs with either J-7Es or even J-7Gs.

34th Transport Division

In order to fulfill the PLAAF's needs for heavy air transport tasks, the Central Military Commission (CMC) issued a 2 May 1952 request to establish a new unit from the North China MRAF's transport brigade, certain elements from the Beijing Xijiao air base and female personnel from the 13th Division. This – at first – 3rd Independent Regiment, was initially placed under the command of the North China MRAF but on 9 February 1953, the PLAAF HQs decided to place it directly under the leadership of the air force.

Left: Another rare image showing two camouflaged J-6Bing fighters at Kunming in 1979.
(via top81.cn)
Right: A rare line-up of both J-7Bs and J-7Es with their serial numbers covered.
(via CDF)

Left: The 33rd Division briefly introduced unit markings in the form of a winged 33 for the 97th and 98th ARs, as seen on this J-7E from the 97th.
(via CMA)
Right: A J-7B assigned to the 99th AR landing. The current status of this unit – now a brigade – is unconfirmed and reports range from it having been disbanded or re-equipped with more modern types.
(via CDF)

The most famous guest transported by this division was surely Chairman Mao, who made his first of 25 flights on 3 May 1956 to inspect the entire country. Three years later on 21 May 1959 a new helicopter regiment was formed on the basis of the 3rd Independent Regiment's helicopter brigade and from the 3rd Training Base in Xuzhou. Equipped with 30 helicopters this unit was based at Xinxiang air base in Henan from June on.

Several years later on 28 August 1963, the Air Force Command ordered, that this 3rd Independent Regiment should be expanded into the 34th Division. This was accomplished on 30 September or 1 October 1963 with jurisdiction over the 100th and the 102nd Regiments. As the division's third regiment, the 101st Regiment was added on 5 December 1964. On 3 May 1969, the 34th Division was expanded from the three established regiments to have a fourth, when the 203rd Regiment was formed. In November 1969 it was relocated to Nanyuan following the 13th School had left the air base. Since then Nanyuan is also home base for the civil carrier China United Airlines (CUA), which used to be part of the 34th Division. Interestingly, it seems as if this division is the sole PLAAF division that does not use the regular designation of Aviation or Air Division but instead – and according to an official note by the PLAAF Command from 11 May 1970 changed its number to 'The 34th Division of the Air Force Aviation'.

Another specialty was, that with the approval of the Central Military Commission (CMC) from 1 September 1980 the PLAAF Command ordered on 9 October 1981 that the 34th Division was reorganised into an independent transport regiment with three subordinated brigades, but still with divisional authority. Consequently in early November 1981 the 100th, 101st and 102nd Regiments became the 1st, 2nd and 3rd Brigades in turn. This however was reversed on 4 March 1988, when again approved by the CMC this Independent Transport Group changed its name again back to the 34th Division and the three brigades again were renamed the 100th, 101st and 102nd Regiments.

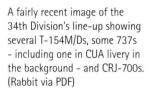

A fairly recent image of the 34th Division's line-up showing several T-154M/Ds, some 737s - including one in CUA livery in the background - and CRJ-700s.
(Rabbit via PDF)

When the 203rd and also the 202nd Regiments were reinstalled is not clear but the helicopters were reorganised somewhere 2016–17 into a dedicated transportation and SAR brigade for the PLAAF HQ. Operational-wise, the 34th Division was actively involved in the Korean War, was always the prime unknot to carry high-ranking political and military leaders and was involved in nearly each and every military operation be that at the Liaodong Peninsula, at the borders to Vietnam, close to India in Tibet or to support the islands in the South China Sea.

Besides the tasks of regular transportation and VIP transport, the 34th Division operates some of the most extensively modified and secretive Tu-154M/Ds and Boeing 737 airborne command posts that remain in PLAAF service.

The PLAAF operated several Hawker Siddeley Trident 1E airliners during the 1970s and one (no. 256) became infamous after the mysterious crash in September 1971 near Öndörkhaan, Mongolia, killing all nine on board, including Chinese Vice Premier and Minister of Defence Lin Biao. (via FYJS Forum)

35th Fighter Division

On 1 July 1965, the 35th Division was formed at the Xingning Shantou air base in Guangdong province with three subordinated units: the 103rd, 104th and 105th Brigades, which were established from brigades drawn from the 9th, 18th and 26th Divisions. All were equipped with J-5 fighters on 21 October 1965 it was placed under the command of the Xingning CP (12th Army). The division was mainly responsible for the protection of Guangdong's eastern airspace and support of army operations in that area.

Since it formation at the early 1990s about 682 combat sorties were flown including the shooting down of 113 high-altitude reconnaissance balloons. Besides that, the division was heavily involved in flood relief and emergency transportation. In the second half of 1967, an additional independent squadron (?) was formed, which was equipped with J-5A.

On 13 March 1976, with the abolishment of the 12th Army, the 35th Division was placed under direct the leadership of the Guangzhou MRAF. In October 1985, the 105th Regiment was withdrawn. Another relocation occurred on 27 November 1993, when the division was transferred from Xingning to Shantou air base and ten years later in November 2003, the 35th Division was disbanded and the 104th AR became the new 25th AR within the 9th Division.

Top left: Besides the regular VIP transports, the 34th Division also operates a few dedicated special-mission types such as Boeing 737 command posts and these Tu-154M/D ELINT aircraft. (via top81.cn)

Top right:
An interesting image that shows the most modern Western airliners in service –
an Airbus A319 ACJ and a Boeing 737-700. Both were aquired for VIP duties. (via CMA)

36th Bomber Division

Only one image of a J-7E loaded with PL-8 AAMs is known. Again, this image shows the typical pre-2005 serial numbers. (via FYJS Forum)

This division has quite a long history even before it became the 36th Bomber Division. In fact it origins back to 15 March 1953, when the PLAAF's 4th Independent Regiment reorganised from the 28th Regiment of the 10th Division in Shijiazhuang, Hebei province. At first equipped with 10 Tu-4 bombers, it began flight training in mid-June as the PLAAF's first heavy bomber unit. In March 1954, the regiment was transferred to Nanyuan air base and in March 1955, it was further transferred to Shaanxi Wugong placed under the command of the Northwest MRAF. In February 1956, the PLAAF organised a test flight conference in Beijing, and decided to use one Tu-4 bomber and several Il-12 transports from the 13th Division to conduct trials on the Wugong-Xining-Yushu-Lhasa route. This was aimed against the rebellion which broke out between March and April 1956 in the northwestern part of Sichuan, where the 4th Regiment was heavily involved with a Tu-4 bomber against rebels in the periphery of Batang and Sichuan. This allegedly included the airdropping of material to ground forces. Similar unrest broke out in the spring of 1958 in some parts of Gannan and Qinghai, and again the 4th Regiment dispatched bombers together with the 25th, the 13th and 26th Division's La-11 brigade, based on Shaanxi Wugong. And yet again in March 1959 similar missions were flown against a rebellion in Tibet in the area of Lhasa and Shannan together with Il-28s drawn from the 8th Division.

Such missions continued until 1961. In the meantime, in order to prepare for the planned Taiwan campaign and especially to crack down nighttime low-altitude harassment by ROCAF aircraft, four Tu-4 bombers were modified (as Tu-4II aircraft) to prepare for night combat and night air defence operations A detachment was transferred to Hebei City and Henan Zhengzhou air base. In April 1960, the first two Tu-16 bomber were acquired via the Soviet Union and transferred from Harbin Pingfang to Shaanxi Wugong, where they were assigned to the 4th Regiment. Finally on 13 April 1965, PLAAF's General Staff ordered to expand the 4th Independent Regiment to the

Before the H-6N was unveiled during the anniversary parade on 1 October 2019, the H-6K was the most advanced bomber in PLAAF service. This example was taking part in the Aviadarts 2019 exercise. (Giovanni Colla)

36th Bomber Division based at Shaanxi Wugong. It had three subordinated brigades, namely the 106th, 107th and 108th which were changed to regiments in May 1969. By then, the 106th Regiment was re-organised into a dedicated PLAAF electronic warfare and reconnaissance regiment and transferred under the Wuhan MRAF. It was equipped with Tu-4 EW aircraft and Tu-16 bombers. In tems of its original mission, a new chapter was opened on 14 May 1965, when the Tu-16 bomber numbered '4251' successfully dropped China's first atomic bomb. Similarly, two years later on 17 June 1967 another Tu-16, numbered '21', successfully tested China's first hydrogen bomb. Finally, in late December 1967 another test was accomplished. Another new chapter was the introduction of the first domestic H-6 bomber within the 36th Division on 28 February 1969.

In October 1969, the division was again put on alert and rated as an air force combat reserve by the Central Military Commission (CMC) and in the 1970s, in order to strengthen the preparations for the Tibet area, the 36th Division sent H-6 bomber twice (in August 1974 and October 1975) to Shigatse in order to verify the use of this type in the Tibetan Plateau. About two years later in August 1976, the division received its first Tu-4 electronic reconnaissance aircraft, which was successfully modified at the PLAAF's 12th Aviation Repair Plant. Additionally, in March 1978, a dedicated group operating WZ-5 UAVs was formed within the 106th Regiment, and this was eventually declared ready in November 1981.

On 16 October 1980, another nuclear test with the airdrop of a nuclear bomb was successfully completed, this time by the 107th AR. Probably the biggest exercise in which the 36th Division ever took part was in September 1981, when 23 H-6 bombers and one Tu-4 electronic jammer participated in the '802' or North China Exercise organised by the Beijing MR in the Zhangbei District/Zhangjiakou. In April 1982, the 106th AR received an additional reconnaissance jamming regiment, equipped with the Tu-4 EW jammer and an high-altitude unmanned reconnaissance aircraft carrier (most likely the WZ-6 drone), which on 17 June was placed under the Wuhan MRAF. Since then, specific data is sparse. In December 1994, the division was identified by the CMC as an emergency mobile combat unit.

Another rare image of several regular H-6H bombers with the original pre-2005 serial numbers but with toned-down markings.
(via CDF)

An H-6H from the 107th AR - albeit with serial numbers corresponding with the 106th AR. Note the characteristic drum-like main radar under the chin and the dark bulbous datalink antenna for the KD-63.
(via Top81.cn)

There is still some confusion regarding the true regimental identity within the 36th Bomber Division, since the 107th and 108th ARs long used non-standard serial numbers. Currently it is unclear if both ARs already fly the H-6K or if they have been renumbered. (via CDF)

In 2004, the 106th AR was disbanded most likely to form an independent aerial survey regiment and the other two were still flying H-6. One of them was long said to be equipped with H-6E and H-6Fs and responsible for the nuclear deterrent role, but that was never confirmed even if it could fit to the mentioned 1994 role. It now flies the H-6H. The final regiment operates a mix of H-6H and updated H-6M – and since January 2017 – also the H-6K. The H-6M are said to go to the re-established 30th AR.

Confusingly, this division wore off-standard serial numbers for long. Probably since the 106th AR was not a bomber regiment, the 107th AR used numbers usually expected to be used by the 106th and similar the 108th AR used numbers expected for the 107th. This is still valid even after the H-6K were delivered, which now have numbers fitting both the 107th and 108th AR, but are said to be only flown in one regiment. It could however be that both regiments are currently under conversion both in the end applied with correct numbers.

37th Fighter Division

The decision to create the 37th Division was made on 29 May 1966 by Central Military Commission (CMC). On 1 August the same year, this was executed at the Langtou air base in Dandong, Liaoning province within the Shenyang MR and under its jurisdiction were the 109th and 111th Brigades. Already on 27 May 1969, the units were transferred from Longtou to Xinjiang with one brigade being based at Ürümqi and another at Malan.

In April 1970, the 110th Brigade was formed, equip the MiG-15bis but already on 5 June all three brigades were renamed the 109th, 110th and 111st Regiments. Between June 1973 and January 1976, the 111th Air Regiment was assigned to the atmospheric sampling mission after ground-based nuclear tests and J-6 were used. On 19 January 1979 another relocating was issued, and the 37th Division was relocated again to the Ürümqi (Dadonggou) air base.

In 1985, a so far unknown independent brigade under the 37th Division was disbanded. Yet another round of base changes was initiated from the mid-1980s on: on 15 January 1987, the 111th Regiment returned to Malan and on 22 April 1989 it was transferred from Malan air base to Korla. At that time the 111th Regiment was still operating J-6. When the three regiments received the J-7 is unclear, but prior to the 2012 modernisations, it emerged as one of the premier PLAAF units.

In April 2012 the 37th Division's three regiments were converted into brigades and subordinated to the newly established Ürümqi Base. The latter facility also took command of the former Lanzhou Military Training Base, at Ürümqi South (Wulumuqi). Since mid-2012 the unit began to operate J-7Bs and JJ-7As, as well as a detachment of Y-8 transports at Jiuquan as the 110th Brigade. The 109th has gained J-8H in 2002 replacing J-6 and a few J-8F followed in 2006. The 110th received J-7G in 2004 replacing J-7B, which were again replaced by JH-7A in 2011. And finally the 111th received J-11B and J-11BS in early 2011 replacing J-7E. Just in April 1989 it has moved from Malan to Korla (Bayingol). Quite surprisingly, in 2016 this brigade also revealed a few examples of the J-11A, which might have replaced the J-11B.

A factory-fresh J-7E operated by the 37th Division but still with the original pre-2005 serial numbers. A few years later the same regiment transitioned from the J-7E to the latest J-7G. (via Top81.cn)

38th Fighter Division

Not much and most of all very vague information is known about this division. Reportedly its predecessor was the PLAAF's Second Aviation Preparation Team in Hangzhou Luqiao in February 1950. In July 1951, it was renamed the PLAAF's Fifth Aviation Preparation Team, which was transferred to Xuzhou City in June 1952. In July 1954, it was renamed the PLAAF Fifth Aviation Preparation School (5th Flight Academy?), which in July 1955 was transferred from the Nanjing MRAF to the Beijing MRAF.

On 16 April 1958 it was reorganised into the PLAAF 1st Training Base at the Jinghai air base in Hebei equipped with 40 MiG-15 fighters and 10 MiG-15U trainers and in January 1959, the MiG-15bis was introduced, when the unit was allegedly based at Yangcun.

In the following several more moves occurred between April 1958 to September 1959 it was located at Jinghai air base in Hebei, between September 1959 to January 1963 at Gaomi in Shandong, between January 1963 and September 1963 it was back at Jinghai from, and at Beijing Tongxian from September 1963 to May 1964 only to be back at Jinghai between May 1964 to August 1968. On 3 August 1968, the 38th Division

Only images of the more recent aircraft flown by the 37th Division are known, including this J-8H from the 109th AR (left) and a J-11BS from the 111th AR (right). All three former regiments are still active today as the 109th, the 110th (flying JH-7A) and the 111th Brigades. (Both via CDF)

Images of the 38th Division's types are again rare and only these early J-6s (left) as well as this radar-equipped J-5A are known.
(Both via CDF)

finally transferred to Yangcun, where the 114th Brigade was formed. Between August 1969 and October 1976, the then 113th AR was upgraded in eight batches to receive J-6 fighters.

In the meantime, between 15 July 1971 and 24 November 1972, the 113th AR was relocated to Fujian Zhangzhou for a combat deployment and by 1982 several surveillance balloons had been shot down. A round of downsizing began on 30 October 1985, when the division's independent brigade was disbanded and the 112th AR was reduced to only three flight brigades (or flight groups), before the 114th AR was also disbanded.

Ultimately, however, the 112th AR was finally disbanded on 30 September 1992 and the 113th AR was renamed the 21st AR, to be reassigned to the 7th Division.

39th Fighter Division

Similar to the 38th Division, also the 39th stem from an educational unit, when in January 1951, the PLAAF's 4th Aviation Preparation Team was established in Xuzhou, Jiangsu province to be renamed in July, as the PLAAF 6th Aviation Preparation Team. This unit was renamed as the PLAAF's 6th Aviation Preparation School (6th Flight Academy?) in July 1954.

In October 1954, this school was transferred from Hangzhou, Zhejiang province to Jilin City, Jilin province, where on 20 July 1958, it was reorganised into the PLAAF 2nd Training Base at Qiqihar, Heilongjiang province with the 3rd and 4th Training Regiments subordinated. The division itself was established only on 1 August 1967 when the 2nd Training Base was converted to the 39th Division at Sanyuanpu air base in Jilin. Subordinated brigades were the 115th and 116th, both equipped with MiG-15bis fighters.

In June 1967 parts of the former 3rd and 4th Regiments were set up to establish a dedicated meteorological flight training brigade to be stationed at Dongfeng in Jilin province. This brigade was established on 9 August 1967 and one year later was renamed the 117th Brigade. In May 1970, the three brigades became the 115th, 116th and 117th Regiments. Similar to the 38th Division, and also the 39th were based at various locations: in October 1967, it transferred to the Fuyang air base in Hunan province, in November 1969, it was located at three different bases around Qiqihar, Heilongjiang province and between November 1967 and August 1968 it was in Fuyang, Hunan province. And finally on 6 July 1969, in order to strengthen the air defence force in the Qiqi-

har area, a brigade was moved from Dongfeng to Qiqihar Sanjiazi air base, and another brigade on July 8, from Sanyuanpu to Hailar.

The 1970s saw several changes: in May 1971 the 115th AR was placed under the authority of the 49th Division and became the 146th AR, in return, the 134th AR of the 45th Division was reassigned as the new 115th Regiment.

Between September 1983 and April 1984, the 117th AR was operationally assigned in war but in October 1985 - again similar to the 38th Division – the downsizing begun, when the 116th AR was withdrawn.

Several more relocations were initiated between 1990 and 1991, when in May 1990, the 115th AR was transferred from Shuangliao to Qiqihar and in May 1991, the 117th AR was stationed at the Lushan air base close to Qiqihar. In 1998, the 39th Division's 115th AR was withdrawn and the 117th AR was transferred to the 21st Division, where in 2003, it became the 62th AR.

This JJ-6 with the construction number '7810' from the 39th Fighter Division is preserved in the entrance area of the China Aviation Museum at Xiaotangshan. (Foxbat.run via CDF)

40th Fighter Division

The 40th Division was formed on 31 July 1969 within the Shenyang MRAF at Liaoning Longtou air base and jurisdiction over the 118th Brigade, which was formed via the original 30th Division's 90th Brigade based at Dadonggou and the 119th Brigade, equipped with J-5 and MiG-15bis fighters.

On 12 March 1984, the 119th AR moved to Liancheng, Fujian province but already on 27 August 1985, the 40th Division was merged with the 30th Division in which turn the number of the 40th Division was deleted.

41st Fighter Division

On 10 August 1969 a new unit was formed within the Beijing MRAF at Gongmiaozi air base in Inner Mongolia with jurisdiction over the 121st and 122nd Brigades. The 121st Brigade was in fact constructed from the 7th Division's 20th Brigade and the 122nd Brigade, from elements of the 11th Aviation School, the 17th Division and other units, whereas an independent brigade – allegedly elements of the 8th Independent Team – which was a dedicated night-fighter brigade – formed the backbone of the new formation.

Sometime in the 1970s, the 121st and 122nd Brigades became regiments and a 123th Regiment was formed. At that time the 41st Division was equipped with J-6 and MiG-15bis fighters and both the 121st and 122nd ARs were stationed at Gongmiaozi air base, while the 123rd AR was stationed at Bikeqi air base.

On 27 August 1985 the 41st Division was disbanded, when the 121st AR at Gongmiaozi and Bikezi/Bikeki air base were reassigned to the 15th Division, only to be later reassigned to the 7th Division with the 122th, the 123th and the Independent Brigade being disbanded.

42nd Fighter Division

According to the operational needs in Guangxi, on 26 August 1969, the 42nd Division was established under control of the Guangzhou MRAF in Guilin, Guangxi. Subordinated brigades were the 124th based on the 9th Division's 26th Brigade and the 125th Brigade, which was formed from the 18th Division's 53rd Brigade, both equipped with the J-5 fighters.

Slightly after April 1970 – the brigades were now regiments – personnel and equipment were deployed from the 124th and 125th ARs to form the 126th AR. In January 1971, the 42nd Division moved from Guilin to Nanning Wuxu air base and during subsequent air defence operations a total of 43 airborne balloons were shot down. Between 19 and 22 January 1974, the Guangzhou MRAF ordered the 124th AR together with other units to transfer to the front line of Hainan Island in order to participate in the operation around the Xisha Islands. The aircraft were organised to conduct aerial photo reconnaissance and combat air patrols around the area. They came back home on 7 June. On 21 January 1977, the 125th AR was transferred from Wusong to Zhangzhou, Fujian province and after the war it returned home on 24 September. Similar, on 13 December 1978 the 42nd Division was again ordered to provide air defence so that in January 1979, the 126th AR was transferred to Huiyang.

Similar missions were performed around May 1981 and around March 1984 and October 1987, when in two separate aerial battles they intercepted Vietnamese Air Force MiG-21s that invaded the PRC's airspace. Finally, until September 1990, the 125th AR was based at Tianyang air base in Changsha.

The more recent history is lesser known: it seems as if on 9 November 1992, the 126th AR lost its number plate and similar unconfirmed, on 14 May 1994, the 124th AR was reorganised. The next step was the reassignment of the 42nd Division under the direct leadership of the Guangzhou MRAF in December 2003. Under the 2012 reorganisations some more changes with the introduction of the brigade structure: the 42nd Division's remaining regiments and the Guangzhou Military Training Base were unified under the command of Nanning Base. In that line the division also regained its third regiment and equipment wise two brigades were modernised in recent years, the 124th gained J-10A in late 2013 and in 2016 the 126th replaced its J-7IIs with JH-7A

Similar to the JJ-6 above, this J-5 from the 42nd Fighter Division is preserved at the China Aviation Museum at Xiaotangshan, in the so called 'MiG Alley'.
(via CDF)

Two J-7IIHs or J-7BHs – which were modified to launch the PL-8 AAM – from the 42nd Division's 125th AR.
(Both via CDF)

43rd Fighter Division

In accordance to urgent operational needs within the Shenyang MRAF, the 43rd Division was formed on 19 September 1969 with at first two subordinated brigades, namely the 127th and 128th Brigades. Therefore on 21 September 1969, the 21st Division's 62nd Brigade was transferred to the 43rd Division and renamed the 127th Brigade, equipped with MiG-15bis. At the same time the 128th Brigade was formed from personnel from the 11th, 20th and 39th Divisions, also equipped with MiG-15bis fighters. The unit was based at Dongfeng, Jilin province and an official inaugural meeting was held on 26 January 1970 at Jilin Ertaizi air base in Jilin. Slightly later on 1 May, the 127th and 128th Brigades became the 127th and 128th ARs and from September 1970 on, the 43rd Division began with air defence operations in Jilin.

In October 1983, the 62nd AR was transferred from the Weihe air base to Luhe and integrated into the 43rd Division. However slightly later the downsizing began, when on 27 September 1985, the 43rd Division's 128th AR (?) and the 47th AR were merged and reorganised into the new 47th AR, which was reassigned to the 16th Division. In parallel, the 127th AR, the 62nd AR from the 21st Division followed suit and both together with the Weihe Air Station were placed under command of the 21st Division.

44th Fighter Division

Established on 24 November 1969, the 44th Division was placed under the command of the Wuhan MRAF in Hubei province, with jurisdiction over the 130th and 131st Brigades. The 130th was established via reassignment of the 19th Division's 55th Brigade

The J-10A was first assigned to the 131st AR at Luliang air base (left) but this regiment is quite often forward deployed to other locations, as here in Tibet (right).
(Both via CDF)

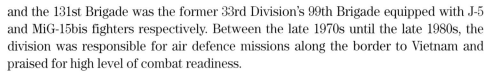

Although not the best quality, this rare image shows several J-6Bing aircraft wearing different colour schemes, as well as some early J-7Bs in the background.
(via CDF)

and the 131st Brigade was the former 33rd Division's 99th Brigade equipped with J-5 and MiG-15bis fighters respectively. Between the late 1970s until the late 1980s, the division was responsible for air defence missions along the border to Vietnam and praised for high level of combat readiness.

By around May 1975, the 44th Division's brigades were renamed regiments and it must have gained the 132nd AR as an additional third regiment. In the years that followed some changes occurred, when on 4 September 1975, the 130th AR was transferred to Fuzhou and on 20 November 1977, the 44th Division's 131st AR – together with the 27th Division – relocated to Kunming Wujiaba in charge of adjust defence. Similar to earlier, in December 1978 it was again responsible for air defence mission against Vietnam.

By 1989, the 131st AR was one of seven regiments equipped with J-6A fighters but during the 1990s all three regiments operated J-7 fighters. Ten years later in 1998, the 132nd AR was disbanded and in July 2004 the 131st AR became the first unit to operate the J-10A.

Since then, reports of its composition were varying and most likely the 132th AR was re-established as the Chengdu MRTB. However this was eventually reversed in 2012 and the division again consisted of three regiments operating J-10A/AS and J-7s. In 2016–17 the 130th AR received J-10A from the 131st AR and the 131st gained new J-10C briefly before both ARs became the 130th and 131st Brigades. In 2014 the 132nd AR relocated from Luliang to Xiangyun and in 2017 it became the 132nd Brigade still acting as a training unit.

45th Fighter Division/Ground Attack Division

It seems as if the 45th Division was set up originally as a fighter division on 24 November 1969 within the Nanjing MRAF at Anhui with two subordinated brigades: the 133rd Brigade by transferring the 14th Division's 44th Brigade, the 134th Brigade by renaming the 26th Division's 77th Brigade. Both were equipped with J-5 aircraft and later on the brigades became regiments and the 135th AR was added.

On 9 May 1976 it was re-formed into a ground-attack division by gaining one regiment each from the 11th and 22nd Divisions, which became the new 133rd and 134th ARs, while the original 133rd, 134th and 135th ARs were transferred to the 49th, 39th and 46th Division respectively. Two years later on 20 November 1978, the 133rd and 134th ARs were transferred the Gansu Dalachi Airbase. Slightly later the unit must have gained Q-5.

The division however was disbanded on 30 September 1992, with two of three regiments disbanded. The 133rd AR was reassigned to the 99th AR within the 33rd Division in Liangping, Sichuan province.

Images of any aircraft from divisions after the 44th are extremely rare, including this example showing two Q-5ls from the 133rd AR.
(via CDF)

46th Fighter Division

On 3 October 1969, the 46th Division was established based on the 9th Independent Brigade and the 47th Brigade of the 16th Division on the Dingxin, Gansu province, with two subordinated brigades: the 136th by renaming the 9th Independent Brigade and the 137th from the 16th Division's 47th Brigade (some sources say the 17th) both equipped with J-6 fighters.

In May 1976 the 45th Division's 135th AR was added as the new 138th AR and in September 1978 the 136th AR was re-established on the basis of the 46th Division's Training Brigade flying MiG-15bis. When however this training brigade was added and when the original 136th AR was transferred or withdrawn is not known.

In 1984, the 46th Division's 137th Regiment organised a campaign on 28 April to carry out combat patrols, in cooperation with the army to recover Laoshan, Yinshan. In 1985, the 46th Division's 136th and 138th ARs were disbanded and the 137th AR was reassigned to the 6th Division as the new 17th AR.

47th Fighter Division

The 47th Division was established on 17 February 1970, at the Yinchuan air base in Ningxia on the basis of the 2nd Division's 5th Brigade and the 32nd Division's 96th Brigade. Its subordinated brigades were the 139th and 140th Brigades, equipped with the J-5 and MiG-15bis fighters. Somewhere later it received J-6 and also must have gained the 141th AR, which on 11 June 1988, was converted into the Lanzhou Training Base.

In 1998, the 47th Division was disbanded and the 140th AR was reassigned to the 6th Division.

48th Bomber Division

The 48th Division was officially established in Fuyang, Hunan province on 4 August 1970, with two subordinated regiments: the 142nd AR based on the original 10th Bomber Division's 30th AR and the 143rd AR, which was formerly the 20th Division's 59th AR. Both were equipped with H-5 bomber. Between 19 and 22 January 1974, the 48th Division was sent to Hainan due to the Paracel crisis where it conducted aerial photographic reconnaissance and theatre patrols over the islands. It returned home on 7 June.

In January 1976 it was placed under direct leadership of the Guangzhou MRAF. In April 1976, the 144th AR was formed. In December 1978, the division was ordered to participate in the evolving Sino-Vietnamese border conflict.

In 1982, the 143rd AR converted to H-6 bombers. Unusually, in January 1984, the 5th AR – then called a reconnaissance regiment – from Guilin was assigned to this bomber division, which was subject to more change in September 1985, when the 142nd AR was finally disbanded again. On 30 September 1992, the PLAAF ordered to disband the 48th Division and its 144th AR, while the 143rd AR was kept and the fate of the 142nd AR is unknown.

Later events were the maiden flight of the HU-6 tanker piloted by the 143rd AR's commander Yu Peiqiang on 6 May 1998 and successfully completing in-flight refueling training with J-8D fighters from the 9th Division's 27th AR. Finally in July 1999, the 143rd AR was transferred to the 8th Bomber Division.

Very early J-6s on the ramp at an unknown base from the 137th AR.
(via CDF)

Another rare image showing a HU-6 with a 48th Bomber Division serial number, before that regiment was reassigned in July 1999.
(via CDF)

Another rare image - and probably the only published example from the 49th Fighter Division - shows J-6 '40208' flown by Liu Zhiyuan during his defection on 19 November 1987, when he flew from Longxi, Zhangzhou, to Ching Chuan Kang Air Base in Taichung, Taiwan.
(via CDF)

49th Fighter Division

The 49th Division was first mentioned on 5 July 1971, but only established officially on 30 December 1971 in Changshu City, Jiangxi province, with the 145th and 146th Regiments subordinated. They were equipped with J-6 and MiG-15bis fighters respectively. Surprisingly, during summer 1971, two changes occurred, namely on 5 July 1971, when the 71st Regiment of the 24th Division was transferred to the 49th Division and renamed 145th AR and on 12 August, when the 115th Regiment of the 39th Division became the new 146th Regiment. In November 1973, the unit moved from Nanchang to Zhangzhou, Fujian province, and the 49th Division was put directly under the leadership of the Fuzhou MRAR in March 1974. From its two bases Fuzhou and Liancheng respectively both regiments were involved in several surveillance balloon shootdowns. A third regiment was added to the division, when on 25 March 1976, the 133rd AR of the 45th Division was transferred as the 147th AR. Several more balloons were shot down between October 1976 and October 1992, where the division was temporarily stationed in Changshu, Jiangxi, while the 147th AR remained at Fuzhou.

In August 1985, the Fuzhou MRAF was withdrawn, and the division reassigned, so that in December 1989, the 145th AR was transferred back to Changshu air base in Jiangxi province. Only three years later however the 49th Division was reorganised again, when on 30 October 1992 the 145th, 146th and 147th ARs were withdrawn.

The 145th AR was transferred to the 14th Division as the new 40nd AR, the 146th AR was also merged with the 14th Division's 42nd AR and – even if not mentioned by name – the remaining 147th AR was transferred to the 26th Division.

50th Bomber Division/Ground Attack Division

Officially established on 1 August 1971 in Guiyang Leizhuang, the 50th Division has two subordinated regiments, the 148th Regiment, which was the former 23rd Division's 69th AR and the 149th AR, which was formed from the 25th Division's 74th Regiment. It was equipped with Tu-2 aircraft and placed under the Kunming MRAF.

During spring 1976, the 50th Division was transferred to Guizhou and on 16 May, it was converted from a bomber to fighter/ground-attack division, when it received the former 84th AR of the 28th Division as the new 148th AR and the 11th Independent Regiment as the new 149th AR. In due course it moved from Guiyang City, Guizhou province, to Lingqiu, Shanxi province, where the 148th and 149th ARs were equipped with the Q-5 and MiG-15bis under the command of the Beijing MRAF. In return, the original 148th and 149th ARs were transferred to the 48th and 25th Divisions respectively, where they were renamed the 144th and 74th ARs.

Somewhere in between also a 150th AR was added, which however on 27 August 1985, together with the 148th AR were disbanded. Only the 149th AR survived and was allegedly transferred on 8 May 1986 to the 8th Bomber Division. Slightly later however in August 1986 a group of Q-5s from the 149th AR were transferred to Huairen, where they conducted joint attack exercises with the PLA Army's 38th Group Army and on 22 September 1998, this regiment relocated to Dingxiang. Finally in April 2005, the 149th AR placed under the 15th Division and renamed the 45th AR.

This is so far the only known clear image of early Q-5s assigned to the 50th Ground Attack Division. At that time, the Q-5s were unpainted.
(via CDF)

This appendix is largely based on a semi-official report published in 2014 to commemorate the PLAAF's 65th anniversary, the *PLAAF 50 Air Divisions History* (中国人民解放军空军航空兵师历史沿革 – 2014-05-13 07:39:27) which was first posted at http://www.plaaf.net/special/hkbs.html and later reposted at http://blog.sina.com.cn/s/blog_a3f74a990101fi67.html

Air Division	Date of Establishment	Location	Note	Re-established or renamed	Current status
1st Fighter Division	1956 March	Anshan, Liaoning	Original 10th Regiment/4th Mixed Brigade		Disbanded; 1st, 2nd and 3rd ARs are brigades, Dalian Base, NTC
2nd Fighter Division	1950 November	Shanghai Longhua	Original 11th Regiment/4th Mixed Brigade		Disbanded; 4th, 5th and 6th ARs are brigades, Nanning Base, STC
3rd Fighter Division	1950 October	Shenyang, Liaoning			Disbanded; 7th, 8th and 9th ARs are brigades, Shanghai Base, ETC
4th Fighter Division	1950 October 1956 April	Liaoyang, Liaoning	Original 10th Regiment/4th Mixed Brigade	Became 1st Division in March 1956; re-established in April 1956, disbanded in 2003; re-established again as transport division in July 2005	Still active, WTC
4th Transport Division	2005 July	Qionglai, Sichuan			
5th Ground Attack Division	1950 December	Kaiyuan, Liaoning			Disbanded; 15th AR became brigade, Jinan Base, NTC
6th Fighter Division	1950 November	Anshan, Liaoning			Disbanded; 16th AR became brigade, Lanzhou Base/WTC; 18th AR became brigade, Ürümqi Base, WTC
7th Fighter Division	1950 December	Dongfeng, Jilin			Disbanded; 19th and 21st ARs became brigades, Datong Base, CTC
8th Bomber Division	1950 December	Siping, Jilin			Still active, STC
9th Fighter Division	1950 December 1956 March	Jilin, Jilin Guangzhou, Guangdong	Transferred to Naval Aviation as 6th NAD in December 1955	Re-established in March 1956	Disbanded; 26th AR became brigade, Nanning Base, STC
10th Bomber Division	1951 January	Nanjing, Jiangsu	Original 12th Regiment /4th Mixed Brigade		Still active, ETC
11th Ground Attack Division	1951 February	Xuzhou, Jiangsu			Disbanded; 31st AR became brigade, Dalian Base, NTC

12th Fighter Division	1950 December	Xiaoshan, Zhejiang			Disbanded; 34th and 36th ARs became brigades, Jinan Base, NTC
13th Transport Division	1951 April	Xinjin Xi'an, Sichuan	Formed out of the very first transport flight		Still active, CTC
14th Fighter Division	1951 February	Beijing Nanyuan			Disbanded; 40th and 41st ARs became brigades, Fuzhou Base, ETC
15th Ground Attack Division	1951 May	Huaide Xi'an, Jilin			Disbanded; 43rd AR became brigade, Datong Base, CTC; 44th AR became brigade, Dalian Base, NTC
16th Fighter Division 16th Specialised Division	1951 February 2012 (?)	Qingdao, Shandong		Became Shenyang MRTB in August 1988 re-formed as Specialised Division in 2012?	Still active, NTC
17th Fighter Division	1951 April 1956 April	Tangshan, Hebei Beijing	Transferred to Naval Aviation as 4th NAD in May 1954	Re-established in April 1956; became Beijing MRTB in August 1988	Disbanded
18th Fighter Division	1951 May	Guangzhou, Guangdong			Disbanded; 54th AR became brigade, Nanning Base, STC
19th Fighter Division	1951 October	Wuhan, Hubei			Disbanded; 55th and 56th ARs became brigades, Wuhan Base, CTC
20th Bomber Division 20th Specialised Division	1951 September 2012/13?	Bengbu, Anhui Guiyang, Guizhou		Disbanded in September 1992; re-formed as Specialised Division in 2012–13	Still active, STC
21st Fighter Division	1951 November	Shanghai Dachang			Disbanded; 61st AR became brigade, Dalian Base, NTC
22nd Ground Attack Division	1951 September	Hengyang, Hunan		Disbanded in October 1992	Disbanded
23rd Bomber Division	1952 January	Nanchang, Jiangxi		Disbanded in August 1985	Disbanded
24th Fighter Division	1952 January	Zunhua, Hebei			Disbanded; 70th and 72nd ARs became brigades, Datong Base, CTC
25th Bomber Division	1952 May	Xi'an, Shaanxi		Disbanded in August 1985	Disbanded
26th Fighter Division	1952 December	Liuzhou, Guangxi			Still active, ETC
26th Specialised Division	2003?	Chongming Shanghai		Re-formed as specialised division in 2003?	

27th Fighter Division	1952 December	Tongxian, Hebei		Became Guangzhou MRTB in June 1988, disbanded in November 2003	Disbanded
28th Ground Attack Division	1952 December	Gucheng, Hebei			Disbanded; 83rd and 84th ARs became brigades, Shanghai Base, ETC
29th Fighter Division	1953 December	Jiaxing, Zhejiang			Disbanded; 85th AR became brigade, Fuzhou Base, ETC; 86th AR became brigade, Shanghai Base, ETC
30th Fighter Division	1960 May	Donggou, Liaoning			Disbanded; 88th, 89th and 90th ARs became brigades, Dalian Base, NTC
31st Fighter Division	1960 March	Yancheng, Jiangsu		Disbanded in August 2003	Disbanded
32nd Fighter Division	1960 April	Jinghai County, Hebei			Disbanded; 95th AR became brigade, Fuzhou Base, ETC
33rd Fighter Division	1960 May	Shanpo, Hubei			Disbanded; 97th, 98th and 99th ARs became brigades, Lanzhou Base, WTC
34th Transport Division	1963 September	Beijing Nanyuan, Hebei		Became an independent transport regiment in September 1980; re-formed again as 34th Division in March 1988	Still active, PLAAF HQ
35th Fighter Division	1965 July	Xingning Airport, Guangdong		Disbanded in November 2003	Disbanded
36th Bomber Division	1965 March	Wugong, Shaanxi			Still active, CTC
37th Fighter Division	1966 August	Dandong, Liaoning			Disbanded; 109th, 110th and 111th ARs became brigades, Ürümqi Base, WTC
38th Fighter Division	1967 June	Jinghai, Hebei	Was the former 1st Training Base	Disbanded in September 1992	Disbanded
39th Fighter Division	1967 July	Liuhe, Jilin	Was the former 2nd Training Base	Disbanded in September 1998	Disbanded
40th Fighter Division	1969 July	Longtou Airport, Liaoning		Disbanded in August 1985	Disbanded
41st Fighter Division	1969 August	Gongmiaozi Airport, Inner Mongolia		Disbanded in August 1985	Disbanded

42nd Fighter Division	1969 August	Guilin, Guangxi			**Disbanded;** 124th, 125th and 126th ARs became brigades, Nanning Base, STC
43rd Fighter Division	1969 August	Dongfeng, Jilin		Disbanded in September 1985	Disbanded
44th Fighter Division	1969 November	Hubei			**Disbanded;** 130th, 131st and 132nd ARs became brigades, Kunming Base, STC
45th Fighter Division	1969 November	Anhui	Re-formed as a ground-attack division in May 1976		
45th Fighter Division	1976 May			Disbanded in September 1992	Disbanded
46th Fighter Division	1969 October	Dingxin, Gansu		Disbanded in 1985	Disbanded
47th Fighter Division	1969 August	Yinchuan Airport in Ningxia		Disbanded in 1998	Disbanded
48th Bomber Division	1970 August	Fuyang, Hunan		Disbanded in September 1992	Disbanded
49th Fighter Division	1971 July	Changshu, Jiangxi		Disbanded in October 1992	Disbanded
50th Bomber Division	1971 August	Guiyang, Guizhou	Re-formed as a ground-attack division in May 1976		Disbanded
50th Ground Attack Division	1976 May			Disbanded in October 1992	

Key

Division still active

Division disbanded, but its regiments became brigades

Division completely disbanded

APPENDIX III

History of the PLAAF serial number system

The PLAAF serial number system is, at first sight, a somewhat complicated issue, especially since it has changed fairly often through the different historical periods. However, it is in fact generally straightforward and follows a broadly structured system that allows – once understood – some very important information to be deduced.

At first, the different periods must be differentiated. Incorrect identification of when a certain aircraft was spotted or photographed could result in misleading conclusions on its parent unit. A first hint – besides the type itself – could be to look how many digits a certain serial number contains. During the early days most aircraft simply had two-digit tactical numbers with no clearly identifiable pattern from which the unit could be deduced.

Three-digit serial numbers numbers are usually only used by PLAAF test facilities and dedicated aircraft on test. Prime examples are those at the CFTE test centre at Xi'an-Yanliang, but also prototypes and development aircraft from factories including SAC and XAC.

Later on the PLAAF introduced four-digit serial numbers, which by all accounts used an 'axax' pattern in which the 'aa' represents the division. However, the type of encryption used – and this was almost certainly based upon a certain system – is not understood. Although a few images exist in which the unit is given, it is so far not possible to conclude upon which system it was based. Especially these four-digit numbers are somewhat complicated. In later periods and up until today, some units – like the old independent regiments, the flight colleges and now flying academies – still use only four-digit numbers, albeit based on a different code system.

Here the system follows the subsequent 'axbx' pattern, where 'a' indicates the flying academy (between '1' and '4') and 'b' indicates the regiment. The 'xx' is reserved for the individual aircraft within that unit. An exception within the four-digit numbers today are aircraft of the first prototype and low-rate initial production batch newly produced before being delivered to the CFTE, where they then receive a three-digit number. Usually these are the first two digits denoting the type of aircraft and an individual, sequential two-digit number. Finally, factory-fresh aircraft – often still in yellow primer – both from CAC and SAC use a four-digit system, where the first two digits denote the production block and the final two the individual aircraft number.

Otherwise, the PLAAF started to use a five-digit serial system for regular frontline units, which replaced the former four-digit numbers. Through the different historical periods, a total of three different systems were used for the 'pre-2005 period', '2005 to 2011–12' and serial numbers 'from 2012 on'.

Pre-2005 period

The first five-digit system was eventually introduced during the late 1960s and remained unchanged until 2005. Most important for identifying the division's number are the first and fourth digits, which combined with a certain code result in the correct number. Unfortunately, and in contrast to the later periods, where a particular system is always valid to deduct the correct division number, the process here is more complicated. Overall, the 'abxax' pattern was introduced in which the two digits 'aa' have to be calculated minus a certain number. While this number was later changed to a common one (namely 11), in this period it was minus one for all numbers beginning with 1, 2 and 4, whereas for all numbers starting with 3 and 5, the 'aa' had to be calculated minus 21. All numbers starting with a 6 were denoted to other units. Otherwise, the second digit 'b' was the indicator of the regiment and until 2005 – by then, the fighters still had only red or blue coloured serial numbers – for the 'b' three numbers ranging from '0' to '2' were in use. The first regiment within a division usually had a '0', the second regiment used a '1' and finally the '2' was reserved for the third regiment. Effectively this meant that a division could consist of 100 serial numbers within each regiment. The final two missing digits numbers three and five – aka 'xx' – were reserved for the individual aircraft within that unit.

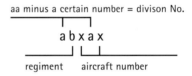

2005 to 2011–12 period

From 2005 until 2012 the regular regiments were subordinated to divisions, which used a revised five-digit serial number system following the established 'abxax' pattern. In this system, the two digits 'aa' are still representative for the division number, and for that period, the division number was covered by a uniform system, in which 11 had to be subtracted from the 'aa' digits to identify the correct number (aa – 11 = division number). The great benefit of the revised serial numbers was that all divisions now followed a common system, thereby correcting the mismatches in the pre-2005 system. Another change was related to the regimental number: when the numbers were

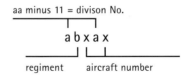

changed to a common yellow – at least for all fighters – the maximum number of codes was reduced to 50 for each regiment. This was accomplished by no longer using the 'b' to denote the regiment, but number blocks of 50 serial numbers of 'bxx' together. In that sense, the second, third and last digit were used together, with numbers ranging from 001 up to 049 for the first regiment, numbers from 050 up to 099 for the second regiment and all numbers from 100 up to 150 for the third regiment.

Usually, the trainers or twin-seaters within the fighter regiments had the last couple of numbers within the range reserved for them. In addition, the military region training bases (MRTBs) and some dedicated special mission or test regiments also used the same pattern, albeit within the 6bxax range. Meanwhile, the flying academies used serial numbers in the 7bxax range.

In parallel to this standard system, dedicated special regiments still retained the four-digit system in use until 2012. However, not all numbers were allocated. Although-before 2005 serial numbers starting with a 3 or 4 – aka '3aax' and '4aax' – were found only on reconnaissance regiments, this changed from 2005 onwards to a '5xax' pattern. The '6xax' pattern was reserved for the 15th Airborne Corps – the later Airborne Forces – and MR HQ transport units. Again, the digit 'a' identified the regiment and 'xx' was the aircraft's individual number within the regiment.

Post-2012 period

From about April 2012 onwards, all of the remaining divisions commonly used the pattern as described above after introducing the yellow serial numbers following an 'abxax' pattern, in which 'aa' minus 11 equals the correct division number (aa – 11 = division number). By looking at the 'bxx' block as a whole, it can be determined which regiment a certain type was assigned to.

On the other hand, early 2012 saw the introduction of brigades, which were transformed from the original regiments with their own serial numbering system. They use a 'bbxbx' pattern, with 'bbb' being the brigade number plus 611. In consequence, the easiest way is to use 'bbb' minus 611 to identify the brigade. With this change, the former military region training bases (MRTBs) were also incorporated in the regular divisions as brigades, and as such adopted their serial numbering system.

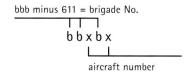

Serial numbers as used by the divisions over the three mentioned periods

Serial number	Pre-2005 period Division or unit	2005 to 2011–12 period Division or unit	Post-2012 period Division or unit
1bx2x	1st Division	1st Division	1st Division
1bx3x	2nd Division	2nd Division	2nd Division
1bx4x	3rd Division	3rd Division	3rd Division
1bx5x	4th Division	4th Division	4th Division
1bx6x	5th Division	5th Division	5th Division
1bx7x	6th Division	6th Division	6th Division
1bx8x	7th Division	7th Division	7th Division
1bx9x	8th Division	8th Division	8th Division
1bx0x	9th Division		
2bx1x	20th Division	10th Division	10th Division
2bx2x	21st Division	11th Division	11th Division
2bx3x	22nd Division	12th Division	
2bx4x	23rd Division	13th Division	
2bx5x	24th Division	14th Division	14th Division
2bx6x	25th Division	15th Division	15th Division
2bx7x	26th Division		
2bx8x	27th Division		
2bx9x	28th Division	18th Division	18th Division
2bx0x	29th Division	9th Division	9th Division
3bx1x	10th Division	20th Division	20th Division
3bx2x	11th Division	21st Division	21st Division
3bx3x	12th Division	22nd Division	
3bx4x	13th Division	23rd Division	
3bx5x	14th Division	24th Division	24th Division
3bx6x	15th Division		
3bx7x	16th Division	26th Division	
3bx8x	17th Division	27th Division	
3bx9x	18th Division	28th Division	28th Division
3bx0x	19th Division	19th Division	19th Division
4bx1x	40th Division	30th Division	
4bx2x	41st Division		
4bx3x	42nd Division		32nd Division
4bx4x	43rd Division	33rd Division	33rd Division
4bx5x	44th Division	34th Division	34th Division
4bx6x	45th Division		
4bx7x	46th Division	36th Division	36th Division
4bx8x	47th Division	37th Division	
4bx9x	48th Division	38th Division	
4bx0x	49th Division	29th Division	

5bx1x	30th Division		
5bx2x	31st Division		
5bx3x	32nd Division	42nd Division	
5bx4x	33rd Division		
5bx5x	34th Division	44th Division	44th Division
5bx6x	35th Division		
5bx7x	36th Division		
5bx8x	37th Division		
5bx9x	38th Division		
5bx0x	39th Division		
6bx1x	1st Flight Academy	Shenyang MR TB	
6bx2x	2nd Flight Academy	Beijing MR TB	
6bx3x	3rd Flight Academy	Lanzhou MR TB	
6bx4x	4th Flight Academy	Jinan MR TB	
6bx5x	5th Flight Academy	Nanjing MR TB	
6bx6x	6th Flight Academy	Guangzhou MR TB	
6xx7b	7th Flight Academy	Chengdu MR TB	
6xx8b	8th Flight Academy	FTTC	
6xx9x		SMTU	
6xx0x			
7bx1x			
7bx2x			
7bx3x			
7bx4x			
7bx5x			
7bx6x	FTTC		
7bx7x	12th Flight Academy		
7bx8x	13th Flight Academy		
7bx9x	50th Division		
1xbx			Harbin Flight Academy
2xbx			Shijiazhuang Flight Academy
3xbx			Xi'an Flight Academy
4xbx			AU FBTB
4xbx			AU FITB
6x0x			Hong Kong
6x1x			15th AC fixed wing
6x2x			15th AC rotary

Abbreviations

AC	Air Corps
FA	Flying Academy
FTTC	Flight Test & Training Center
MRTB	Military Region Training Base
NTS	Navigator Training School
SMTU	Special Missiles Testing Unit
AU FBTB	Aviation University Flight Basic Training Base
AU FITB	Aviation University Flight Instructor Training Base
fixed wing	aircraft
rotary	helicopters

中国人民解放军空军

INDEX

Military Regions/MRAF

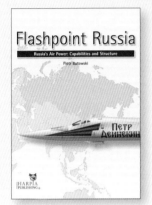